THE KEY

STUDENT STUDY GUIDE

English 10 Academic

THE KEY student study guide is designed to help students achieve success in school. The content in each study guide is 100% aligned to the provincial curriculum and serves as an excellent source of material for review and practice. To create this book, teachers, curriculum specialists, and assessment experts have worked closely to develop the instructional pieces that explain each of the key concepts for the course. The practice questions and sample tests have detailed solutions that show problem-solving methods, highlight concepts that are likely to be tested, and point out potential sources of errors. ***THE KEY*** is a complete guide to be used by students throughout the school year for reviewing and understanding course content, and to prepare for assessments.

Canadian Cataloguing in Publication Data

Rao, Gautam, 1961 –
THE KEY – English 10 (2009 Edition) Ontario

1. English – Juvenile Literature. I. Title

Published by
Castle Rock Research Corp.
2340 Manulife Place
10180 – 101 Street
Edmonton, AB T5J 3S4

5 6 7 FP 10 09 08

Printed in Canada

Publisher
Gautam Rao

Contributors
Brigitta Braden
Kelly Durin Laffin
Lois Westerlund

Dedicated to the memory of Dr. V. S. Rao

THE KEY—GRADE 10 ENGLISH ACADEMIC

THE KEY consists of the following sections:

KEY Tips for Being Successful at School gives examples of study and review strategies. It includes information about learning styles, study schedules, and note taking for test preparation.

Class Focus includes a unit on each area of the curriculum. Units are divided into sections, each focusing on one of the specific expectations, or main ideas, that students must learn about in that unit. Examples, definitions, and visuals help to explain each main idea. Practice questions on the main ideas are also included. At the end of each unit is a test on the important ideas covered. The practice questions and unit tests help students identify areas they know and those they need to study more. They can also be used as preparation for tests and quizzes. Most questions are of average difficulty, though some are easy and some are hard—the harder questions are called *Challenger Questions*. Each unit is prefaced by a ***Table of Correlations***, which correlates questions in the unit (and in the practice tests at the end of the book) to the specific curriculum expectations. Answers and solutions are found at the end of each unit.

KEY Strategies for Success on Tests helps students get ready for tests. It shows students different types of questions they might see, word clues to look for when reading them, and hints for answering them.

Practice Tests includes one to three tests based on the entire course. They are very similar to the format and level of difficulty that students may encounter on final tests. In some regions, these tests may be reprinted versions of official tests, or reflect the same difficulty levels and formats as official versions. This gives students the chance to practice using real-world examples. Answers and complete solutions are provided at the end of the section.

For the complete curriculum document (including specific expectations along with examples and sample problems), visit www.edu.gov.on.ca/eng/curriculum/secondary.

THE KEY *Study Guides* are available for many courses. Check www.castlerockresearch.com for a complete listing of books available for your area.

For information about any of our resources or services, please call Castle Rock Research at 905.625.3332 or visit our website at http://www.castlerockresearch.com.

At Castle Rock Research, we strive to produce an error-free resource. If you should find an error, please contact us so that future editions can be corrected.

TABLE OF CONTENTS

KEY Tips for Being Successful at School

NOTES

KEY FACTORS CONTRIBUTING TO SCHOOL SUCCESS

In addition to learning the content of your courses, there are some other things that you can do to help you do your best at school. Some of these strategies are listed below:

KEEP A POSITIVE ATTITUDE. Always reflect on what you can already do and what you already know.

BE PREPARED TO LEARN. Have ready the necessary pencils, pens, notebooks, and other required materials for participating in class.

COMPLETE ALL OF YOUR ASSIGNMENTS. Do your best to finish all of your assignments. Even if you know the material well, practice will reinforce your knowledge. If an assignment or question is difficult for you, work through it as far as you can so that your teacher can see exactly where you are having difficulty.

SET SMALL GOALS for yourself when you are learning new material. For example, when learning the parts of speech, do not try to learn everything in one night. Work on only one part or section each study session. When you have memorized one particular part of speech and understand it, then move on to another one, continue this process until you have memorized and learned all the parts of speech.

REVIEW YOUR CLASSROOM WORK regularly at home to be sure that you understand the material that you learned in class.

ASK YOUR TEACHER FOR HELP when you do not understand something or when you are having a difficult time completing your assignments.

GET PLENTY OF REST AND EXERCISE. Concentrating in class is hard work. It is important to be well-rested and have time to relax and socialize with your friends. This helps you to keep a positive attitude about your school work.

EAT HEALTHY MEALS. A balanced diet keeps you healthy and gives you the energy that you need for studying at school and at home.

HOW TO FIND YOUR LEARNING STYLE

Every student has a certain manner in which it seems easier for him or her to learn. The manner in which you learn best is called your learning style. By knowing your learning style, you can increase your success at school. Most students use a combination of learning styles. Do you know what type of learner you are? Read the following descriptions. Which of these common learning styles do you use most often?

Linguistic Learner: You may learn best by saying, hearing, and seeing words. You are probably really good at memorizing things such as dates, places, names, and facts. You may need **to write and then say out loud** the steps in a process, a formula, or the actions that lead up to a significant event.

Spatial Learner: You may learn best by looking at and working with pictures. You are probably really good at puzzles, imagining things, and reading maps and charts. You may need to use strategies like **mind mapping and webbing** to organize your information and study notes.

Kinaesthetic Learner: You may learn best by touching, moving, and figuring things out using manipulation. You are probably really good at physical activities and learning through movement. You may need to **draw your finger over a diagram** to remember it, **"tap out" the steps** needed to solve a problem, or **"feel" yourself writing** or typing a formula.

SCHEDULING STUDY TIME

You should review your class notes regularly to ensure that you have a clear understanding of all the new material you learned. Reviewing your lessons on a regular basis helps you to learn and remember ideas and concepts. It also reduces the quantity of material that you need to study prior to a test. Establishing a study schedule will help you to make the best use of your time.

Regardless of the type of study schedule you use, you may want to consider the following suggestions to maximize your study time and effort:

- Organize your work so that you begin with the most challenging material first.
- Divide the subject's content into small, manageable chunks.
- Alternate regularly between your different subjects and types of study activities in order to maintain your interest and motivation.
- Make a daily list with headings like "Must Do," "Should Do," and "Could Do."
- Begin each study session by quickly reviewing what you studied the day before.
- Maintain a routine of eating, sleeping, and exercising to help you concentrate better for extended periods of time.

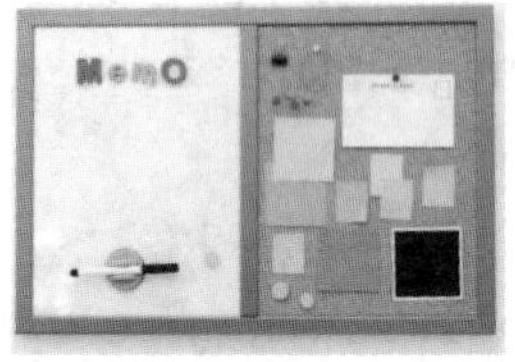

CREATING STUDY NOTES

MIND-MAPPING OR WEBBING

- Use the key words, ideas, or concepts from your reading or class notes to create a *mind map* or *web* (a diagram or visual representation of the given information). A mind map or web is sometimes referred to as a *knowledge map*.
- Write the key word, concept, theory, or formula in the centre of your page.
- Write down related facts, ideas, events, and information and then link them to the central concept with lines.
- Use coloured markers, underlining, or other symbols to emphasize important information, such as relationships between ideas or specific aspects of a timeline.

The following mind map is an example of an organization tool that could help you develop an essay:

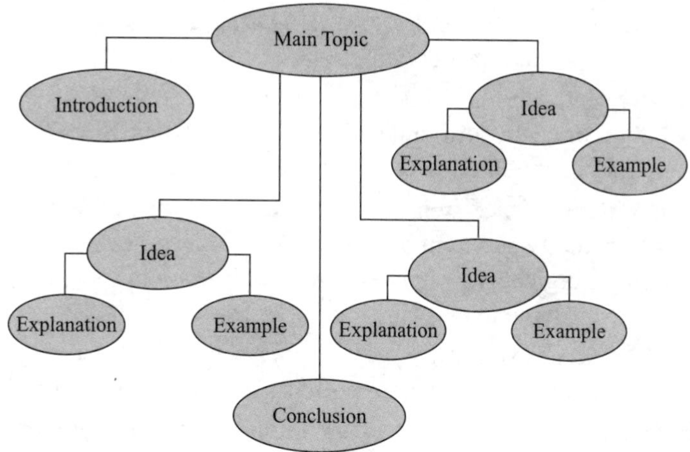

Index Cards

To use index cards while studying, follow these steps:

- Write a key word or question on one side of an index card.
- On the reverse side, write the definition of the word, answer to the question, and any other important information that you want to remember.

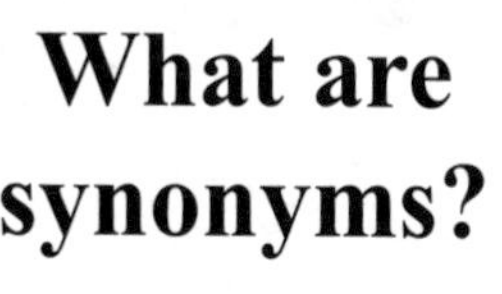

What are synonyms?

Synonyms are words that have the same or almost the same meaning.
E.g., coarse = rough

Symbols and Sticky Notes—Identifying Important Information

- Use symbols to mark your class notes. For example, an exclamation mark might be used to point out something that must be learned well because it is a very important idea. A question mark may highlight something that you are not certain about, and a diamond (◊) or asterisk (*) could highlight interesting information that you want to remember.
- Use sticky notes when you are not allowed to put marks in books.
- Use sticky notes to mark a page in a book that contains an important diagram, formula, explanation, etc.
- Use sticky notes to mark important facts in research books.

MEMORIZATION TECHNIQUES

- **ASSOCIATION** relates new learning to something you already know. For example, to remember the spelling difference between *dessert* and *desert*, recall that the word *sand* has only one *–s*. So, because there is sand in a desert, the word *desert* only has one *–s*.
- **MNEMONIC DEVICES** are sentences that you create to remember a list or group of items. For example, the first letter of each word in the phrase "**E**very **G**ood **B**oy **D**eserves **F**udge" helps you to remember the names of the lines on the treble clef staff (E, G, B, D, and F) in music.
- **ACRONYMS** are words that are formed from the first letters or parts of the words in a group. For example, *radar* is an actually acronym for Radio Detection and Ranging, and *MASH* is an acronym for Mobile Army Surgical Hospital. **HOMES** helps you to remember the names of the five Great Lakes (**H**uron, **O**ntario, **M**ichigan, **E**rie, and **S**uperior).
- **VISUALIZING** requires you to use your mind's eye to imagine a chart, list, map, diagram, or sentence as it is in your textbook or notes, on the chalk board or computer screen, or in a display.
- **INITIALISMS** are abbreviations that are formed from the first letters or parts of the words in a group. Unlike acronyms, initialisms cannot be pronounced as a word themselves. For example, IBM is an initialism for International Business Machines, and PRC is an initialism for the People's Republic of China.

KEY STRATEGIES FOR REVIEWING

Reviewing textbook material, class notes, and handouts should be an ongoing activity. Spending time reviewing becomes more critical when you are preparing for tests. You may find some of the following review strategies useful when studying during your scheduled study time:

- Before reading a selection, preview it by noting the headings, charts, graphs, and chapter questions.
- Read the complete introduction to identify the key information that is addressed in the selection.
- Read the first sentence of the next paragraph for the main idea.
- Skim the paragraph and make note of key words, phrases, and information.
- Read the last sentence of the paragraph.
- Repeat this process for each paragraph and section until you have skimmed the entire selection.

KEY Strategies for Success: A Checklist

Review, review, review: review is a huge part of doing well at school and preparing for tests. Here is a checklist for you to keep track of how many suggested strategies for success you are using. Read each question and then put a check mark (✓) in the correct column. Look at the questions where you have checked the "No" column. Think about how you might try using some of these strategies to help you do your best at school.

***KEY* Strategies for Success**	**Yes**	**No**
Do you know your personal learning style—how you learn best?		
Do you spend 15 to 30 minutes a day reviewing your notes?		
Do you study in a quiet place at home?		
Do you clearly mark the most important ideas in your study notes?		
Do you use sticky notes to mark texts and research books?		
Do you practise answering multiple-choice and written-response questions?		
Do you ask your teacher for help when you need it?		
Are you maintaining a healthy diet and sleep routine?		
Are you participating in regular physical activity?		

NOTES

Class Focus
Reading and Literature Studies

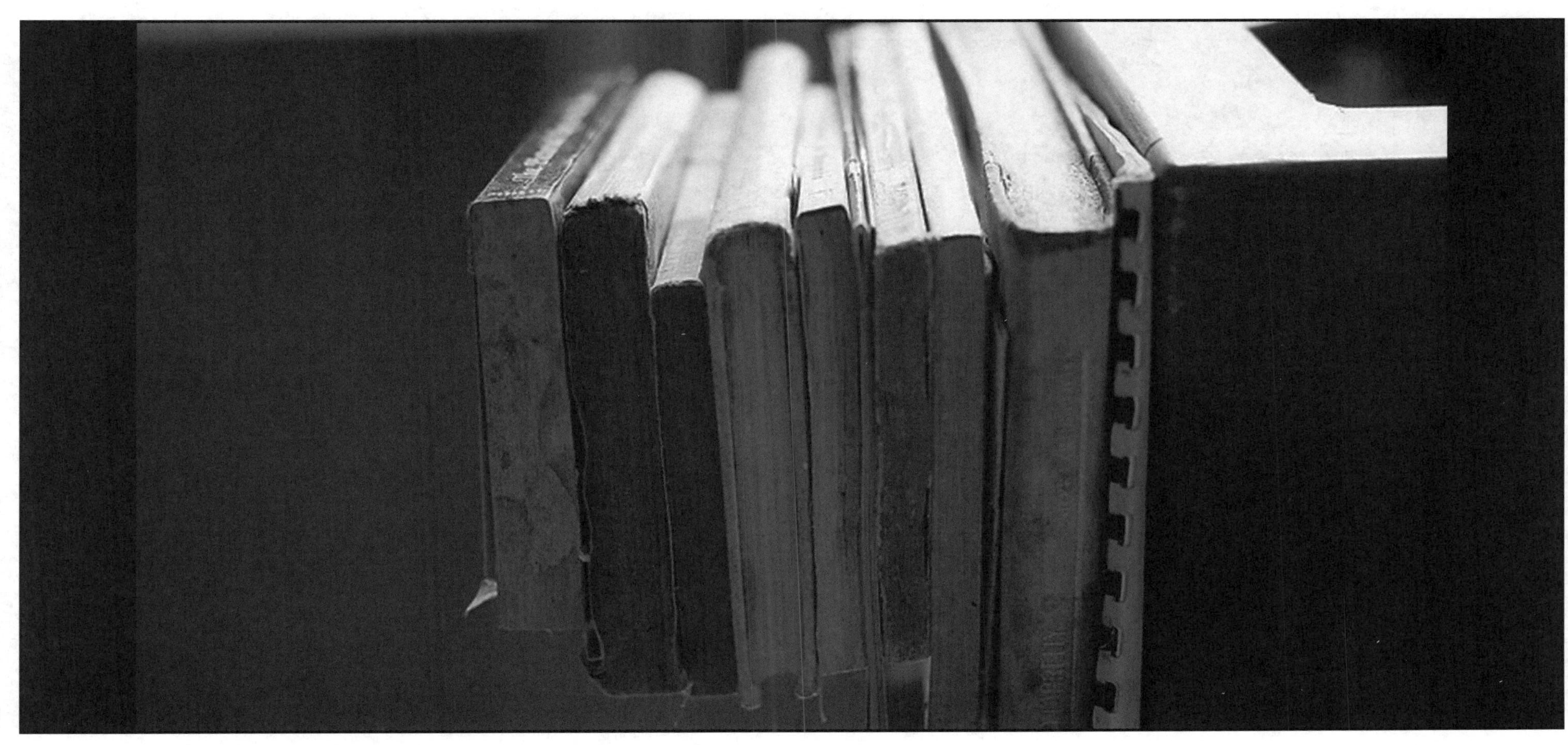

TABLE OF CORRELATIONS

General Expectation	Specific Expectation	Practice Questions	Unit Test
Students are expected to:			
10R1.0 read and demonstrate an understanding of a variety of literary, informational, and graphic texts, using a range of strategies to construct meaning. (Reading for Meaning)	10R1.1 read a variety of student- and teacher-selected texts from diverse cultures and historical periods, identifying specific purposes for reading. (Variety of Texts)	11, 36, 39, 40	
	10R1.2 select and use appropriate reading comprehension strategies before, during, and after reading to understand texts, including increasingly complex texts. (Using Reading Comprehension Strategies)		
	10R1.3 identify the most important ideas and supporting details in texts, including increasingly complex texts. (Demonstrating Understanding of Content)	19, 27, 28, 34, 46, 50	1, 8, 9, 11, 17
	10R1.4 make and explain inferences about texts, including increasingly complex texts, supporting their explanations with well-chosen stated and implied ideas from the texts. (Making Inferences)	10, 13, 14, 16, 20, 21, 22, 23, 48, 51, 55	4, 7, 20

	10R1.5	extend understanding of texts, including increasingly complex texts, by making appropriate connections between the ideas in them and personal knowledge, experience, and insights; other texts; and the world around them. (Extending Understanding of Texts)	32, 35, 52, 56	
	10R1.6	analyse texts in terms of the information, ideas, issues, or themes they explore, examining how various aspects of the texts contribute to the presentation or development of these elements. (Analysing Texts)	7, 8, 12, 33, 44, 49	12, 25
	10R1.7	evaluate the effectiveness of texts, including increasingly complex texts, using evidence from the text to support their opinions. (Evaluating Texts)	43	16, 23
	10R1.8	identify and analyse the perspectives and/or biases evident in texts, including increasingly complex texts, and comment on any questions they may raise about beliefs, values, identity, and power. (Critical Literacy)	2, 6, 53	6, 10, 19, 26

10R2.0 Recognize a variety of text forms, text features, and stylistic elements and demonstrate understanding of how they help communicate meaning. (Understanding Form and Style)	10R2.1 identify a variety of characteristics of literary, informational, and graphic text forms and explain how they help communicate meaning. (Text Forms)	7	3, 18
	10R2.2 identify a variety of text features and explain how they help communicate meaning. (Text Features)	38, 41, 42	
	10R2.3 identify a variety of elements of style in texts and explain how they help communicate meaning and enhance the effectiveness of the texts. (Elements of Style)	1, 3, 9, 17, 26, 29, 31, 37, 45, 54	2, 13, 14, 15, 21, 22, 24
10R3.0 Use knowledge of words and cueing systems to read fluently. (Reading With Fluency)	10R3.1 automatically understands most words in a variety of reading contexts. (Reading Familiar Words)	15, 30, 47	
	10R3.2 use appropriate decoding strategies to read and understand unfamiliar words. (Reading Unfamiliar Words)	4, 5, 18, 24, 25	5
	10R3.3 identify and use a variety of strategies to expand vocabulary (Developing Vocabulary)	57, 58	

ANALYSING FOR MEANING

The main function of writing is to communicate meaning. Finding out the meaning of a text you are reading is not always easy, and it is important to discover different strategies of finding meaning in a variety of texts. Analysing the meaning of a poem will involve different techniques than analysing the meaning for a research essay. The following section of your *KEY* will show you how meaning is communicated in different forms of writing and will give you some strategies as to how you can best analyse meaning. This section will also show you how to best communicate the meaning you intend in your own writing.

10R1.1 read a variety of student- and teacher-selected texts from diverse cultures and historical periods, identifying specific purposes for reading

A Purpose for Reading

Reading without a purpose is like going on a road trip without a map. You find yourself wasting a lot of time because you are not sure where you are going.

One of the most important steps to take before reading is to establish your purpose. The reason you are reading a text can help you decide how to read it. Perhaps you are doing research, reading instructions, reading for meaning, or reading for fun.

When you have a purpose for reading, you can keep a closer eye on your progress and know to stop when something is not quite right. Sometimes you need to revisit the purpose, and at other times, your purpose changes.

10R1.2 select and use appropriate reading comprehension strategies before, during, and after reading to understand texts, including increasingly complex texts

Reading Comprehension Strategies

Reading comprehension strategies help you to make sense of what you read. The following strategies highlight how being a thoughtful reader and taking your time as you read is important. The following section provides some specific reading strategies, explanations, and examples that show you how to use these strategies for reading prose, poetry, and visual texts.

Previewing

Previewing means taking a brief overview or glance at the parts of the text that stand out to you. When previewing, take a look at the reading selection and think about what stands out. Are there headings or titles? Are there graphs or charts? Are there any pictures? Are there captions that describe the pictures? If the passage has any of these things, make a little note in your mind to pay close attention to them as you read.

It is an excellent idea to preview a new text, such as a textbook, before you receive any reading assignments. You can learn helpful information about a course and its content before you ever begin. Here are some possible previewing activities to try with textbooks or any book:

- Look at the publication date. Is it important that this particular text is current?
- Look over the table of contents. How is it organized?
- Does the text have a glossary?
- Is there an index?
- Leaf through the text to check the graphics: pictures, diagrams, charts, maps, and so on. How will these aid your learning?
- Skim through at least one chapter:
    - How is it organized?
    - Are vocabulary terms listed at the beginning?
    - Are the subheadings in a larger, bolded font?
    - Are key words bolded?
    - Are there questions or comments in the side bars to help you understand the text as you read?
    - Is there an overview paragraph at the beginning of the chapter?
    - Is the chapter summarized at the end?
    - Is there a chapter review?
    - Does the text include an answer key?

Using Prior Knowledge

Build on your background knowledge and experiences to help you understand any text you read. Take your time reading and use what you already know about something to make the text you are reading clearer. To do this, make connections between what you know and what you read by asking yourself the following questions:

- Does this story remind me of any other stories or texts?
- What do I already know about the topic I am reading about?
- Is there something in this text that is similar to something I already know?

Predicting and Questioning

Try to predict what you will learn or what will happen next as you read. Using your background knowledge and clues from the text, you can form hypotheses (predictions) as you read. You should be able to support your predictions with facts from the text.

The following steps form an example of how you can predict what will be in a text:

1. Before you start reading, ask "I wonder…" questions.
2. Predict what the story will be about, perhaps based on its title.
3. If there are headings or chapter titles, think about what ideas or subjects are being touched upon before reading further.
4. As you read, stop and predict what might happen next.
5. When you are finished reading, ask yourself if your predictions are correct. If they were not, consider why.

A Purpose for Reading

As with the strategies discussed earlier in this section, what you do before you start to read can add to your reading experience. One of the most important steps to take before reading is to establish your purpose. The reason you are reading a text can help you decide how to read it. Are you reading to research information for an essay, answer questions for an assignment, or locate the phone number, hours of operation, and address of a new clothing store? How you go about reading for any of these different tasks will change with your purpose.

When you have a purpose for reading, you can keep a closer eye on your progress. You know when to stop and turn around when something is not quite right. Sometimes you need to revisit your purpose, and at other times your purpose changes.

Monitoring for Meaning

Monitoring for meaning refers to checking your understanding of the material that you read. Think about whether or not the text makes sense to you, and think about the broader meaning of the story. Keep in mind that it is perfectly acceptable to have difficulty with or be confused about some part of a text. Monitoring for meaning means to think about what you understand as well as what you do not understand.

To practice monitoring for meaning, you can ask yourself the following questions as you read:

- Do I understand what I just read?
- What is happening in the story?
- How do the important ideas and details relate to each other?

When you are finished reading, think about any questions you still have. These questions can help you pinpoint parts of the text you may have had trouble with.

Visualizing

Visualizing is a process in which what you are reading can be like watching a movie. Writers convey information with words. As you read, you can use these words to create pictures in your mind that show what is happening in the text. Usually, visualizing is something natural that happens for the reader. Visualizing in this way can help you remember information more easily than by words alone, and it can deepen your understanding of the text. Through visualization, you can create images of the characters, settings, and events of a story.

To practice visualizing while reading, try the following techniques:

- Pause frequently and describe any picture in your mind.
- After reading a passage, draw a picture of what you see in your mind.
- Work backward. This could include looking at a wordless picture book and creating a story to match the pictures.

Inferring

Inferring is a part of everyday life. When you wake up, you make inferences, or assumptions, about what is going to happen throughout the day. You brush your teeth, get dressed, and perform other morning tasks because you infer that you are going to school. Suppose that, in the middle of breakfast, you learn that it is a snow day and school is cancelled. Now you immediately start thinking of what else to do and make inferences about your options for the day. Reading is the same way. When you open up a book, you immediately make assumptions about the text based on what kind of book it is, if you know other books by the writer, how the cover of the book looks, etc. You will make different inferences about a textbook than you would about a novel or an instructional manual.

The inferences you make are based on your life experiences and what you have already read and understand. Your background knowledge and the information in the text create meaning beyond what is directly stated in the text. Inferences may include conclusions, predictions, and new ideas.

To practice inferring while reading, ask yourself the following questions:

- What do I think this story is about?
- How do I think the character feels?
- Why did I think that would happen?
- How did I know that?
- What does the writer actually say?

Importance

Determining what is important in a text is particularly useful for non-fiction and informational texts. You can save time by distinguishing between what is vital information in a text and what may be less important. By identifying important ideas and themes, you can set aside less important information.

To practice determining what information is most important in a text, try the following techniques:

- While reading, look for clues in the format of the text that might indicate importance. Pay attention to the first and last lines of a paragraph, the title, any headings or subheadings, captions, framed text (text with a box drawn around it), quotation marks, font size, and font style (underlined text, italicized text, bold text).
- Pay particular attention to pictures, illustrations, charts, and diagrams; they may provide you with important information.
- As you read, focus on remembering information that appears to be "must-know" information.
- After reading, think about what was the most important information you learned.

Synthesizing

Synthesizing is the ability to put various elements together to form a whole. It allows you to sort through information to make sense of it.

To practice synthesizing, ask yourself the following questions while reading a text:

- What was the writer's purpose for writing this piece?
- What is the main idea of this story?
- What clues helped me to determine the main idea?

- How do the different parts of this story connect with one another?
- Has my thinking changed after reading this piece?
- Can I think of a different title for this piece?

Figure it Out

If you are having trouble understanding something you are reading, different strategies can help. As you use these strategies, they will become more and more familiar to you. In time, you will probably use these strategies without even realizing it. Over time, reading strategies can become second nature to how you read. The following list describes some strategies that can help your reading comprehension:

- Reread: sometimes a second reading is all that it takes. If you cannot make a picture in your mind or you do not understand what you have just read, try reading it again.
- Skip ahead: sometimes you need to move on. If you do not understand something you have just read, skip ahead and continue reading. There may be information later on that helps you to understand the section that you are having trouble with. You can always go back and reread difficult sections later.
- Context clues: use familiar words surrounding an unfamiliar word to help you determine the unfamiliar word's meaning.
- Picture clues: use information from pictures to help make sense of what you have read.
- Ask for help: ask a teacher, parent, classmate, or sibling for help when you have tried your own strategies and still do not understand something.

Following are some questions to ask before, during, and after reading a piece of text.

Before Reading

- Are there headings, charts, graphs, vocabulary, or questions that I can preview?
- What is my purpose for reading?
- What will I be doing with the information I read?
- What do I already know about the topic?
- What reading strategies should I use to read this text?
- How is the text organized?
- What questions do I have before reading this text?
- Can I turn headings or subheadings into questions?

During Reading

- Am I meeting the purpose I set out for reading?
- Am I making sense of what I am reading?
- Do I understand what I am reading?
- Do I have a clear visual image in my mind's eye?
- Is what I am reading what I expected?
- Are some parts different or similar to my predictions?
- What is the main idea of the text so far?
- What kind of graphic organizer would I use to begin organizing the ideas?
- What did I visualize in my mind about these ideas while I was reading?
- Is the information in the text similar to other passages that I have read?

After Reading

- Do I need to reread any parts that were difficult?
- What new information did I learn, and how does it fit into my background knowledge?
- What else do I still need to know about the topic?
- What are my thoughts about what I have read? Do I agree or disagree? Why?
- Do I like what I have read? Why or why not?

In cases where you are not permitted to mark the text itself, you can put the symbols or reading comments on sticky notes, which can be removed later.

Remember, the purpose of every reading strategy is to help you better understand what you read. Any strategy that becomes an automatic part of your reading contributes to your success in school and in life and allows you to pursue academic goals with confidence.

10.R.1.3 identify the most important ideas and supporting details in texts, including increasingly complex texts

Understanding Content

When you are reading, understanding the main idea of a work is important to tie in all of the information you are reading. A main idea connects the details of a text together. Often, the main idea is in the title or in one to two strong sentences near the beginning or the end of the passage. The main idea of a piece of writing is always supported by details that describe or explain the main idea. Look at the two examples below, and notice how the supporting details support the main idea in each article.

TSUNAMIS (MAIN IDEA)

<u>Tsunamis are caused by underwater earthquakes and volcanic eruptions, and they are the largest waves of all</u> (**main idea**). Earthquakes occur when two **tectonic plates** collide or slide past each other. When an earthquake occurs under the ocean, the ocean bottom shakes. This movement causes the water above to become **displaced**. Waves of energy spread out in all directions from the sources of the vibrations in ever-widening circles. As the tsunami approaches the shore, the waves rub against the seafloor. **Friction** causes the waves to slow down and build from behind, creating a huge volume of water that crashes onto the shore.

All the other sentences support the main idea that tsunamis are caused by underwater earthquakes and volcano eruptions.

ROGUE WAVES (MAIN IDEA)

Sometimes, groups of large ocean waves caused by a storm slam into a powerful ocean current passing in the opposite direction.$_{(1)}$ When this happens, several storm waves pile up to form gigantic waves called rogue or freak waves.$_{(2)}$ These waves can be more than 100 feet (30 metres) tall and can bury cargo ships beneath the sea.$_{(3)}$ Rogue waves are most common off the coasts of Japan, Florida, and Alaska.$_{(4)}$ Currently, a project known as WaveAtlas monitors the oceans with satellites.$_{(5)}$ Over the next few years, oceanographers hope to analyze these satellite images to help them better understand why freak waves occur.

In this paragraph, sentences 1 and 3 are details supporting exactly what rogue waves are, while the other sentences give further informative details about rogue waves.

Main Ideas and Details in Informational Text

There are various strategies for identifying and recording main ideas and supporting details in informational text. Three common methods are to create a chart or graphic, to make a timeline, or to make an outline. Read the following passage and review the example of an outline that follows. Think about how you might use an outline to organize the information in this passage.

CLIMBING THE HIGH PEAKS

If you have ever scrambled up a rocky cliff, followed a trail to the top of a hill, or gasped at the beauty of the Rockies, you can probably understand why people climb mountains. It's difficult, dangerous, and—some say—deranged. But there is a certain kind of person who thinks it's the best adventure of all.

The greatest challenges for mountain climbers lie in Tibet and Nepal. There the Himalayan chain of peaks rises skyward, with Mount Everest the highest at 8840 m. Traditionally, these remote Asian countries did not allow Europeans to enter, so the first climbers had to disguise themselves as Nepalese herdsmen, Buddhist pilgrims, or Tibetan merchants.

Early in the twentieth century, permission was granted for an occasional British expedition to enter Tibet for the purpose of exploring the Himalayas. From this time on, conquering the high peaks has become the goal of adventurers from around the world.

The mountains themselves, of course, offered their own difficulties to climbers. First of all, there were the steep glaciers. Parties of climbers crossing these stretches of ice had to beware of falling into deep crevasses. They dodged almost daily avalanches. High altitudes caused breathing problems, headaches, and worse. Worst of all, ferocious storms could—and sometimes did—sweep the climbers and their equipment right off the steep ridges.

Essential to the success of most expeditions in the Himalayas has been the assistance of the Sherpas. These mountain people are used to high altitudes, can carry 115-kg loads day after day, and can even walk barefoot in the snow. They have earned the nickname of "tiger" from visiting climbers. The most famous of the tigers—Tenzing Norquay (or Norgay)—was one of the first men to reach the summit of Mount Everest.

Continued

The story of that climb, which took place in 1953, is an exciting one. It was the most elaborate expedition up to that time. The leader, Colonel John Hunt, arranged to have five tonnes of equipment carried up to the highest possible point on the mountain. It took 362 porters to carry all the boxes from Darjeeling in northeastern India. Thirty-four experienced Sherpas came along when the glaciers were reached. The climbers established a series of camps on the mountainside, each a little higher than the last. They spent plenty of time at each level to get used to the high altitude. All of these people were necessary, but only two would be chosen to climb to the top.

The first attempt to reach the summit from Camp IX (the highest point that could be reached carrying heavy loads) was made by Tom Bourdillon and Charles Evans. They got to within 100 m of the summit, then turned back, sick with exhaustion and disappointment.

Next to try were Edmund Hillary of New Zealand and Tenzing Norquay, the Sherpa. They spent the night alone in Camp IX, huddled in their tent at 8504 m. At 6:30 the next morning, May 29, 1953, they set out on their famous journey. Armed with a nylon rope, ice axes, oxygen tanks, and crampons for walking on snow, they kicked steps across the steep snow slope. At times the ridge was as narrow as a knife-blade, and cornices of snow hung over the edge. As the snow became harder, the men had to cut out each step with their axes. And the oxygen would last less than five hours longer. They had to reach the summit by 11:30 or else turn back. At one point, Tenzing almost stopped breathing as ice clogged his oxygen tubes.

An hour after this incident, Hillary suddenly stopped. Just ahead of him, a tower of rock 12 m high rose straight up from the ridge. He thought they had been beaten. Then he saw a wide crack that led all the way up.

It was the last major obstacle. After pushing and kicking their way to the top, they realized that there was yet more snow climbing, but they were too close to stop. They cut step after weary step into the ice. Finally, at 11:30 exactly, Tenzing and Hillary were standing together on the highest point of the earth's surface—looking down! While Hillary took photographs, Tenzing buried gifts for his Buddhist gods.

The following outline is an example of one you could make for the passage "Climbing the High Peaks." Making an outline can help you determine the main ideas and how they are supported by relevant details.

OUTLINE FOR "CLIMBING THE HIGH PEAKS"

I. Tibet and Nepal greatest challenges to mountain climbers
- **A.** Himalayas are world's highest mountains
- **B.** They are in a remote part of Asia
- **C.** Until early 20th century, no Europeans were allowed to climb

II. Difficulties for climbers
- **A.** Glaciers and crevasses
- **B.** Avalanches
- **C.** High altitude problems
- **D.** Storms

III. For climbs to be successful
- **A.** Sherpas were needed
  - **1.** Tenzing Norquay—a famous Sherpa—First to climb Everest
- **B.** Proper equipment needed
  - **1.** Sunglasses
  - **2.** Oxygen mask and bottle
  - **3.** Down parka
  - **4.** Ice axe
  - **5.** Crampons
  - **6.** Pack
  - **7.** Nylon over boots

IV. 1953 ascent of Everest
- **A.** Header John Hunt
  - **1.** Arranged equipment to be carried up mountain
  - **2.** Established camps on mountain
  - **3.** Ensured time was spent acclimatizing
- **B.** Actual attempts at summit
  - **1.** 1st attempt by Bourdillon and Evans failed
  - **2.** 2nd attempt by Hillary and Tenzing succeeded
    - **a)** May 29, 1953
    - **b)** Started at 6:30 A.M.
    - **c)** Reached the summit at 11:30 A.M.
    - **d)** Hillary took photos
    - **e)** Tenzing buried gifts for Buddha

Creating an outline of a text you have read will help you remember the facts of the text.

10R1.4 *make and explain inferences about texts, including increasingly complex texts, supporting their explanations with well-chosen stated and implied ideas from the texts*

10M1.2 *interpret media texts, including increasingly complex texts, identifying and explaining the overt and implied messages they convey*

10M1.5 *identify the perspectives and/or biases evident in media texts, including increasingly complex texts, and comment on any questions they may raise about beliefs, values, identity, and power*

Making Inferences

As you read fiction and non-fiction, you will draw conclusions and make inferences from the information in the text. Your responses to the text should always be supported by relevant aspects from the text itself or from your experiences in reading and in life.

Interpretation of Media Text

Media text refers to texts, information, and messages that are deliberately packaged for large or public audiences. Newspapers, magazines, all forms of advertising, artwork, and photographs are examples of media text. Messages hidden in the visual images of advertising are not only subtle but are also open to interpretation. For instance, why is a cartoon family of bears used to sell toilet paper? The following example illustrates how the same media text can be interpreted in a variety of ways.

Media Text Interpretations

Consider *The Scream*, Edvard Munch's famous painting from 1893. This painting has appeared as a writing prompt in a student writing text. *The Scream* was probably chosen because it seems to demand an interpretation. The four examples that follow the image of the painting demonstrate some different interpretations of the same painting.

Der Schrei (*The Scream*)

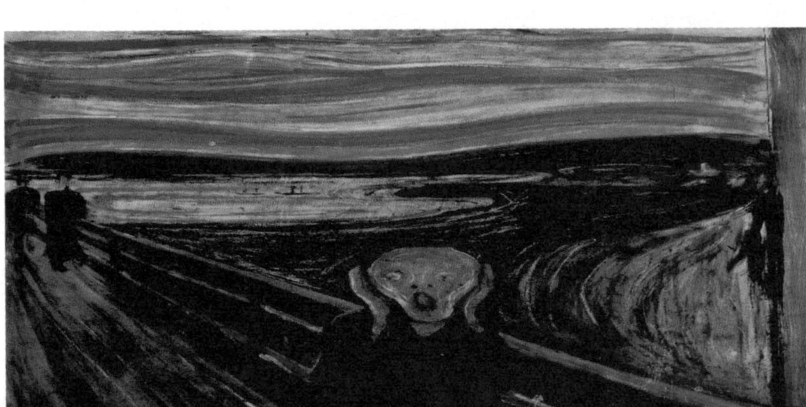

Interpretation 1—Artist Edvard Munch (1864–1944)

I prided myself on being a symbolist painter. I tried to paint a single state of mind, a tension-filled canvas of an emotional moment in life, when the emotion at the time was the dominant thing. This is one piece from a series I painted called "Frieze of Life," and I painted several variations of this emotion, which could be labelled "fear," "despair," or "anxiety." In my language, this painting was titled Der Schrei (The Scream). Notice the emotion is front and centre in the body language and facial expression of the figure on the bridge. My figure has no gender. That is a deliberate impression on my part. So is the fact that the figure is placed at the focal point in the foreground, with the background of lesser consequence. Is the figure on a bridge, a dock, or a country road? That is for you to decide.

Interpretation 2—Novelist Stephen King

What a great painting! What amazing possibilities for suspense and drama. In my favourite writer's genre, which happens to be horror fiction, I could easily use this painting as part of a cover design for a new novel. My female character, Desmonida, has been hearing voices ever since her sister Helene disappeared. Someone keeps emailing her with strange clues. She keeps searching, searching… the last email ordered her to come alone, to an abandoned lighthouse at the end of a rickety, unused bridge near a deserted, stony beach. As Desmonida approaches the end of the bridge, the voices grow louder, more insistent… Dare she enter the lighthouse? What will she find? Why didn't she tell at least one person where she was going? The bridge creaks warningly, and the gulls scream hoarsely and agonizingly overhead… her throat is tightening with fear and she is suffocating…

Interpretation 3—Boutique Owner Maureen Kozak

I am quite excited about the new inventory for my shop that I ordered from that big gift show in Toronto last week. Especially my "Scream" pieces. I had never heard of the artist or his work until the painting was stolen from the Munch Museum in Oslo. I was impressed when I read what it was worth in the paper. That would be quite a few years of profits for my shop! Anyhow, the painting has achieved renewed fame and notoriety through the theft (and eventual recovery, thank goodness), so I think the stained glass pendant and clutch handbag with the painting on the front will sell well at my Whyte Avenue shop this summer—even with the young crowd. They like the artsy items, especially if there is an interesting story to go with them.

Interpretation 4—Grade 10 Student Carl Brownlee

Ms. Bonner showed us a PowerPoint about *The Scream* at the beginning of writing class, and now we have to write some kind of poetic response to the painting. I feel like writing some lyrics that I can maybe put to music when I get home … probably rap or hip hop, I'm thinking. For me, the painting captures how we teenagers feel sometimes … peer pressures, doubts, loneliness, fears about the uncertain future, impossible goals and expectations, deaths of relationships…closing in and choking us with anxiety. This is really going to let me express some strong emotions and feelings. I hope Ms. Bonner just reads it to herself. This is pretty personal.

The following examples can help you reach conclusions or inferences by using the clues in texts.

In Prose

In the following narrative, "I Am a Native of North America" by Chief Dan George, you could make several inferences about Chief Dan George and his father, supported by stated or implied ideas in the text. Some questions about possible inferences follow this example.

Example

I AM A NATIVE OF NORTH AMERICA

In the course of my lifetime I have lived in two distinct cultures. I was born into a culture that lived in communal houses. My grandfather's house was eighty feet [24 m] long. It was called a smoke house, and it stood down by the beach along the inlet. All my grandfather's sons and their families lived in this large dwelling. Their sleeping apartments were separated by blankets make of bull rush reeds, but one open fire in the middle served the cooking needs of all. In houses like these, throughout the tribe, people learned to live with one another. And children shared the thoughts of the adult world and found themselves surrounded by aunts and uncles and cousins who loved them and did not threaten them. My father was born in such a house and learned from infancy how to love people and be at home with them.

And beyond this acceptance of one another there was a deep respect for everything in nature that surrounded them. My father loved the earth and all its creatures. The earth was his second mother. The earth and everything it contained was a gift from See-see-am … and the way to thank this great spirit was to use his gifts with respect.

I remember, as a little boy, fishing with him up Indian River and I can still see him as the sun rose above the mountain top in the early morning … I can see him standing by the water's edge with his arms raised above his head while he softly moaned … "Thank you, thank you." It left a deep impression on my young mind.

And I shall never forget his disappointment when once he caught me gaffing for fish "just for the fun of it." "My Son," he said "The Great Spirit gave you those fish to be your brothers, to feed you when you are hungry. You must respect them. You must not kill them just for the fun of it."

This then was the culture I was born into and for some years the only one I really knew or tasted. This is why I find it hard to accept many of the things I see around me.

—*by* Chief Dan George

INFERENCE QUESTIONS

- What kind of environment did Chief Dan George grow up in? How did his environment and his actions in life affect his beliefs?
- What did Chief Dan George's father teach him about life, about nature? What are some words you could use to describe his father's character?
- What kind of relationships has Chief Dan George had with spirituality? Has he always thought of nature and his heritage in the same way? What changes have taken place in his mind?

Being curious is the first step in making inferences. You probably know a lot more about a text than you may think, and asking questions is the first step to unlocking that information.

10R1.5 *extend understanding of texts, including increasingly complex texts, by making appropriate connections between the ideas in them and personal knowledge, experience, and insights; other texts; and the world around them*

USING WHAT YOU READ EVERY DAY

Books are powerful and have the ability to change your thoughts and actions. When you read a book, you are adding the information and experiences of a writer to your body of knowledge. The information you receive from reading does not stay inside the pages of books; it becomes a part of how you interact with the world. After you read a book on pollution, for example, you are likely to begin to look at everyday things differently. If you see someone throwing out a pop can into the garbage rather than the recycling bin, the information you learned in that book will spring to your mind. Activities that might not have bothered you before, such as littering or driving a car, may seem more negative now that you have read that book. The knowledge that books give allows you to experience the world with a new perspective.

The ultimate goal of most writers, whether they write to inform, explain, persuade, or entertain, is to have their readers connect with and understand what they have written in a personal way. When you make connections in text, you are remembering or internalizing what you read. You make connections by doing the following things:

- accessing prior knowledge you may have that can help you understand new material
- expressing a new insight or way of looking at an issue or topic by reading a related story, poem, or article
- feeling empathy with a character because of a similar problem or personal experience in your own life
- remembering a movie, play, or other novel that has a related plot or theme to what you are reading

10R1.6 *analyse texts in terms of the information, ideas, issues, or themes they explore, examining how various aspects of the texts contribute to the presentation or development of these elements*

10M2.2 *identify conventions and/or techniques used in a variety of media forms and explain how they convey meaning and influence their audience*

Analysing Texts

Analysing texts that you read involves thinking about how those texts explore or present information, ideas, issues, and themes.

How Themes are Presented and Reinforced

As you read through the following poem, an underlying theme becomes evident—a potentially productive life being wasted by someone that is living too much in the lorry days of their past. Try to make note of particular phrases in the poem that either suggest or reinforce this theme.

EX-BASKETBALL PLAYER

Pearl Avenue runs past the high-school lot,
Bends with the trolley tracks, and stops, cut off
Before it has a chance to go two blocks,
At Colonel McComsky Plaza. Berth's Garage
Is on the corner facing west, and there,
Most days, you'll find Flick Webb, who helps Berth out.

Flick stands tall among the idiot pumps—
Five on a side, the old bumble-head style,
Their rubber elbows hanging loose and low.
One's nostrils are two S's, and his eyes
An E and O. And one is squat, without
A head at all—more of a football type.

Once Flick played for the high-school team, the Wizards.
He was good: in fact, the best. In '46,
He bucketed three hundred ninety points,
A country record still. The ball loved Flick.
I saw him rack up thirty-eight of forty
In one home game. His hands were like wild birds.

He never learned a trade, he just sells gas,
Checks oil, and changes flats. Once in a while,
As a gag, he dribbles an inner tube,
But most of us remember anyway.
His hands are fine and nervous on the lug wrench.
It makes no difference to the lug wrench, though.

Off work, he hangs around Mae's Luncheonette.
Grease-gray and kind of coiled, he plays pinball,
Sips lemon cokes, and smokes those thin cigars;
Flick seldom speaks to Mae, just sits and nods
Beyond her face towards bright applauding tiers
Of Necco Wafers, Nibs, and Juju Beads.

—*by* John Updike

Following is an analysis of some lines and phrases in the poem in order to observe how they may suggest or reinforce the theme.

- The quotation "Flick stands tall among the idiot pumps" suggests that Flick is far above what he does for a living, much too talented to be spending his days manning gas pumps. The word "idiot" also expresses the meaningless, mindless futility of Flick's present life.
- The quotations "He was good: in fact, the best… His hands were like wild birds" show Flick's amazing talent as a player, but the inclusion of the word "once" in the line above the phrase "In '46" immediately following indicate that the glory days are a thing of the past.
- In the quotation "He never learned a trade, he just sells gas," the words "never" and "just" reinforce the theme of wasted opportunities.
- The lines "Flick seldom speaks to Mae, just sits and nods…toward bright applauding tiers" reinforce the idea in the theme of a person dwelling on the achievements of his past and dreaming only instead of tackling real goals.
- The last line of "Of Necco Wafers, Nibs, and Juju Beads" reinforces the empty reality of a wasted life. Flick is looking off into space at the cheering crowds from his remembered past, while the actual scene above his vacant gaze contains shelves of junk food for sale.

Writers are usually very careful to choose the exact words they want to express a given idea. The next time you are analysing a text, think about how individual words work to convey a message. An analysis like the one above is helpful to understanding the text's themes and intended meaning. Analysing text in poems allows you to see beyond the words in a text to images, moods, and themes that those words express.

Use of Style to Create Tone and Mood

A writer's style of writing and tone help to create the mood of a given work. As you read more, you will be able to recognize how style, tone, and mood all work together to have an effect on the text.

1. Tone

A writer's tone is the overall attitude that the writer has toward what is written. Tone is established by the writer's word choice, or diction. The tone conveys the writer's attitude toward the story or characters. It sets the mood of the writing; it must always be appropriate to the purpose and audience. The tone of a story can be, for example, serious, light-hearted, sad, emotional, formal, or informal. Because writers cannot use a speaker's tone of voice, they create their tone through the choice and arrangement of words, punctuation, sentence length, and so on.

In an excerpt from Edgar Allan Poe's "The Tell-Tale Heart," the writer's serious tone allows the reader to see the narrator's insanity. The more the narrator talks about how serious and unemotional his decision is to murder the old man for seemingly no real reason, the better the reader can understand that the narrator is not in his right mind.

from "THE TELL-TALE HEART"

True!—Nervous—very, very dreadfully nervous I had been and am; but why *will* you say that I am mad? The disease has sharpened my senses—not destroyed—not dulled them. Above all was the sense of hearing acute. I heard all things in the heaven and in the earth. I heard many things in hell. How, then, am I mad? Hearken! And observe how healthily—how calmly I can tell you the whole story.

It is impossible to say how first the idea entered my brain; but once conceived, it haunted me day and night. Object there was none. Passion there was none. I loved the old man. He had never wronged me. He had never given me insult. For his gold I had no desire. I think it was his eye! Yes, it was this! One of his eyes resembled that of a vulture—a pale blue eye, with a film over it. Whenever it fell upon me, my blood ran cold; and so by degrees—very gradually—I made up my mind to take the life of the old man, and thus rid myself of the eye forever.

—*by* Edgar Allan Poe

Poe's tone is seen in his attitude toward the narrator in the story. The narrator uses eccentric, strange, and defensive language, which reveals that the writer perceives the character to have those characteristics.

2. Mood

While tone describes the writer's attitude toward the story, mood is the atmosphere of a piece of writing that is felt by the reader. Mood is not often stated outright; rather, writers carefully choose their words, phrases, and images in order to lead their readers to guess at and feel the mood. In the following passage, you can tell that the narrator is frustrated and angry through the use of repetition, through word choice, punctuation, and the use of sarcasm.

Garbage

Garbage! Garbage! Garbage! Why is there so much garbage and waste? Do people think it will disappear on its own? I work hard to recycle and reuse, yet garbage heaps up on us all the time! There is no end to it!

The mood of a story can be angry, sad, frightening, suspenseful, enthusiastic, scary, etc. You can use a variety of words to describe mood. One famous opening line to a story, "It was a dark and stormy night," does not contain enough description to establish a mood of, say, fear and terror. To create this kind of mood, you would need to add more creative descriptions.

For example, in the following paragraph from *Island of the Blue Dolphins*, Scott O'Dell creates a mood of eeriness, suspense, and loneliness. As a reader, you wonder what is going to happen, and you can feel the narrator's loneliness and sadness.

It was a morning of thick fog and the sound of far off waves breaking on the shore. I had never noticed before how silent the village was. Fog crept in and out of the empty huts. It made shapes as it drifted and it reminded me of all the people who were dead and those who were gone. The noise of the surf seemed to be their voices speaking.

In this passage, it is the writer's style of writing—the short, simple sentences and the tone that is established through the choice of words such as "thick fog," "waves breaking," and "fog crept in and out… It made shapes"—that create the mood you experience as you read.

In summary, tone and mood are closely related, but are separate aspects of style. Tone is the writer's apparent attitude toward their subject, their characters, or their readers. The writer's tone, depending on aspects such as subject matter, use of formal or informal language, and characterization, may come across to you, the reader, as serious, light, cynical, sympathetic, indifferent, or passionate.

Mood, on the other hand, describes the atmosphere that the reader feels while reading a text. Mood, ideally, should be transmitted so that you feel connected to an atmosphere that is morbid, optimistic, sinister, thoughtful, suspenseful, romantic, and so on.

10R1.7 *evaluate the effectiveness of texts, including increasingly complex texts, using evidence from the text to support their opinions*

10M1.3 *evaluate how effectively information, ideas, issues, and opinions, are communicated in media texts, including increasingly complex texts, and decide whether the texts achieve their intended purpose*

Evaluating Texts

As you evaluate the many different types of text that you read, both at school and during your personal time, your critical thinking skills will enable you to use text effectively and confidently for a great variety of purposes. You will be asking yourself questions such as the following:

- Why is this story so believable?
- Why is this argument so convincing?
- Why is this poem so appealing?
- Why is this ad so effective?

On the surface, these are simple, direct questions. However, answering them by providing supporting evidence from the text can become fairly complex. Certain elements of a text contribute to a reader finding that text appealing. Following are some explanations of those aspects of text, which will in part explain why some texts appeal to you or convince you more than others.

Believable Stories

The attempt by a writer to make a story realistic to readers by using real-world details is called *verisimilitude*. The word may remind you of the word *verify*. *Verisimilitude* quite literally means "similar to the truth." An example of verisimilitude would be fiction that deals with current events or real political leaders. A work of fiction that includes details of the city of Ottawa, for example, including Parliament Hill, would be using verisimilitude. By including details about the real world that the reader is familiar with, the reader can relate to the characters and situations in the plot more easily.

Realistic Plot

A believable plotline is very important to the success of a story. If something does not ring true for readers, it is likely that they will not enjoy the text. This is why writers write what they know. It is easier for them to get all the little details right if they are based on reality. For example, writers for crime television series often use plot ideas from actual events in the news.

Realistic Setting

Having a realistic setting is particularly important in works of historical fiction, such as the Charles Dickens novel *A Tale of Two Cities*. The two cities in this story are London and Paris, and the time of the setting is during the French Revolution. Although the novel is a work of fiction, the story is made realistic and convincing through descriptions of real places, such as the Bastille, and of events that actually took place, such as the public executions during the 18th century.

Realistic Characters

Characters are made realistic through their actions, manner of speaking (dialect), thoughts, and description. Many writers develop characters with which readers can identify in terms of age, gender, cultural background, hobbies, religious beliefs, ambitions, motivations, and personality. An example of a popular fictional character is Anne from the novel series *Anne of Green Gables*. She is such a popular character that fans of L.M. Montgomery's series come to visit the inspiration for Anne's house in Prince Edward Island. The house is now a huge tourist attraction. For readers, it supports ideas about the character they have come to know and care about through the books.

Realistic Situations

In real life, not every story has a happy ending. This is true of realistic stories as well. In the novel *The Parent Trap*, identical twin girls try to get their parents back together. With humorous twists and turns in the plot, the girls manage to reunite their parents. However, this is not a very realistic ending to a story.

Convincing Arguments

How do you know if an argument is logical or true? Many arguments can sound convincing but may not be true. Sometimes a writer writing an argument may not reveal all of the information to you about a subject so that you will be more convinced by his or her position. There are several aspects to consider in order to evaluate the level to which an argument or viewpoint as stated in text is convincing. Never just assume one point of view is correct. Look at all sides of an issue.

Another important part of learning whether or not an argument is good is by looking at where the argument comes from, who has written the argument, etc. If the argument is written on a blog on the Internet, it is more likely to have a bias than a major newspaper.

Fact and Opinion

Facts are statements that can be proven true. You can use experiments, research, or observations to prove facts. Opinions are statements that express personal beliefs. Opinions cannot always be proven. Sometimes, it is difficult to tell the difference between fact and opinion, and sometimes it is very obvious. As the reader, you must try to separate the two. Almanacs, encyclopedias, and atlases are examples of books that are usually reliable sources of factual information.

Factual statements are ones that can be proven to be true. Much of what people read is not necessarily verified, but readers usually accept it because it appears to be true or others say the information is true. Magazine, books, newspaper, the Internet, websites, bulletin boards, and blogs, for example, should not be entirely trusted until the knowledge and experience of the writer has been verified.

People often also reach faulty conclusions because the evidence they use may be based on either faulty observations or observations that maybe prejudiced, wishful, or imaginative.

Determining the Reliability of Sources

Not everything that is stated with authority is fact. Generally, you would tend to think that information you find in encyclopedias is fact. There are many other resources, such as eyewitness accounts, newspaper accounts, supermarket tabloid accounts, and the Internet. These sources are often less reliable than reference materials you can find at the library. Information on the Internet often has errors or bias.

How do you determine what makes a resource reliable as a source of information? When is the information valid and authentic? What kinds of sources will mostly provide accurate information?

It is important to be critical of what you read, particularly when the information you are reading claims to be factual or truthful. Evaluate the facts stated carefully. Decide what evidence is convincing and what might need verification. Look for biases that suggest a particular viewpoint or opinion, even when the bias is not directly stated. If a newspaper, for example, reports mostly stories and articles that cast a particular politician or political party in a negative light, you could probably draw the conclusion that the paper does not support the policies of that politician or her or his party. It is a good idea to either not read a newspaper that has a bias or to balance your knowledge of issues by reading a variety of news sources.

10R1.8 identify and analyse the perspectives and/or biases evident in texts including increasingly complex texts, and comment on any questions they may raise about beliefs, values, identity, and power

Critical Literacy

Being able to identify perspectives and biases in texts will strengthen your critical literacy skills. You will be better equipped to comment on questions and issues related to beliefs, values, and identity. After perspectives and biases are explained, you will find some examples that illustrate how they apply to texts that you read.

Bias and Stereotyping

Bias and stereotype are both rooted in prejudice. The following section explains how bias and stereotyping in text is important to recognize and analyse from a balanced point of view.

Biases

Bias is an unconscious or natural tendency to adopt a preferred view on something. It may be unspoken, but is often expressed in attitude or behavior. It can certainly be positive, as in having an inner pride in being Canadian, which would be a pro-Canada bias, or having a bias to cheer for your home team no matter what. However, there are negative biases, such as

- **anti-youth bias**, which refers to assumptions made about young people
- **anti-aging bias**, which refers to assumptions made about older people, which can include misconceptions that they are obsolete because of their age
- **anti-authority bias**, which makes a person view teachers, parents, policemen, or other authority figures with hostility and suspicion
- **racial prejudice**, which makes a person dislike or hate anyone who looks different from their own ethnic group

Other biases include political biases, gender biases, economic biases, and religious biases. Negative biases prevent people from being tolerant of other people and different viewpoints.

Stereotypes

Stereotypes are overly generalized beliefs about individuals or groups. These generalizations are based on preconceived notions that may be the result of a personal bias or from being misinformed. Stereotypes paint a whole group of individuals with the same brush and do not acknowledge uniqueness and individuality. They create mistaken assumptions; for example, that tall people must be good basketball players, people wearing glasses must be smart, or that unemployed people must be lazy.

Racial stereotypes, particularly in areas where there is a concentration of a visible minority ethnic group, may, unfortunately, be passed on to a younger generation by adult family members. An example of this is the United States prior to the Civil Rights Movement. At that time, many white Americans were in solidarity with black Americans to change laws that were discriminating against them. The results of the protests were fully integrated schools of mixed races and basic freedoms for black Americans, such as the right to sit where they want on public transportation, use public restrooms and drinking fountains, and eat in restaurants of their choice.

It is important to be mindful of stereotypes when you read texts of any kind. Advertising and editorial writing often includes stereotypes. Watch for bias or slants no matter what type of medium is being presented to you. Bias can occur through omission—when an advertiser or a reporter deliberately chooses to include some facts and omit others. The bottom line is that stereotyping and bias come from opinions based on fear, not fact. The best action you can take is to read as much as you can about a topic in order to get a lot of information. Different sources about a topic will probably have different opinions and different facts that are featured. When you read as much as you can about a topic, you are giving yourself a balanced picture of that topic. Many writers will expose you to stereotypes and biases intentionally in order to educate you about respecting individuality, tolerating differences, and forming your own (hopefully unbiased) opinions.

Analysing a text is a complex process. Finding meaning in a text often means relating that text to your life, to information you have already read, and examining smaller parts of a text. One of the great things about literature is that one text can mean different things to different people. It is important to form opinions that are informed when you analyse a text. This section of your *KEY* has shown you how using a variety of methods to analyse a text can ensure that the meaning you find in a text is balanced and enriching.

ON 10R2.1 identify several different characteristics of literary, informational, and graphic text forms and explain how they help communicate meaning

Form and Style

When you want to find out how a work has been written, you will have to analyse the form and style of that work. Form and style are connected to each other. The form of a text refers to how it has been written from a broader perspective: for example, how a text is structured, whether or not it is poetry or prose, and how long a text is. The style of a text refers to how it has been written from a closer perspective. For example, style can refer to the type of words that are used, or the tone or mood of the text.

In this section of your KEY, you will learn about the most common forms of writing, as well as about different aspects of style. Learning to identify form and style will help you analyse writing on different and important levels.

Text Forms

Text is intended to communicate ideas. Text, as you know, comes in a variety of forms that are designed to suit the ideas that a writer wants to communicate. Literary forms of text are published works that are usually in the form of poetry or prose. They can entertain and give readers insight into the emotions and experiences of others.

Text appears in many different forms. The following chart shows three categories of text and some examples of each. More detail is provided in the following sections about the items with asterisks beside them.

Literary Text Forms	Informational Text Forms	Graphic Text Forms
• poem • play – musical – screenplay • short story • novella • novel	• history – biography – autobiography – memoir – newspaper article • essay • letter • diary • journal • reference – text book – manual – consumer document – workplace document – public document – memorandum – electronic magazine	• advertisement – poster – cartoon • comic book • graphic novel • graphic organizer

Literary Text Forms

The form of a text gives you an idea of the type of ideas you should be looking for. For example, if you wanted to present facts about a current events issue that interested you, you probably would not choose the form of a poem to write about it. Chances are you would choose an essay or an oral presentation. Poems and novels are usually more expressive, whereas essays tend to be more factual or objective. Following are some definitions, descriptions, and examples of different literary text forms that you may have encountered in class.

Poems

Poetry can be created in a number of forms that follow pattern guidelines, such as limericks, epics, ballads, odes, and sonnets. What a poet wants to write about and how they want to write it often change the structure or form of the poem.

Poetry has special characteristics, just as plays, short stories, and essays do. These special characteristics distinguish poetry from other written texts.

Poetry Characteristics and Examples

1. Forms and patterns
   a) Some poems have specific, set patterns
   - haiku
   - imerick
   - tanka
   - ballad

   b) Some poems have no specific set pattern
   - free verse
2. Rhyme—there are many rhyming patterns:
   a) Rhyming couplet
   - rhyme two lines together

   b) Alternate rhyme
   - rhyme every other line

   c) Free verse
   - no rhyme
3. Rhythm—nearly all poems have some rhythm
   - gentle, soft rhythm
   - strong, forceful rhythm
   - repetitive rhythm

Some of the very first stories ever told were in verse. Long before books existed, people sat around their campfires chanting about their brave deeds and of the great events they had witnessed. Over time, these chants were written down as epic or narrative poems. The best way to read narrative poetry is out loud so that you can enjoy both the story and the way it is told.

A sonnet is a poem of fourteen lines following a set rhyme scheme and a logical structure. Some are written in an octave (8 lines) followed by a sestet (6 lines), while others are written in 12 lines ending with a couplet, such as the following example written by William Shakespeare.

Example

2

When forty winters shall besiege thy brow
And dig deep trenches in thy beauty's field,
Thy youth's proud livery, so gazed on now,
Will be a tottered weed, of small worth held:
Then being asked where all thy beauty lies,
Where all the treasure of thy lusty days,
To say, within thine own deep-sunken eyes
Were an all-eating shame and thriftless praise.
How much more praise deserved thy beauty's use,
If thou couldst answer, 'This fair child of mine
Shall sum my count and make my old excuse,'
Proving his beauty by succession thine.
This were to be new made when thou art old
And see thy blood warm when thou feel'st it cold.

—*by* William Shakespeare

Informational Text Forms

Informational texts are non-fiction, which means that they are based on reality or facts, although they may contain opinions believed or expressed by the writer. They are also generally presented in a prose style of writing, which means in sentences and paragraphs. It is important to be careful with non-fiction or informational texts. Although they usually make a claim to reality or unbiased writing on a subject, they are not always without bias. Non-fiction can have a writer's slant just as fiction can.

Letters

Letters generally begin with an inside address and date and use conventional greetings and closings, such as "Dear ____" and "Yours Sincerely." Letters may be personal and informal (friendly letter) or formal (business letter). Each has a slightly different format. It is common for opinion essays to appear in a newspaper as letters to the editor.

Reference Books

Reference books contain specific, non-fiction information. Examples of reference books are encyclopedias, dictionaries, thesauruses, atlases, and almanacs.

Consumer Documents

A consumer document provides important information about products and services. These documents take different forms, such as consumer reports, warranties, recall announcements, and advertisements.

Workplace Documents

Most workplaces have specially designed documents suited to that particular workplace. These include application forms, contracts, safety policies, dress codes, emergency procedures, Internet use rules, and email policies.

Public Documents

A public document is often provided through a government office or agency and contains information that supports public safety and welfare. Examples of public documents are clean air, safe water, and highways acts; littering laws; driver's handbooks; and library policies.

Memorandums

A memorandum is often brief and is addressed to a limited group, such as the employees of a company. It is limited to essential information and is frequently sent in the form of an inter-office email.

Electronic Magazines

The Hockey News is an example of a popular sports magazine that can be read online. For a free preview, you just need to follow links listed on the home page, such as "New, Features, Salaries, Schedules, Stats, Teams, Players, Standings, and Fan Corners." A full subscription, of course, is not free. Those who post electronic magazines generally want readers to subscribe to the whole text of the magazine for a fee.

Other examples of online magazines are

- *Consumer Report*, which provides performance and quality statistics on many products
- *Macleans*, which is called Canada's national "news" magazine

Some people prefer electronic versions of their favorite newspapers and magazines. They save paper and can browse sections at their leisure throughout the day.

Graphic Text Forms

Graphic text forms rely heavily on drawings and illustrations or showing information using graphic organizers, such as charts or plot diagrams. There are a variety of forms of graphic text. Some forms are legitimate means of conveying art or entertainment, and other forms are used primarily for organizing statistics or other information. Using visual aids in addition to text to convey meaning gives a work more depth and can often explain information in a way that text alone cannot.

Advertisements

Text advertisements are mostly found in newspapers, magazines, and posted in public places, such as buses and on billboards. The Internet is, as you know, full of advertisements that range from pop-up ads to ads that are built into the design of a website. Companies even pay search engines so that their company website will show up on the first page of a person's search.

Graphic Novels

Graphic novels are also known as picture novels. A graphic novel is a full-length novel in which the action and characters have been drawn by an artist to complement the narrative text, which is framed in captions and word balloons similar to a regular comic book. A comic book really differs from a graphic novel only in length.

Graphic novels, in one form or another, have been around since the 1940s. They are not really a new or recent trend. At that time, a series of stories from classical literature were published in a comic book format called *Classics Illustrated*, with well-known titles such as *Robinson Crusoe* and *Treasure Island*. The intention was to entice young readers to read literature that they might be reluctant to read in full-length novel form.

By 1975, graphic novels were gaining broader acceptance as a genre. In 1986, a graphic novel called *Maus* by Art Spiegelman won the Pulitzer Prize for the category of Letters, Drama, or Music. You may have read a graphic novel or two yourself, such as *5 Shots* by Jemir Johnson or *Diary of a Wimpy Kid* written by Jeff Kinney. A selection of graphic novels can be found at your school or local library.

ON 10R.2.2 identify a variety of text features and explain how they help communicate meaning

Text Features

Organizational Features of Books

Informative books are organized with features that help you find information quickly. After you have read a book, these features can also help you recall or find the information that you need again. Here are some features with which you should be familiar.

A **title page** tells you the topic of the book and its writer or editor.

The **table of contents** is found at the front of a book, usually just after the title page. It lists the book's chapters or divisions in order from first to last. The starting page number of each chapter is also given. You can skim a table of contents from top to bottom to find out where a particular chapter begins and how long it is.

Example

Chapter 1 – Under the Sea..............................1
Chapter 2 – Fish, Fish, Fish!............................17
Chapter 3 – Why We Like Diving......................28
Chapter 4 – Underwater Machines....................36

A **preface** or **foreword** is an introduction that sometimes includes helpful or positive features of the book.

The **visual layout** of a book refers to how the book is put together, whether it contains pictures and diagrams, etc.

The **appendix** is a section found at the back of some information books containing extra information to help you understand the material such as notes, charts, maps, or diagrams.

An **index** is an alphabetical list of the important topics in an information book. It tells you which pages have information on each topic.

A **glossary** is often found at the back of a non-fiction book. It lists and explains the meanings of words in the book that are important or that you may not already know. While reading a book with a glossary, you can quickly check the meaning of a word without getting out a dictionary.

Chapter organizers are arranged according to the order of the content. Organizing and presenting material using many different styles can help you learn difficult material. These features also help you navigate through a chapter. This is especially useful if you want to read only certain kinds of material from each chapter as you study for an exam.

Visuals as an Organizational Feature

When you read cartoons, you are also interpreting the visual clues that convey meaning. Facial expressions and body language contribute to meaning as much as the text in dialogue and thought balloons. When you read the caption under a picture in your social studies text and connect it to the picture, you better understand the meaning that is being illustrated. You can easily recognize the value of visuals in science books, math texts, and manuals. Diagrams make complex systems or processes easier to understand, whether you are trying to solve a problem or are figuring out the functions on your new cell phone.

Visuals enhance communication and convey meaning within text. Whether you are researching a topic or reading in a textbook, do not underestimate the power of any visuals that are included.

Text Layout Used to Enhance Meaning

The manner in which text is laid out or presented on a page adds to and can change the meaning of the text itself. Concrete poetry is an example of how text layout affects meaning. Concrete poetry, sometimes called "shape" poetry, uses configurations of words that are related to the subject of the poem. In the first example, only 14 words are used to reflect on insolence. *Insolence* means bold rudeness or open disrespect, usually toward an authority figure. The poet's message becomes more powerful when the attitude of insolence can be read in the poem as descending rungs on a ladder, "wrong by wrong" (word play on "rung by rung"), to the bottom. Instead of climbing up toward goals of success, the wrong attitudinal choices follow the words of the poem downward in the direction of probable failure.

INSOLENCE

and
the
young
man
laughed
as he
climbed
down
the
ladder
wrong
by
wrong

—*by* Nanci Neff

Using such dramatic visual features is usually most appropriate in poetry assignments, but visual tools can be used in less obvious ways in other texts as well. Newspapers use many visual tools to keep readers interested.

ON 10R2.3 identify a variety of elements of style in texts and explain how they help communicate meaning and enhance the effectiveness of the text

Elements of Style

Different elements of style in text communicate meaning and enhance the effectiveness of the text. For the purposes of this section, style refers to a particular or characteristic manner of writing to achieve deliberate effects in the text or responses in the readers.

Figurative Language

Figurative language creates imagery and affects the senses of the reader. Imagery occurs when a writer paints a picture in the mind of the readers by appealing to their senses of smell, taste, touch, sight, and hearing. For example, the sentence "The wind whistled through the dancing leaves of copper and gold as the storm howled its fury in glow of twilight" should paint a picture in your mind.

A **simile** occurs when a writer compares two or more things or ideas using *like* or *as*.

Examples

With his smug grin, he looked as sly as a fox.
Her eyes sparkled like diamonds in the sunlight.

A **metaphor** occurs when a writer compares two or more things or ideas directly, without using the words *like* or *as*. A metaphor can occur within a sentence, a paragraph, or throughout an entire piece of writing. For example, in the sentence "The stars were diamonds in the sky," the stars are being compared to diamonds.

Personification is a literary device that gives human characteristics to an animal or inanimate (non-living) object.

Example

The silver grin on the Man in the Moon held secrets we could only guess.

Alliteration occurs when initial consonant sounds are repeated in adjacent or nearby words.

Examples

<u>s</u>oared <u>s</u>moothly above the <u>s</u>tadium
<u>b</u>ellowed <u>b</u>rokenly
<u>t</u>arnished the <u>t</u>winkling <u>t</u>imelessness

Onomatopoeia occurs when a word actually seems to sound like what it represents.

Examples

swoosh, buzz, thwack, crackle

Hyperbole is an extreme exaggeration.

Examples

I ate a mountain of pancakes for breakfast.
After I swallowed the chilli, my mouth was on fire.

Figurative language is used in prose (stories, article) as well as in poetry. Pay close attention to the underlined phrases in the following paragraph.

Out in the bay, treacherous currents sizzle and leap among the underlying rocks with the relentless (1) purpose of a hungry dragon. Which unsuspecting ship will be (2) on the menu today? (3) Like a spoiled child, the waves demand (4) their favorite meal, the creaking timbers of a vessel too weak to escape the (5) cruel, crunching (6) jaws of the ravenously hungry sea.

The figurative and metaphorical uses of words in the paragraph are explained below.

1. "Purpose of a hungry dragon" is a metaphor that compares the sea with a dragon.
2. "On the menu" is a metaphor that compares the sea with a restaurant.
3. "Like a spoiled child" is a simile that compares the sea with a child in the middle of a temper tantrum.
4. "Their favorite meal" is a metaphor that compares the waves with customers ordering food at a restaurant.
5. "Cruel, crunching" is alliteration, which is the repetition of the beginning consonant sound.
6. "Jaws" is a metaphor that compares the frightening waves with the jaws of a monster dragon.

Symbolism

Symbolism is used to enhance a theme, suggest a mood, or create an effect. Symbolism occurs when a writer uses an object, a situation, or an action to suggest another meaning. A writer might use a tiger to symbolize strength or fierceness. Another writer might use a lamb to suggest peace and gentleness. Symbols usually occur throughout a story. Generally, if an image or word is used three times or more in a story, there is a good chance that it is important enough to be a symbol in the story.

The following list provides a number of symbols that are commonly found in literature. Knowledge of these "universal" symbols can help you find more meaning in the literature that you encounter in school, regardless of the type (genre) or cultural source of the literature.

Common Symbols in Literature

Water – fertility, life-giving, rebirth, purification, and redemption
Stagnant or polluted water – corruption, evil
Fire – destruction, purification, passion, death
Earth – baseness, fertility
Air/wind – spirits, freedom, inspiration
Sun – wisdom and vision, power, life-giving, regeneration
Sunrise – birth, rebirth, joy, hope
Sunset – death
Mountains – obstacles, achievement, aspirations, awe, glory
Storms – death, evil, inner turmoil
Roads, ships, trains, railroads, etc. – journeys, changes
Fork in the road/crossroads – choices, decisions
Doors/gates/arches – escape, opportunities, utopias, fantasy worlds, freedom
Bridges – transitions, crossing over

Walls/fences/hedges – barriers, dividing lines, prisons
Windows – freedom, longing, imprisonment
Mirrors – illusion, unreality, passage to other worlds
Birds/sky – freedom
Circle – wholeness, unity
Gardens – Eden, paradise, innocence, fertility
Desert – spiritual aridity, death, hopelessness, sterility
Lamb – innocence, Christ
Sheep – conformity
Black – evil, death, despair
White – innocence, good, redemption
Red – war, anger, blood, vengeance, love, passion
Green – growth, renewal, life, nature, envy
Yellow – sun, happiness, cowardice, betrayal

ON 10R3.1 automatically understand most words in a variety of reading contexts

Reading Familiar Words

By Grade 10, you are in a position to understand most of the vocabulary you encounter in text, whether it is personal text online, literature you read at school, or the more subject-specific vocabulary used in textbooks and research references.

Subject-Specific Terminology

You are required to read all the time in a variety of subjects while you are a student. Most of these subjects are presented in units. Most units, no matter what the subject is, will have some terms that you will have to learn. Before you can master the unit, you must understand central vocabulary terms. Often, subject-specific terminology is introduced at the beginning of a new unit or chapter.

For instance, before beginning a poetry unit, most English teachers will review terms like *sonnet*, *lyric*, *metaphor*, *onomatopoeia*, and so on, because these terms are often used with respect to poetry.

Terminology can have a totally different meaning from one subject to another. Here are a few examples, using the subjects of math and science:

Word/Term	Math	Science
base	side or face of a polygon from which an altitude rises	chemical compound that acts with an acid to form a salt
formula	equation that shows a general relationship	chemical or physical equation
power	notation of a number with a base and an exponent, such as a^n where a is called the base and n is called the exponent	mechanical or physical energy
transformation	any mapping of a figure resulting in a change in position, shape, size, or appearance of the figure	the process of metamorphosis, as in caterpillar to butterfly

Subject-specific words that are important are often

- bolded in math, social studies, and science textbooks
- defined at the beginning of a new chapter
- defined at the bottom of the page or at the back of the textbook
- used by the teacher on the board, overhead, or for assignments

Learning new words helps you to better understand and remember information, ideas, and concepts.

Some strategies for adopting new words are to

- add them to your personal vocabulary list
- learn the meaning of the words in the content area
- practice spelling them correctly, even if you have to check back in the textbook
- use them in answers and assignments
- give them a permanent home in your "mental computer" (brain) so you can retrieve them as needed

It is important to master the subject-specific terminology used in specific content areas if you want to avoid the frustration that goes along with not understanding what the teacher is trying to explain. Take a look at the following tips.

Learn the words first

Before plunging into new learning, learn any terms that will help you comprehend the information better. Use the glossary; see if the term is defined in the text; list the terms beside their meanings in your notes for quick reference.

Review old words

Learn or review the terms while you are learning the unit. Most subject-specific terminology is not language you use every day, so just learn it as you need it. Refresh your memory as needed during the unit or course. Then review them later when you need them, such as for a final exam.

ON 10R3.2 *use appropriate decoding strategies to read and understand unfamiliar words*

Understanding Unfamiliar Words

What should you do when you encounter an unfamiliar word as you are reading?

When you read, you automatically decode words. *Decoding* means identifying or understanding meaning. As you read a passage, the familiar words are quite easy to decode because the meaning you know fits appropriately into the sentence or context. If automatic decoding does not work for a particular word or if the word is unfamiliar, some of the decoding strategies described below may help you to understand the word as it is being used in the passage. Understanding the words you read improves your reading comprehension.

Decoding

- Read the whole sentence to see if you can guess the meaning of the unknown word. Does your guess make sense, or do the other words in the sentence give you a clue to what the unknown word might be?
- Look for root words. For example, the root word of *simplify* is *simple*.
- Look for compound words. Compound words are made up of two parts; for example, *some* and *thing* becomes *something*.
- Look for word families or chunks within the word. For example, *infatuate* can be broken into easy chunks, like *in-fat-u-ate*.
- Sound out the word.
- If possible, look the word up in a dictionary.
- If you are unable to figure out the word, skip the word and try to understand what is being said in the sentence without the word.

The following passages will help you use different strategies in more detail: using knowledge of word order and parts of speech; using context clues to substitute a word that makes sense in the context; using knowledge of roots, prefixes, and suffixes; and sounding words out phonetically.

Word Order and Parts of Speech

Knowing what part of speech the word is can help you understand or recognize how it is being used. Following are the basic parts of speech you may be asked to identify.

Noun

A noun is a person, place, thing, or idea.

There are two types of nouns: *common* and *proper*.

Common Noun: a *general* person, place, thing, or idea. Examples of common nouns are *dog*, *house*, *car*, and *woman*.

Proper Noun: a *particular* person, place, thing, or idea. Examples of proper nouns are *Samuel*, *Europe*, and the *Olympic Games*.

Pronoun: takes the place of a noun. Examples of pronouns are *I*, *we*, *me*, *anybody*, *that*, *this*, and *us*.

Adjective: modifies or describes a noun or pronoun. Examples of adjectives are *red* car, *large* television, and *loud* speaker.

Verb

A verb shows action or state of being. Examples of verbs are *run*, *is*, *think*, *sleep*, *grow*, and *played.*

There are two types of verbs: *regular* and *irregular.*

Regular Verb: the verb's past tense and past participle forms end in *-ed.* Examples of regular verbs are *played*, *jumped*, and *hunted.*

Irregular Verb: modified in different ways than a regular verb. Examples of irregular verbs are *run* (*ran*), *slide* (*slid*), and *grow* (*grew*).

Infinitives

In English, verbs are often listed in their infinitive form; that is, preceded by the word *to*. Examples of infinitives are *to run*, *to climb*, *to seek*, and *to study*.

An infinitive can be used as a noun in a sentence; for example, "Sometimes, *to speak* is an unwise choice." (The infinitive *to speak* is used as the noun subject of the sentence.)

Participle

A participle is basically a verb used as an adjective. A participle ending in *-ing*, or present participle, is the most common; for example, "*Arriving* late, Norma quickly took her seat." (*Arriving* modifies the noun, *Norma*.)

You will also encounter past participles; for example, "*Having arrived* late, Norma quickly took her seat." (*Having arrived* modifies the noun, *Norma*.)

Adverb

An adverb modifies or describes a verb, adjective, or another adverb. Examples of adverbs are "She ran *quickly*," "I *rarely* eat pizza in the morning," and "This is an *extremely* interesting book."

Preposition

A preposition is a word placed in front of a noun or pronoun to connect it to another part of the sentence. Examples of prepositions are *to*, *for*, *over*, *by*, *at*, and *from*.

Conjunction

A conjunction joins words, phrases, clauses, and sentences. Examples of conjunctions are *and*, *or*, *but*, *either*, and *or*.

Interjections

An interjection expresses some form of emotion. Examples of interjections are "*Ouch*! That hurts" and "*Oh*, I don't know."

Knowing what part of speech a word is and then recognizing its syntax or word order in a sentence pattern can help you to decode a word's meaning. First of all, look at the form of the following words used for different parts of speech:

Verb	Noun	Adjective	Adverb
beautify	beauty	beautiful	beautifully
depend	dependant	dependable	dependably

Now look at how these words might be used in sentences:

The students *beautified* the field behind their new school by planting trees and shrubs.

Figure it out: *Beautified* is a verb, and the suffix *-ified* usually refers to the changing or acting upon of something. The word must mean the students made the grounds more beautiful by planting trees.

You will be a *dependant* until you turn 18.

Figure it out: *Dependant* is a noun. You know the meaning of the verb *depend*, so *dependant* must mean a person who relies on adults for their care because they are not self-sufficient.

Using Context Clues to Substitute a Different Word

When you are having trouble understanding a word, try looking at the context clues in the surrounding words of the sentence. Often, there will be other words in the sentence that you understand and that add to the meaning of the sentence. There will also be words that you will struggle with. Once you have an idea of the context of the word, try substituting a different word into the sentence to see if it makes sense. If the new word agrees with the meaning of the sentence, chances are the word you were struggling with means something similar to the new word you substituted.

Examples

Glancing *dispassionately* at his list of instructions, Gordon, with a casual shrug of his shoulders, took his time leaving the office.

Figure it out: The context, especially these words *glancing* and *casual*, suggest that Gordon does not care. Try substituting *carelessly* or *indifferently* for *dispassionately*. Do these words work?

In her white furs, emerald jewellery, and shimmering silver gown, the countess made her *ostentatious* entrance into the Grand Ballroom as the strains of the first waltz wafted from the orchestra pit.

Figure it out: The context of jewels, expensive clothing, and the Grand Ballroom suggest possible substitutions like *showy* or *extravagant* for *ostentatious*. Do these substitutions make sense?

Substituting might not give you the exact definition of a word, but it will get you close. Use the words you know to help you with the words you do not know. Use a dictionary to confirm that your guess is correct. The dictionary will give you a precise answer, but guessing and substituting are important stages of understanding the meaning of a word.

Roots, Prefixes, and Suffixes

Many scholars think that in prehistoric Europe, there may have been a common language called proto-Indo-European. However, as people moved around over many hundreds of years seeking food and grazing lands, they became isolated from each other and, as a result, developed their own languages.

The three main branches of the proto-Indo-European language that have most influenced the development of English are the Germanic, Italic, and Hellenic languages.

The Germanic language branch had the greatest influence on the English language, but Italian, Latin, French, Spanish, and Greek have all contributed to the development of the English language. To this day, the English language continues to change and grow as it absorbs new words and phrases.

Many English prefixes and suffixes are derived from Greek and Latin. These words become altered, and can often lead to new words being invented.

A *prefix* is defined as one or more syllables added to the beginning of a root word to form a new word. Here are a few examples of prefixes derived from Greek and Latin.

Latin Prefix	Meaning	New Word
ante-	before	anterior, antemeridian (A.M.)
ben-, bon-	good, well	benefit, bonanza
bi-	two	bicycle, binary
mal-	bad, ill	malfunction, malnutrition
migr-	to move, travel	migrate, migration
Greek Prefix	**Meaning**	**New Word**
anti-	against	anticlockwise, anticlimax
auto-	self	automatic, automobile
hemi-	half	hemisphere, hemicycle
tele-	far off	telephone, telepathic
poly-	many	polygon, polygraph

Suffixes have the special job of changing the root word to another part of speech; for example, a verb, a noun, an adjective, or an adverb. Here are a few examples of Latin and Greek suffixes with their purposes.

Latin Suffix	Purpose	Meaning
-age	forms a noun	belongs to (storage)
-ance	forms a noun	state of being (appearance)
-ible, -able	forms an adjective	capable of being (possible)
-ive	forms an adjective	belonging to/quality of (attractive)
-ly	forms an adverb	like/to the extent of (happily)
-ate	forms a verb	to make (alienate)
-fy	forms a verb	to make (simplify)
Greek Suffix	**Purpose**	**Meaning**
-y	forms abstract noun	state of (e.g., happy)
-ism	forms noun	act/condition (e.g., nationalism)
-ic	forms adjective	having the nature of (e.g., pathetic)

As you can see, there are more Latin suffixes than there are Greek. As the English language developed, many prefixes, suffixes, and root words from both Latin and Greek were joined together, and the resulting English word is derived from both languages.

Adding a prefix to a root word changes its meaning. For example, the prefixes *pre-*, *post-*, and *ante-* all change the time frame of a root word. *Pre-* and *ante-* both mean *before*, while *post-* means *after*. Look at the following root words and how their meanings change when a prefix is added:

Root	Meaning	*Prefix*+Root	New Meaning
condition	state of person or thing	*pre*condition	something necessary for a result to occur
view	act of seeing or looking	*pre*view	an advance showing
chamber	a room, especially a bedroom	*ante*chamber	a waiting room
script	handwriting	*post*script	a note added to a letter that has already been signed

A suffix also adds meaning to a root word or changes it slightly.

The suffixes *-ic*, *-tic*, *-ical*, and *-al* mean "having to do with." When one of these suffixes is added to a root word, the new word takes a different form, including a different spelling. Look at how a suffix affects a root word. Notice also how the spelling of each word is altered and how each root is changed from a noun to an adjective.

Root	Meaning	Root+*Suffix*	New Meaning
economy	financial system	econom*ic*	to do with the economy
drama	plays and theatrical art	dramat*ic*	overtly expressive or emotional
analyse	examine carefully	analyt*ical*	logical or reasoning
structure	a building or other constructed object	structur*al*	part of a structure

Root words from Greek and Latin can sometimes appear to be prefixes and suffixes, but they are actually the roots or main parts of the words. Following are some examples of Greek and Latin root words.

Root	Origin	Meaning	Derivations
bio	Greek	life	*bio*graphy, *bio*logy, micro*bio*logy
lab	Latin	to work	*lab*our, *lab*oratory, e*lab*orate
phone	Greek	voice, sound	*phono*graph, tele*phone*, micro*phone*
port	Latin	to carry	*port*able, trans*port*, trans*port*ation

If you take the time to learn the meanings of commonly used prefixes, suffixes, and root words, you can better identify the meanings of words that use them. This knowledge allows you to break unfamiliar words into meaningful chunks that can be decoded or figured out.

Look at the following examples to help you understand this concept. Remember that prefixes (*pre* = before) are placed before the root word and suffixes (*suf*- under) are placed after the root word.

atheist = *a-the-ist a* = (without), *theo* = (God), *ist* = (one who) = one who does not believe in God

incredible=*in-cred-i-ble*=in (not), *credibilis* (deserving of belief)=seems to be impossible or unbelievable

circumnavigation=*circum-navigate-ion*=*circum* (around), *navigate* (to travel), *ation* (state of)=the act of travelling around the world

ON 10R3.3 identify and use a variety of strategies to expand vocabulary

Personal Dictionaries

A personal dictionary is a list of words and phrases you encounter at school or on your own. If you keep the list words and their definitions in a coil notebook or binder, the list is flexible and can grow as you progress through high school and beyond. Any words that you think are important or you might like to use in your own writing are words that can go into the dictionary. Words your teacher emphasizes are also good words to record in your dictionary. A personal dictionary is great because it is individualized: words you may know well and use often do not need to be in the dictionary.

Occasionally you should flip through your list, especially when planning a piece of writing. Try using the words in your dictionary in your everyday speech. The more you use a word, the better you will remember it in the long term. Actually using the words and phrases will help to internalize some of the vocabulary.

Word quizzes and games, crossword puzzles, and game shows that test language knowledge are all useful and fun methods to increase your vocabulary.

Slang

Slang words are often used by a certain group of people, such as teenagers. Slang differs from jargon in the sense that slang is regarded as very casual language, whereas jargon is usually used by professionals to discuss something specific. Slang expressions tend to come and go. For example, in the 1950s, a "hot rod" referred to a powerful car, while today the term is used very rarely and may not be used to refer to a car.

Jargon

Jargon refers to a specialized set of words and phrases commonly understood by a group, such as members of a profession, hobby, or field of study. The following chart shows some examples of jargon words and how they can have different meanings depending on the subject area or discipline the word is being used for.

Jargon Word	Group	Meaning to Group
goal	teachers students hockey players government committee	curriculum outcome life or academic ambition score deadline to eliminate homelessness
trade	stockbrokers skilled workers hockey players 12-year-old boys	stock market activity occupation sent to another team exchange hockey cards
deal	bridge players business men advertisers	passing out cards closing an agreement bargain for consumers

For example, imagine going to the dentist. After examining your teeth and X-rays, she tells you that you have a "cavity on your 1-3." You most likely would not know what she is talking about. She is using jargon that is specific to dentists. Your dentist would have to say you have a "cavity on your top right canine tooth" so you would understand.

Jargon is common among different professions and can be confusing to someone who does not belong to the special group for whom the jargon has meaning.

English and Other Languages

English is a language of borrowed words. The majority of English words have been derived from Greek, Latin, or Anglo-Saxon. As the English language spread throughout the world by travel, trade, and settlement, many other cultures have contributed words to it.

Phrases

French, Latin, and Spanish phrases have become common in the English language. The following examples are used commonly in everyday speech:

French

à la carte: according to the menu, ordering individual items from the menu as opposed to complete dinners

bon voyage: have a good trip

c'est la vie: such is life

toute de suite: immediately

Latin

e pluribus unum: one from many

ad nauseum: to the point of disgust

mea culpa: my fault

status quo: the way things are

sub rosa: secret or confidential

Spanish

hasta la vista: see you later

mi casa es su casa: my house is your house

Multiple-Meaning Words

Words can have more than one meaning and can often have meanings that are quite different from each other. The word *break*, for instance, can be used multiple ways: break the glass, coffee break, "Give me a break," break some news, break the silence, etc.

Homographs or *multiple-meaning words* are words that share the same spelling but have different meanings. Sometimes the words are pronounced differently, but when you read them, you can determine their meaning from the context.

Examples

well (noun) – a hole drilled into the earth
well (adverb) – in good health

I was feeling *well* enough to help my father drill a new *well*.

sound (adjective) – untroubled, strong, secure, sensible, free from injury
sound (noun) – something heard as noise or musical tones
sound (verb) – to carefully find out someone's thoughts or feelings
sound (noun) – a narrow passage of water

I was awoken from a *sound* sleep by the *sound* of the distant drums from across Puget *Sound*.

These sentences demonstrate that you can usually figure out the meaning of a word that has more than one possible meaning when you see the word in context.

METACOGNITION

The word *metacognition* refers to thinking about how you think; this process includes thinking about how you learn. As you discover and think about strategies that work best with your individual learning style, you will become a more confident and productive learner. It is important to think about your learning and to ask yourself questions about how it works for you. Do you work better in groups or on your own? Do you memorize things visually? What kind of reading do you like to do best? The more time you spend analysing how you think, the better able you will be to pinpoint areas you excel at, as well as areas you have trouble with.

The following section of your *KEY* gives you many examples and guidelines on metacognition. The examples are designed to show how an individual student performs metacognition activities. Keep in mind that the way you think and learn is unique, so different methods may appeal to you more than others. Learning what appeals to you is also a part of metacognition.

ON 10R4.1 describe a variety of strategies they used before, during, and after reading; explain which ones they found most helpful; and identify detailed steps they can take to improve as readers.

Reading Metacognition Checklist

The following examples are of questions you can ask that use metacognition to examine your learning.

- What is the best way to approach this learning task?
- At this point, how well do I understand information, concepts, characters, etc.?
- How can I maintain my motivation to complete what I have started?
- Am I using the best tools for this learning task?

The checklist below shows different strategies you can use to get the most out of your reading. More importantly, it helps you think about how you approach various reading tasks. You could use this checklist several times during the school year to help you understand or change your approach.

Using the Checklist

Put check marks in the “Most Effective for Me” column next to each of five strategies that work best for you.

- Write a number beside each check mark showing how effective the strategy is for you (1 is most effective, 5 is least effective).
- Think of logical reasons for the order you have chosen.
- Discuss and compare your top five most effective strategies with a peer.
- Collaborate to identify the top five strategies from both of you and describe the best uses for each strategy.
- List five ways that you and your peer can become better readers.

READING METACOGNITION CHECKLIST

Thinking About My Reading Strategies	Most Effective for Me	Use Most Often	Use Sometimes	Should Try
Before Reading I *preview* (look over exams, texts, stories, articles, and assignments) to determine: • What is involved in this text? • What is my purpose for reading? • How should I approach this? • How should I read (speed, etc.)?				
I think about my *prior knowledge*—what I already know that might be relevant to the topic or task in front of me.				
I *visualize* or try to picture the characters, setting, what I hope to find out, etc.				
While Reading I *check back* to verify a definition, information about a character, etc.				
I use *vocabulary strategies* like context clues, root words, prefixes, and suffixes to understand unfamiliar words and phrases.				
I make point form notes or *graphic organizers* when I need to remember plots, key ideas, etc.				
I pause while reading and *predict* what I think will happen next in the story.				
I *tag text* with sticky notes or mark parts I find confusing so I can ask about it later.				
I use a *highlighter*—when I am allowed—to mark the text (notes, handouts, etc.) for key phrases and important ideas.				
I write *notes*, *questions*, and *comments* in margins if I am allowed. Sometimes, I use these later on to clarify information.				
I ask questions such as the following to *monitor my understanding* of what I read: • Does this make sense to me? • What exactly is the writer saying? • What is the narrator's point of view? • Do I agree? Why or why not?				

Thinking About My Reading Strategies	Most Effective for Me	Use Most Often	Use Sometimes	Should Try
When the text does not state something directly, I make *inferences* and draw *conclusions* from my reading.				
I deliberately use *skimming* and *scanning* skills when appropriate, such as to locate a specific answer or idea in the text.				
I *adjust my reading rate* as needed, slowing down for detailed information, etc.				
I *pay attention* to diagrams, pictures, charts, and graphs—anything that may help me make more sense of the text.				
After Reading I *summarize*, using notes or a graphic organizer.				
I write my thoughts, questions, and reactions in a *personal response journal*.				
I *share with a peer* in the following ways: • in written form, like a double response journal, in which we write back and forth • by discussing informally within a share-pair or small group • by explaining a newly-learned concept I try to *support my own opinions* and *show respect* for the opinions of others.				
I write *critical responses* to text when invited to do so. I try to include comments on the form, purpose, writer's viewpoint, historical context, mood, imagery, etc. When possible, I point out comparisons to other texts or draw from my personal experiences to deepen my response.				

Sample Applications of Metacognition

The following section shows you some strategies that involve metacognition. Journals, visual charts, and literature circles/book clubs are all great methods of making yourself more aware of how you read. Some of these may be more useful to you than others. Figuring out which methods work best for you will give you insight into your learning style.

Personal Response Journal

A personal response journal can be a great record of what you read. A journal can also be a good starting point to get ideas for homework assignments. A journal entry should include the date, title, and name of the work that you describe. The entry should express your connections with the text. How does the work connect to your experiences? How does it relate to your opinions?

The following example shows a poem and one student's personal response journal entry regarding that poem. The personal response describes that student's individual experience with the poem. To practice metacognition, try writing your own response to this poem.

Example

DRAGON NIGHT

Little flame mouths,
Cool your tongues.
Dreamtime starts,
My furnace-lungs.

Rest your wings now,
Little flappers,
Cave mouth calls
To dragon nappers.

Night is coming,
Bank your fire.
Time for dragons
To retire.

Hiss.
Hush.
Sleep.

—*by* Jane Yolen

Personal Response Journal Entry: "Dragon Night" by Jane Yolen

> February 27, 2008
>
> Although this poem seems to be written as a lullaby for baby dragons, it means something different and very personal to me. Of all the poems we studied in our September poetry unit, this is my absolute favourite. It brought back lots of memories of the summer, sitting with my family on the deck of our cottage at Muskoka Lake, relaxing and looking at the lake. As I read the poem, I thought of tiny flashes of light down by the lakeshore—fireflies flicking their mini-lanterns on and off. The poem has lots of summer/evening imagery. I felt quiet and relaxed by the end of the poem.

The great thing about journal entries is that you do not have to worry that you are being too casual with your language. Even though the entry may be casual and talk about your own life experience, the information about your opinions can be used to write something more formal later on. Keeping a journal about what you read is a great tool for keeping track of your learning.

Venn Diagrams and Other Visuals

A Venn diagram is useful for comparing and contrasting two different types of text. It can also help you compare and contrast the strategies you use to read them. Look at the following comparison of a poem and an advertisement, and think about the ways you would approach each of them as a reader.

Example

Venn Diagram: Poems vs. Advertisements

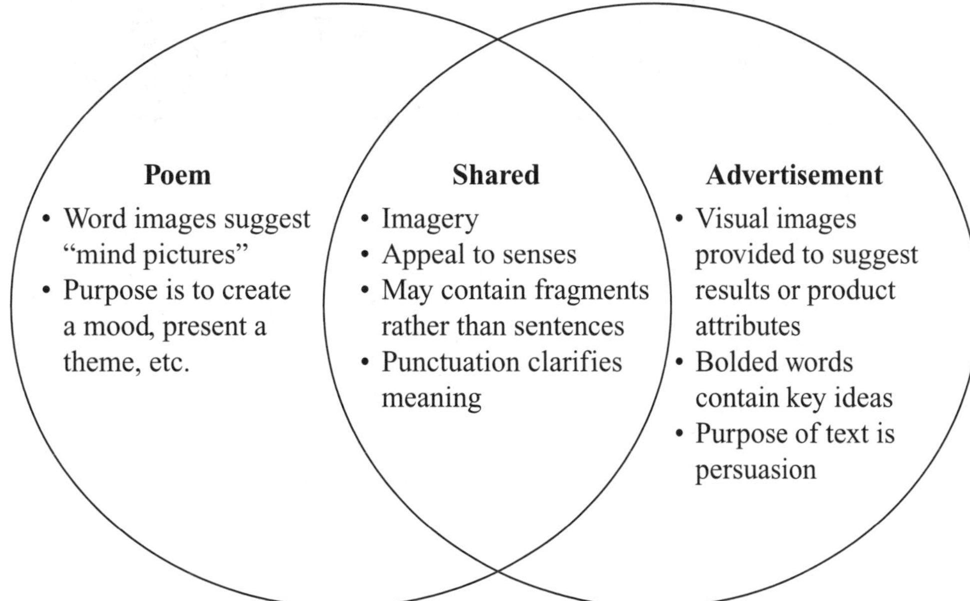

Poem
• Word images suggest "mind pictures"
• Purpose is to create a mood, present a theme, etc.
Shared
• Imagery
• Appeal to senses
• May contain fragments rather than sentences
• Punctuation clarifies meaning
Advertisement
• Visual images provided to suggest results or product attributes
• Bolded words contain key ideas
• Purpose of text is persuasion

One purpose of a poem is to create mind pictures. Slowing down to think about the meaning of the images that a poem creates is important. An advertisement, on the other hand, is meant to grab your attention and get its message across right away. It would be a disadvantage of an advertisement if it compelled you to slow down and think about its meaning. Advertisements tend to be as simple as possible to grab your attention.

Literature Circles and Book Clubs

A literature circle or a book club may help you better understand a novel. It can also be a fun way to talk with classmates about literature in a more casual way than in the classroom. Everyone interprets literary works a little differently. By talking to others freely about your impressions of a text, you can learn about different ways of looking at it. You also gain a better understanding of your own opinions by having to express them to others.

ON 10R4.2 identify a variety of their skills in listening, speaking, writing, viewing, and representing and explain how the skills helped them read

Skills That Aid Reading

Now that you are in Grade 10, you have developed a variety of communication skills that both help you as a reader and improve as you read more. As your reading improves, for example, your ability to state your opinions aloud also improves. Honing your skills in presenting ideas in different media, such as plays or poster art, can improve your skills in summarizing or understanding concepts as you read.

Communication Tools

Being able to communicate using one tool will boost your ability to communicate using another. The following examples show different communication tools and how using them will improve your reading overall.

Listening and Reading

When good readers read out loud, they use several tools to make their reading effective: clear articulation, appropriate tone and expression, pacing, rate of reading, and pauses. As you acquire these skills through listening, you can use them when you read out loud.

As you listen to peers in a small group setting, you can

- clarify things you missed or misunderstood
- hear a description of an experience that you might not have known or thought about
- discuss views and opinions arising from the same text, and learn to use text to support your own viewpoint
- consider the viewpoint of a peer, which could be just as well supported in the text as your own opinion

Speaking and Reading

As you share your insights and viewpoints from your reading, you will

- improve your reading comprehension
- learn to support your viewpoint using text statements and inferences
- improve your oral reading skills as you read aloud

In a pair or a small group, express your ideas from your reading. In a peer group there is no pressure to use precise or formal language. You can feel free to explain your ideas in a more casual setting. Discussion is used to shape your ideas, so they do not have to be perfectly formed at this time.

Writing and Reading

When you write a response to your reading, you can craft a thoughtful response that uses words you take time to decide upon. Written responses are also an efficient way for you to answer questions from a text and to reread parts of it—both strategies used by effective readers.

Viewing and Reading

Viewing material can enrich your reading experience by adding a visual component. When characterization, costumes, and settings in a film are true to the descriptions in a book that it is based on, the stories can come to life in a new way. Viewing a film version of a book may help you associate better with the characters in the book. Sometimes you might find that the film version is not how you imagined it as you read it. Perhaps the actors do not look the way you imagined the characters to look, or the setting is different than you pictured it. Sometimes readers become resentful if a movie does not seem true to a novel.

It is important to keep in mind that the film version of a novel is the interpretation of the people who made the film. One of the best things about reading is that you, in a sense, have the power to create the same visuals in your mind that a director does when making a movie. You direct the movement and appearance of a book in the same way that a director might. In order to better understand your interpretation of a novel, you could adapt portions of a story to a dramatic form. This will enhance your effectiveness as a reader as you review the story for accurate dialogue and consistent character portrayal.

Presenting Ideas Using Different Media

When you present ideas in a different medium, you can understand the ideas in a text better. After reading a book, taking ideas from it and addressing them in a play or on a poster can give you a better understanding of the book's focus and themes. Presenting a text in a new way can highlight aspects of a book's theme, mood, character qualities, or symbolism that you might not have thought about otherwise. For example, a poster or a collage could be used to show the dominant theme in a novel using nothing but pictures cut from magazines.

Applying Skills: Using Research in Projects

Research is a vital part of writing formal papers. Metacognition can be applied to your research in order to see where you can improve your researching techniques. In the following fictional account, two students were given a news article about a local issue and were asked to use research to clarify and extend their understanding of the article and the issues it presents. As you read about their assignment, try and think about how you might go about researching this issue if it were your own assignment. How might the techniques you would use be different from the ones used by the fictional students in this example?

The students were given two weeks to work on a project about current events. They were asked to identify an issue raised in a news article they were given, track the issue for two weeks, consider perspectives and possible outcomes, and afterwards, engage their classmates in the issue.

The article was about an airport safety issue arising from a recent crash landing at Pearson International Airport (Toronto) that could have resulted in a tragic loss of lives. According to the news item, an Air France jet carrying 309 passengers and crew had landed halfway down the runway during a summer rainstorm. Overshooting the 90-metre buffer zone at the end of the runway, the plane careened over a bank and finally came to a stop. Fortunately, before the damaged aircraft burst into flames, everyone on board was safely evacuated and removed from danger. The accident was caused by human error, but the issue arising from this incident involved passenger safety and accident prevention. After reading the information, the students felt that the runway buffer zone should be extended to 300 metres, the required length at most major European airports.

The students decided to use a kind of tracking log to record what they did to clarify or extend their understanding of this story and the issues it raised.

This is what they recorded over their two-week assignment:

Class Project: The Pearson Airport

1. We collected stories on the topic from the newspaper, television, and Internet for about two weeks. We ended up with a total of 21 news items.
2. We recorded facts or messages common to all of the stories, such as
   - the Pearson runway has a 90-metre buffer zone
   - the weather conditions were severe
   - the pilot landed halfway down the runway
   - incidents such as this happen more frequently than is commonly believed.
3. We looked for public reactions on the newspaper and television websites and on the editorial page of the newspaper. We recorded repeated responses, such as
   - safety is of major concern
   - the expense of extending the runway is worth possibly saving lives
   - Pearson airport should have the same standards as the rest of the world.
4. We watched for different opinions on the issue and found opinion articles from
   - the Airline Pilots' Association
   - the Ontario Department of Tourism
   - city and provincial governments (about who would bear the cost of the runway upgrade).
5. Based on all that we found, we tried to predict an outcome—the runway extension would be built over the next two years, funded by the province.
6. We watched to see if the issue was resolved in two weeks. It wasn't, but the matter was under review by a transportation committee.
7. We summarized our findings and prepared our class presentation.
8. After our presentation, we will allow a brief time for discussion on our issue. We will then ask Miss Fergusen to review business letter format and take us to the computer lab to write letters to the Transportation Safety Board of Canada, to be forwarded to the Honourable Lawrence Cannon, Minister of Transport, Ottawa. The purpose of the letters will be to request mandatory lengthened buffer zones for major Canadian Airport runways by 2010.

   Our Concluding Comments:

   Through reading, research, and discussion, we clarified and extended our understanding of an important and newsworthy safety issue. We came to have a strong personal interest in the outcome of this issue because, like most Canadians, we will use air travel throughout our lives. If a short-sighted decision is made, we ourselves could someday be victims.

Research is critical to writing non-fiction text. The more you learn about an issue, the better able you will be to form an opinion that is informed and balanced. Finding information that is accurate and does not have a bias can be difficult. As you become a better researcher, understanding information and how to find good information will become easier.

Use metacognition the next time you are researching for a project. Think about areas of research you may have missed and how you could effectively use the research you have found.

READING AND LITERATURE STUDIES—PRACTICE QUESTIONS

Read the following passage to answer questions 1 to 12.

A PURPLE WORLD

Waterton Lakes—When the sun sets behind these mountains you can almost see them begin to breathe. It's a trick of the light, really, something created by the encroaching purple darkness, distance, and an indefinable desire for magic.

The Old Ones believed that this was a strong spirit time. The grandfathers and grandmothers whose spirits reside within these trees, rocks, rivers and mountains would come alive again and around those ancient tribal fires their songs would be sung and the drums would echo the heartbeat of the universe to welcome them.

My *mishomi*s, Ojibway for grandfather, described this time and the mountains breathing as the universe giving a collective shrug. It was his way of saying that the earth is alive.

The earth is alive. It was ironic to be perched on a rock at the edge of a small, rushing river in the back country of southern Alberta's most beautiful park, while Environment Week (June 3–9, 1991) rolled into gear across the country. Here, amid the rough and tangle of pristine creation, the thought of as pecial week designed to focus attention on the earth as a living, breathing entity was an elegant redundancy.

In the Indian way of seeing, the land, and all things that move upon it, is alive and therefore sacred. Humankind's relationship to the earth and its life-forms has always been that of an equal. The honor of one is the honor of all. If you cared enough to consider the guardianship of yourself and your family, it followed that you care enough to consider the guardianship of the earth.

Here, in the gathering darkness, in the middle of what the whiteman so loosely terms *wilderness*, it was good to consider these things.

There was never a term for wilderness in native tongues. Wilderness is a European term that simply means something that can't be controlled. For the Indians there was never any need or desire to control, to fear or to abuse something which you were a part of. There was only a need, and a responsibility, to preserve it. So the destruction of forests, the damming of rivers, the depletion of resources and the extinction of animals has always been mystifying to the aboriginal peoples.

It all comes down to the idea of one heartbeat. A spiritual connectedness to those things that surround us and a realization that the reverse of the honor of one philosophy, logically, is the dishonor of all. This is spiritual, this is truth, this is Indian.

But the establishment of a spiritual connection to the earth isn't enough. It's a good foundation for an individual or a society, but the aboriginal peoples believed that a feeling could only become a belief and a principle if it were acted upon. So it was necessary for every tribal member to practise the idea of guardianship for all things.

Young people were taught the principles of respect and waste management virtually from the moment they could understand. Life was sacred and since all things were seen to be alive, respect meant taking and using only that which was necessary. If a life-form needed to be used, nothing was wasted. There were no landfills in pre-settlement North America.

Continued

It was good for me, an urban-based aboriginal person, to remember these things. Life in the city and existence in a cosmopolitan society has a sly way of taking you away from the philosophies and traditions of centuries. It's not long before the frantic sweep of modern living erases the recollections of the wisdom of the Old Ones.

So for me, sitting there watching the world become a purple place was a vital reconnection to the environmental foundations of my people's view of the world.

Walking along the parched bed of a mountain stream made it easy to imagine this place as it must have been two or three hundred years ago—untrammelled and free. These same rocks that have sat untouched for generations have their stories and it's becoming open enough to realize this and to listen for them that instigate the reconnection.

One week devoted to refocusing on environmental concerns isn't enough for anyone. Seven days to be reminded of the fact that the earth is a living, breathing entity won't halt the continued rape and plunder of finite resources; nor will it guarantee a collective mindset geared towards environmental protectionism. But it's a start.

What it takes is a walk upon the land. Learning to see these things that exist here with something other than your eyes. Leaving the material trappings behind awhile and allowing yourself to become a part of the sweep and grandeur of the planet; allowing your heartbeat to echo the universal heartbeat.

When you do that, you learn to see the mountains, begin to breathe in the falling darkness. You learn to accept the responsibility that comes with being a part of creation and you begin to understand, as the Old Ones understand, that the honor of one thing is the honor of all.

—*by* Richard Wagamese

1. Richard Wagamese's description of twilight is used **mainly** to create

A. personification that supports the main idea

B. imagery that characterizes unity of native people

C. a metaphor that reflects the writer's artistic sensitivity

D. alliteration that increases reader interest through sound

2. For the writer, it is important to be "Here, in the gathering darkness" because this experience

A. erases the tension of life in the city

B. reconnects him to his people's beliefs

C. causes him to think of the earth's lost resources

D. reminds him of the simple pleasures of walking upon the land

3. The tone of the statement, "This is spiritual, this is truth, this is Indian" is **best** described as one of

A. criticism

B. arrogance

C. confidence

D. sentimentality

4. As it is used in the phrase "existence in a cosmopolitan society has a sly way of taking you away," the word that is **closest** in meaning to "cosmopolitan" is

   A. vulgar

   B. foreign

   C. enlightened

   D. sophisticated

5. When the writer imagines the land as "untrammelled and free," the word "untrammelled" means

   A. picturesque

   B. unexplored

   C. unspoiled

   D. powerful

6. The quotation "But it's a start" **best** indicates that the writer's attitude is one of

   A. trust in the beliefs of the Old Ones

   B. disillusionment about the indifference of society

   C. depression about the loss of irreplaceable resources

   D. reconciliation to the difficulties of changing human behaviour

7. In the context of the entire essay, the phrase "material trappings" contrasts **most strongly** with the phrase

   A. "tribal fires"

   B. "collective shrug"

   C. "spiritual connection"

   D. "environmental concerns"

8. The Old Ones' belief that "the honor of one thing is the honor of all" **best** reflects the idea that

   A. all things are interconnected

   B. unity between peoples is essential

   C. wilderness is a complex concept in Native spirituality

   D. ancient messages are a source of wisdom and intelligence

9. In context, the words that **best** suggest an apparent contradiction in terms are

   A. "indefinable desire"

   B. "elegant redundancy"

   C. "cosmopolitan society"

   D. "environmental protectionism"

10. The writer's comments throughout the essay **best** characterize him as

A. honest and practical

B. perceptive and sincere

C. shrewd and aggressive

D. egotistical and sophisticated

11. The **main** purpose of this essay is to encourage people to

A. become aware of the principles of waste management

B. listen to the important spiritual lessons of the Old Ones

C. accept responsibility for being part of the natural world

D. understand nature as it was two to three hundred years ago

12. The theme of the essay is **best** embodied by the quotation

A. "Here, amid the rough and tangle of pristine creation"

B. "It all comes down to the idea of one heartbeat"

C. "These same rocks that have sat untouched for generations have their stories"

D. "What it takes is a walk upon the land"

Read the following passage to answer questions 13 to 27.

CIRCUS IN TOWN

It was Jenny's first circus. A girl in purple tights, erect on a galloping horse, a redcoated brass band, a clown, an elephant ripped through the middle. "And did you see the elephant?" she asked her brother Tom, who had found the piece of poster in the street when he was in town marketing the butter and eggs. "Was it really there? And the clown?"

But the ecstatic, eleven-year-old quiver in her voice, and the way she pirouetted[1] on her bare toes as he led the horse out of the buggy shafts, made him feel that perhaps in picking up the poster he had been unworthy of his own seventeen years; so with an offhand shrug he drawled, "I could see the tents and things but I didn't bother going over. Good shows never stop off at the little towns." And then, in a softer voice, as if suddenly touched by her white eagerness, "Everybody said it wouldn't amount to much. A few ponies and an elephant or two—but what's an elephant?"

She wheeled from him, resenting his attempt to scoff away such wonders. The bit of poster had spun a new world before her, excited her, given wild, soaring impetus to her imagination; and now, without in the least understanding herself, she wanted the excitement and the soaring, even though it might stab and rack her, rather than the barren satisfaction of believing that in life there was nothing better, nothing more vivid or dramatic, than her own stableyard.

Continued

[1] pirouetted—twirled

It was supper-time, her father just in from the field and turning the horses loose at the water-trough, so off she sped to greet him, her bare legs flashing and quick like the pink spokes of a wagon wheel, her throat too tight to cry out, passionate to communicate her excitement, to find response.

But the skittish old roan Billie took fright at the fluttering poster, and her father shouted for her to watch what she was doing and keep away from the horses. For a minute she stood quite still, cold, impaled by the rebuff; then again she wheeled, and this time, as swiftly as before, ran to the house. A wave of dark heat, hotter than the summer heat, struck her at the door. "Look—" "she pierced it shrilly—what Tom brought me—a circus," and with the poster outstretched she sprang to the stove where her mother was frying pork and eggs and potatoes.

There was no rebuff this time. Instead, an incredible kind of pity—pity of all things on a day like this. "Never mind, Jenny." A hot hand gentle on her cheek a minute. "Your day's going to come. You won't spend all your life among chickens and cows or I'm not the woman I think I am!" And then, bewilderingly, an angry clatter of stove-lids that made her shrink away dismayed, in sudden dread of her father's coming and the storm that was to break.

Not a word until he had washed and was sitting down at the table. Then as the platters were clumped in front of him he asked, "What's wrong?" and for answer her mother hurled back, "Wrong? You—and the farm—and the debts—that's what's wrong. There's a circus in town, but do we go? Do we ever go anywhere? Other children have things, and see things, and enjoy themselves, but look, look at it! That's how much of the circus *my* girl gets!"

Jenny dared to be a little indignant at the scornful way her mother pointed to the piece of poster that furtively she had hung over one of the kitchen calendars while waiting for her father. A beautiful poster—a band and half an elephant—and she felt exasperated and guilty that there should be a quarrel about it, her father looking so frightened and foolish, her mother so savage and red.

But even had she been bold enough to attempt an explanation it would have been lost in the din of their voices. Her mother shouted about working her fingers to the bone and nothing for it but skimping and debts. She didn't mind for herself but she wanted Jenny to have a chance. "Look at her clothes and her bare feet! Your own daughter! Why don't you take hold—do something? Nothing ahead of her but chickens and cows! Another ten years—can't you just see the big, gawky know-nothing she's going to be?"

Jenny gulped, startled. Ten years from now it was a quite different kind of young lady she intended to be. For a moment there was a sick little ball of consternation down near her midriff, a clammy fear her mother might be right—and then she was furious. So furious that for the next minute or two the quarrel passed over her. She wasn't gawky and she wasn't know-nothing. She was farther on in school than any other girl her age. She could do fractions and percentages and draw the map of North America with her eyes shut. Her mother to talk, who only last Sunday when she was writing a letter had to ask how to spell "necessary"!

But suddenly the din between her mother and father split apart, and it was Tom speaking. Tom unruffled and magisterial, rising to his seventeen years and the incumbency of maintaining adult dignity at their table. "Can't you hold on and let us eat in peace? We've heard all that before. Jenny and I are hungry."

Jenny shivered, it was so fine and brave of Tom, but there was a long, terrible minute while she watched her father's face to see what was going to happen. Two or three years ago, she remembered, for just such bravery, Tom had been sent reeling through the door with a welt across his face.

Continued

But today, instead of the oath and whack of knuckles, there was Tom's voice again, steady and quiet, a little scornful. "Come on, Jenny, you're not eating anyway. We'll go out and leave them to it."

It was dangerous, she thought swiftly—taking sides was always dangerous, parents weren't to be flouted—but she couldn't help herself. Her pride in Tom was uncontrollable, mastering her discretion. Eyes down, bare feet padding quick and silent, she followed him.

They walked gravely across the yard and sat down on the edge of the water-trough, as if their destination had been agreed upon before they started. "It's too bad all right you couldn't go to the circus," Tom consoled her, "but everybody said it wouldn't be worth the money. And maybe some Saturday night before long you can come to town with me."

She glanced up puzzled, impatient. Pity again! If only they would just keep quiet and leave her alone—join her, if they liked, to see the circus.

That was all, for she wasn't wishing yet. It was too soon. There was a sudden dilation of life within her, of the world around her—an elephant, a brass band in red coats, half a poster blown from a billboard—and to recapture the moment of its impingement against her was all she wanted, to scale the glamour and wonder of it, slowly, exquisitely, to feel herself unfurl.

"There's Dad now, starting for the barn," Tom nudged her. "Better go and finish your supper. I don't want any more." Neither did she, but to escape him she went. Uneasily, apprehensive that when she was alone with her mother there might be a reckoning for her having taken sides with Tom. And she was afraid of her mother tonight. Afraid because all at once she felt defenceless, perishable. This sudden dilation of life—it was like a bubble blown vast and fragile. In time it might subside, slowly, safely, or it might even remain full-blown, gradually strengthening itself, gradually building up the filmy tissues to make its vastness durable, but tonight she was afraid. Afraid that before the hack of her mother's voice it might burst and crumple.

So when she found the kitchen deserted, her mother down cellar putting food away, there was a cool, isolated moment of relief, and then a furtive[2] poise, an alert, blind instinct for survival and escape. She glided across the kitchen, took down the poster from where it still hung over the calendar, and fled with it to the barn.

There was a side door, and near it a ladder to the loft. No one saw her. She lay limp in the hay, listening to her heart-beat subside, letting the little core of pain in her breast that had come from running slip away through her senses, like the cool grains of wheat that sometimes she sat in the granary trickling through her fingers. It was a big, solemn loft, with gloom and fragrance and sparrows chattering against its vault of silence like boys flinging pebbles at a wall. And there, in its dim, high stillness, she had her circus. Not the kind that would stop off at a little town. Not just a tent and an elephant or two. No—for this was her own circus; the splendid, matchless circus of a little girl who had never seen one.

"You'll catch it," Tom said when he found her, "hiding up here instead of helping with the dishes."

Catch it she did, but for once the threats of what would happen next time failed to touch her. The circus went on. All night long she wore her purple tights and went riding Billie round and round the pasture in them. A young, fleet-footed Billie. Caparisoned in blue and gold and scarlet, silver bells on reins and bridle—neck arched proudly to the music of the band.

—*by* Sinclair Ross

---

[2] furtive—stealthy, secretive

13. For Jenny, the circus **most likely** represents an

A. opportunity to succeed

B. escape from the arguments she hears

C. enchantment that is missing from her life

D. experience that she can share with her brother

14. Bringing Jenny the torn circus poster **most likely** reveals Tom's

A. curiosity

B. tolerance

C. condescension

D. thoughtfulness

15. The word closest in meaning to *ecstatic* is

A. hysterical

B. anxious

C. thrilled

D. happy

16. When Tom wonders if he "had been unworthy of his own seventeen years" after giving Jenny the circus poster, it **most strongly** suggests that he is

A. questioning his own judgement

B. envious of Jenny's enthusiasm

C. shocked by Jenny's reaction

D. reluctant to admit his defeat

17. Jenny's mood, described by the phrase "white eagerness," is **most effectively** contrasted with the phrase

A. "soaring impetus,"

B. "sudden dilation"

C. "filmy tissues"

D. "furtive poise"

18. In this context, the phrase "even though it might stab and rack her" **most strongly** reveals Jenny's acceptance of

A. pain as a partner to joy

B. work as a part of reality

C. danger as an aspect of caution

D. dissatisfaction as a result of resentment

19. Jenny contrasts the world represented by the circus with the world of

A. the town

B. the pasture

C. her classroom

D. her stableyard

20. When Jenny's parents argue, Jenny becomes angry with her mother because her

A. brother is forced to criticize both of her parents

B. mother causes Jenny to question her image of herself

C. father is made to feel guilty about the family's poverty

D. parents appear to care more about their problems than for Jenny and her brother

21. The mother's argument with the father **most clearly** reveals that she is feeling

A. critical of their children

B. despair about their children

C. desperate for companionship

D. frustrated with doing her husband's chores

22. Tom's maturity is revealed **most clearly** when he

A. scolds Jenny in the hayloft

B. speaks up at the supper table

C. consoles Jenny at the water trough

D. downplays the appeal of the circus

23. When Tom tries to console Jenny, the reason she responds to Tom with impatience is that she wants to

A. escape her family

B. be cherished and respected

C. see the wonders of the circus

D. savour the excitement she is feeling

24. Which of the following quotations **best** reveals the meaning of the phrase "dilation of life"?

A. "The bit of poster had spun a new world before her, excited her, given wild, soaring impetus to her imagination"

B. "A wave of dark heat, hotter than the summer heat, struck her at the door"

C. "But even had she been bold enough to attempt an explanation it would have been lost in the din of their voices"

D. "She could do fractions and percentages and draw the map of North America with her eyes shut"

25. In this context, the meaning of the phrase "impingement against" is **closest** in meaning to the phrase

A. impact upon

B. temptation of

C. imprinting on

D. confrontation with

26. The simile "like a bubble blown vast and fragile" **most strongly** suggests that Jenny's dream is

A. unlimited

B. delicate

C. foolish

D. elusive

27. Which of the following quotations **best** conveys Tom's influence in Jenny's world?

A. " 'Look—' she pierced it shrilly—'what Tom brought me—a circus' "

B. "Jenny shivered, it was so fine and brave of Tom, but there was a long, terrible minute"

C. "Her pride in Tom was uncontrollable, mastering her discretion"

D. " 'You'll catch it,' Tom said when he found her, 'hiding up here instead of helping with the dishes' "

Read the following passage to answer questions 28 to 35.

OF FROGS AND FAIRY GODMOTHERS

When the warm breath of April moves across our ponds, the first frogs begin to stir, poking small snouts out of the mud, sleepily swimming to a bank, and lying there to soak up the sun, which will soon regenerate them, send their blood surging on its way, and inspire them to lift their voices in the songs that we hear on warm evenings: the long-drawn notes of the toads like the bowing of a cello, the bright chirping of spring peepers, the deep, resonant bass of green frogs, all the more marvelous because this is perhaps the most ancient music in the world, changed little if at all from the music of amphibians who were singing long before the first bird flew, or the first dinosaur went sniffing among the tree ferns in the age of reptiles.

We are lucky to have toads and frogs and newts and salamanders in our part of the world, our small sanctuary in Nova Scotia, on the shore of the Bay of Fundy. So far we have escaped the apocalypse that has overtaken the amphibians in so many places where they were once plentiful. Whatever it is that is killing off the world's frogs has not reached us yet, or anyway not at lethal levels.

Continued

Lambs Lake on South Mountain, where we sometimes swim in summer, has a population of bullfrogs as well as green frogs and leopard frogs. Sometimes you can see myriads of their great, fat tadpoles in rocky pools near the shore. My daughter Leah, watching their activity, thought she might transfer a few of them to our ponds, where they might grow and breed and add their voices to the frog chorus. We had done this earlier with the tiny tadpoles of the spring peepers. But after thinking it over, I suggested leaving them where they were. I doubt that bullfrogs would be content to stay in ponds as small as ours. Likely, on reaching maturity, they'd take off, searching for broader waters. Besides this, if they reached adulthood in our ponds, they'd likely eat the smaller frogs, and newts, and perhaps some of the small snakes as well. I think something like this happened when Leah brought home a semi-wild Muscovy drake caught in a nearby tidal creek. After this voracious bird had spent a few months in our largest pond, there wasn't a tadpole in sight, and newts, too, seemed very scarce. Fortunately we had other ponds where small amphibians could flourish undisturbed by ducks.

The emergence of the frogs, a cardinal event of spring, seems always to have fascinated people. In ancient times peasants saw them rising from the mud of the river Nile, and supposed they were not just walking from sleep, but being created anew, that the mud, in fact, was giving birth to them—an idea that now strikes us as absurd. It is not a long time, however, since people believed that rotting meat could generate flies, that a rotting fish might turn into maggots, or even that the carcass of a lion might produce a swarm of honeybees. "Spontaneous generation" was accepted as a fact until Louis Pasteur, in a long series of experiments, disproved it in the 1860s, some ten years after Wallace and Darwin had published their theory of evolution.

Frogs belong to an ancient branch of the animal kingdom, direct descendants of the fishes. Originally, amphibians had scales, but all modern ones have lost their scales, just as elephants, whales, manatees, and humans have lost their fur. They seem to be vulnerable little animals, soft-bodied, not very fast, eagerly gobbled up by snakes, herons, and ducks, and even by some house cats. Being egg layers, they can reproduce rapidly if nothing stops them, but that's just where they are now most vulnerable. Their eggs can be destroyed by polluted water, by acid rain, or by excessive doses of ultraviolet B pouring down from a sky drastically altered by human insanity.

Frogs look rather humanlike. When they swim they seem to be doing the breast stroke. They are rather neckless and broad-bodied, but they have hips, knees, ankles, five toes on each foot, and legs as graceful as any dancer's. It is remarkable how this body type has persisted, though frogs and humans are separated by some quarter of a billion years of evolution. Insects, meanwhile, have adopted shapes as fanciful as anything we might imagine on the planets of Alpha Centauri, birds have turned themselves into flying flowers, and dolphins have become imitation fish. Humans and frogs look much the way they did when they first began to climb and hop. Like us, frogs have survived the great natural disasters that have visited the world time and again in the past quarter of a billion years, disasters that caused most earthly creatures to become extinct. Now, in the midst of what may be another great extinction, they may be facing their greatest crisis. But then, we may be, too.

Even in other parts of the Atlantic Provinces frogs seem to be in great trouble. They all but disappeared from Newfoundland, for example, and none of the field biologists there seemed to have an explanation. Their near extinction was not a "natural population fluctuation" as some people at first suggested. The green frog used to be a very common animal on the Avalon and Bonavista Peninsulas. Then they were gone—not completely, but almost. The cause in Newfoundland was not destruction of habitat, because there has been little habitat destruction there in recent decades. Surface pollution had reduced populations in many places, and might have been a factor in a few Newfoundland waterways, but certainly not in most, and certainly not in Labrador, where frogs have also been dying out.

Continued

Acid rain? Disease? Weakened immune systems? None of it seemed to be a satisfactory explanation.

Ultraviolet radiation (especially ultraviolet B, the part of the spectrum most directly linked to skin cancer) kills the eggs of some species of amphibians. The Arctic ozone hole is therefore suspected of being the chief culprit in the disappearance of frogs from the northernmost parts of their range. This is certainly the cause in high mountain lakes near the Pacific coast, where pollution of air and water is not a problem, but where the ultraviolet level has always been high, and is now critically high because of ozone depletion. Field biologists studying mountain frogs in the far west discovered that species laying eggs in areas open to the sky were declined because few of their eggs were hatching. Those laying eggs in the shade cast by vegetation or overhanging banks were doing much better.

It is tempting to look for a single, simple cause of a universal phenomenon like the die-off of the small amphibians, but often the causes are multiple and complex, rather than single or simple. In Nova Scotia we cannot blame the decline of the frogs solely on elevated levels of ultraviolet, because the decline is most apparent on the eastern side of the province, the Atlantic slope, where ultraviolet levels are no more elevated than in central and western regions. What else may be killing them off? We cannot be sure, but the most likely culprit is acid rain, which affects lakes and rivers draining into the Atlantic much more severely than those draining into the Bay of Fundy. The nearly worldwide population crash of small amphibians may well be an indicator of what lies in store for bigger and harder creatures such as ourselves if we continue throwing wastes and poisons into the air and water, for though not all the data are complete, we know that ozone depletion, putrefaction of lakes and rivers, acid rain, and sewage pollution are all symptoms of a single problem—massive destruction caused by human irresponsibility and corporate decisions that profits are more important than lives—whether we're talking about the lives of frogs, newts, salamanders, or people.

Here on the shore of Annapolis Basin the merchants of death have not yet triumphed. The chorus of spring pepper, the cello notes of the toads, the percussion of the green frogs, the *basso profundo* of the bullfrogs combine to lift up our hearts, to give us hope and reassurance that life is still fighting the good fight, hope that in the end it might triumph over corporate greed and the global market.

Just as we do not believe, today, that frogs emerge from mud without having burrowed into it first, so we believe that no living thing is a creation of the non-living world. *Ex nihilo nihil fit*, to quote an axiom ascribed to Lucretius. Not only did we discard the idea that living things might emerge from non-living matter, but also the idea that the universe was created *ex nihilo*, out of nothing, as theologians had insisted.

But now cosmologists have revived the idea of such creation, with the added refinement that god is removed from the picture. The universe is said to have created itself *ex nihilo*. A "quantum fluctuation," we are told, might have inflated itself by means of a Lagrangian mathematical formula until it became a hundred billion trillion stars. Where the Lagrangian formula came from is another question. And in any case, as Huck Finn said, anybody who could believe that would suck eggs. It is an explanation in exactly the same class as a fairy godmother waving her wand. Except, of course, that there's no fairy godmother. Just a self-created wand. Take your choice: god, magic, or a Lagrangian.

Continued

No one has asked the frogs' opinion, but if you pay attention to them, they have words of wisdom for you just the same. We on this planet are "all in the same boat" and not nearly so all-fired smart as we thought we were back in the cocky days of the 1950s, before the world had so obviously started to fall apart. As I've mentioned, some people suspect that we may be in the midst of another great extinction, like the one that killed off the dinosaurs, this time not caused by comet, meteorite, drifting continents, or massive volcanic eruptions, but by the arrival of an animal with too much technical cleverness and not nearly enough intelligence to go with it.

—*by* Harold Horwood

28. The first paragraph of the essay describes the frogs'

A. habitat

B. summer rituals

C. search for food

D. awakening from hibernation

29. The writer's emphasis on the sounds the frogs make as they wake up in the spring has the effect of

A. getting the reader to hear them more closely

B. reinforcing his main point about the value of the frogs

C. helping the reader to appreciate their complexity and diversity

D. shifting the reader's focus from how unpleasant many of them look

30. In the phrase "the apocalypse that has overtaken the amphibians," the word "apocalypse" emphasizes the idea that

A. frogs are in their last days

B. protection could save the frogs

C. weapons are devastating the frogs

D. whole populations of frogs have been wiped out

31. The phrase "the warm breath of April" contains an example of

A. personification

B. symbolism

C. imagery

D. simile

32. The reason the writer decides against introducing the tadpoles of the large frogs into his pond is **best** expressed through which of the following principles of nature?

A. The ones that eat the most survive

B. There's no place like home

C. Pond life can be cruel

D. Survival of the fittest

33. The fourth paragraph, which begins by describing the "emergence of the frogs," focuses on

A. faulty science

B. the frogs of the Nile

C. a bullfrog's appetite

D. revelations about "spontaneous generation"

34. The writer states that frogs are rendered **most vulnerable** as a result of the fact that they

A. lay eggs

B. have a slow gait

C. have soft bodies

D. swim in unusual patterns

35. The **most notable** of the similarities the writer describes as existing between frogs and humans is that both species have

A. a love of singing

B. the potential for extinction

C. a similar way of swimming

D. the ability to impact their environments negatively

Read the following passage to answer questions 36 to 43.

THE JOY OF FAMILY VACATIONS

When most people look back on their childhood years, somewhere tucked away in the dusty files of their brains, they find the memory of a family vacation. On the outside, this cherished moment in time seems to be one of the greatest adventures of childhood, but when people take a second look at the event, they see a completely different picture.

Let us first take a jaunt down memory lane, to relive the day when the initial family vacation announcement occurs. The parents have their children seat themselves in the living room and then proclaim, "We have some exciting news for you!"

The children's eyes light up as they excitedly ask, "What, what is it?"

Finally, the suspense is broken, and the parents' reply with big, happy smiles on their faces, "We're driving out to Vancouver to spend our summer vacation!" The kids naturally all jump for joy and squeal with excitement.

Does it seem like forever until the day of departure? Each day, the children get out their calendars and place a big "X" on the date that has just gone by. The countdown begins, and the tension level of the household creeps up and up. The parents bicker over whether the playpen will fit into the trunk of the car and discuss whether the youngest son still needs to bring along his portable potty. Sooner or later frustration sets in and one adult shouts, "I'm not going. You can take the kids and go by yourself!" In the end, the adults cool down, the car is packed, the pets are bid farewell, the over-burdened vehicle is started, and the family vacation begins.

Continued

In the first fifteen minutes of the travelling holiday, one child asks, "Are we there yet?" while a second individual announces, "I have to go to the bathroom." At first the parents reply with voices that are kind and understanding, but patience runs out after about two to three hours, and soon the replies become, "Sit back in your seats and be quiet! Leave your sister alone!" When things really get to the adults, they put a technique called selective hearing into practice. They apparently cannot hear anything that the children are saying as though there is an invisible glass wall separating the back seat from the front seat of the car.

Many hours later, everyone but the driver is asleep, the destination is finally reached—the relatives' house. Somehow, no matter how accommodating relatives are, they seem to tire of their new house guests rather rapidly. Most of the vacation is thus spent without the relatives—visiting the ocean, the mountains, the zoo, the aquarium, and walking to fast food restaurants.

Unfortunately for the children, all good things must come to an end, and it is soon time to return home. Good-byes are said, the little ones shed tears, and pretty soon the family is on the road again. Two hours later, the youngest child plaintively asks, "Where's my night-night?" Both adults look at each other, and panic fills their faces. The car is pulled over, and a frantic search for the child's blanket begins. Since it is not in the car, it must be back at the relatives' home. The family returns to Vancouver; the blanket is retrieved, and the little group once again begins its homeward journey.

After many trials, the family returns to their own home and the parents promise themselves never to attempt another vacation together. But time heals all wounds, and as the next summer rolls around, another family vacation becomes a reality.

—*by* Natalie Cooper

36. The **main** purpose of the first sentence of the passage is to

A. create a factual and realistic tone

B. develop the narrative by revealing a vital fact

C. promote understanding through characterization

D. introduce a familiar topic by using a generalization

37. The single sentence of paragraph 3 serves **mainly** to

A. create an informal tone

B. provide an example of dialogue

C. emphasize the children's suspense

D. contrast the parents with the children

38. An error in punctuation that needs to be corrected is evident in the quotation

A. "we have some exciting news for you"

B. "finally, the suspense is broken"

C. "the parents' reply with big, happy smiles"

D. "we're driving out to Vancouver"

39. The **main** effect of paragraph 5 is to

A. indicate the parents' confusion regarding trip preparations

B. convey the writer's desire to remain at home with the pets

C. illustrate the parents' commitment to the family's vacation

D. reveal the writer's humorous understanding of family stress

40. The **main** purpose of paragraph 6 is to

A. describe the setting

B. develop the humour

C. create balanced sentence structure

D. demonstrate grammatical effectiveness

41. Which of the following revisions will correct the punctuation error in the first sentence in paragraph 7?

A. Many hours later, everyone but the driver is asleep; the destination is finally reached—the relatives' house.

B. Many hours later everyone, but the driver is asleep, the destination is finally reached—the relatives' house.

C. Many hours later everyone but the driver is asleep the destination is finally reached—the relatives' house.

D. Many hours later everyone, but the driver, is asleep, the destination is finally reached—the relatives' house.

42. The writer organizes her composition by using

A. spatial order

B. contrast of ideas

C. chronological order

D. degree of importance

43. Which of the following quotations **best** indicates the writer's awareness of her audience?

A. "Does it seem like forever until the day of departure?"

B. "When things really get to the adults, they put a technique called selective hearing into practice"

C. "Unfortunately for the children, all good things must come to an end"

D. "After many trials, the family returns to their own home"

Read the following passage to answer questions 44 to 58.

ONE MAN'S CEILING IS ANOTHER MAN'S FLOOR

There's been some hard feelings here
About some words that were said
There's been some hard feelings here
And what is more
There's been a bloody purple nose
And some bloody purple clothes
That were messing up the lobby floor
It's just apartment house rules
So all you 'partment fools
Remember: one man's ceiling
is another man's floor
Remember: one man's ceiling
is another man's floor

There's been some strange goin's on
And some folks have come and gone
And the elevator man don't work no more
I heard a racket in the hall
And I thought I heard a fall
But I never opened up my door
It's just apartment house sense
It's like apartment rents
Remember: one man's ceiling
is another man's floor
Remember: one man's ceiling
is another man's floor

And there's an alley
in the back of my building
Where some people congregate in shame
I was walking with my dog
And the night was black with smog
When I thought I heard somebody
Call my name

—*by* Paul Simon

44. The "apartment house" is a metaphor for

A. the world

B. slum housing

C. desperate poverty

D. a competitive business

45. The admonition “One man’s ceiling is another man’s floor” could be interpreted as meaning that

A. everyone has their own perspective

B. tenants should respect the rights of other tenants

C. for every person who is successful, another fails

D. human beings live too closely crowded in large cities

46. In the second verse, the speaker discusses how he

A. misses the former residents of the apartment house

B. does not want to get involved in the violence that he hears

C. wants to act as a witness for the events that transpired in the hall

D. believes that the residents of the apartment house deserve their privacy

47. The phrase “apartment house sense” refers to the act of

A. fighting in the lobby

B. paying the rent on time

C. minding one’s own business

D. watching through the peephole in the door

48. The **most likely** reason the “elevator man don’t work no more” is that

A. he does not want to work in a dangerous environment

B. he was fired for giving someone a bloody nose

C. he messed up the lobby floor

D. the elevator is broken

49. A recurring theme in this poem is

A. the struggle against drug addiction

B. the tribulations of urban life

C. violence against women

D. unemployment

50. The poem **most clearly** criticizes society’s

A. unwillingness to take responsibility for others

B. refusal to deal with poor living conditions

C. inability to mediate in racial conflicts

D. tendency to migrate to urban centres

51. The last two lines in the poem illustrate the speaker's

A. alertness

B. paranoia

C. frustration

D. antagonism

52. The phrase "It's just apartment house sense / It's like apartment rents" refers to

A. unreasonable rent increases

B. guidelines for survival in the inner city

C. a rental contract between landlord and tenant

D. rules that apply to anyone who does not own their own home

53. Evidence in the poem suggests the speaker is **probably**

A. the owner of the building

B. a tenant in the apartment

C. a visitor to the building

D. the apartment manager

54. The expression "One man's ceiling is another man's floor" can **best** be described as

A. a proverb

B. a limerick

C. an anecdote

D. an admonition

55. Where in a large city is the speaker's apartment building **probably** situated?

A. On a busy downtown street

B. In the industrial area

C. In a poorer quarter

D. On the outskirts

56. The people in the alley **most likely** "congregate in shame" because they

A. have many things in common

B. are engaged in illicit activities

C. have little hope for a good life

D. are unhappy inside the apartment

57. The phrase “going’s on” can **best** be defined as

A. incidents

B. accidents

C. problems

D. breakdowns

58. The statement “There’s been some hard feelings here” **most likely** means that people living in the apartment are

A. angry

B. intolerant

C. having difficulty

D. expressing their emotions

READING AND LITERATURE STUDIES—UNIT TEST

Read the following passage to answer questions 1 to 7.

YOU HAD TWO GIRLS

You had two girls—Baptiste—
One is Virginie—
Hold hard—Baptiste!
Listen to me.

The whole drive was jammed
In that bend at the Cedars,
The rapids were dammed
With the logs tight rammed
And crammed; you might know
The Devil had clinched them below.

We worked three days—not a budge,
"She's as tight as a wedge, on the ledge,"
Says our foreman;
"Mon Dieu! boys, look here,
We must get this thing clear."
He cursed at the men
And we went for it then;
With our cant-dogs[1] arow,[2]
We just gave he-yo-ho;
When she gave a big shove
From above.

The gang yelled and tore
For the shore,
The logs gave a grind
Like a wolf's jaws behind,
And as quick as a flash,
With a shove and a crash,
They were down in a mash,
But I and ten more,
All but Isaàc Dufour,
Were ashore.

Continued

[1] *cant dogs*—or cant hooks; short, heavy poles with a spike and a swiveling hook at one end; used to twist a log
[2] *arow*—in a row; a line of men with cant dogs are twisting the logs to free them and loosen the jam

He leaped on a log in the front of the rush,
And shot out from the bind
While the jam roared behind;
As he floated along
He balanced his pole
And tossed us a song.
But just as we cheered,
Up darted a log from the bottom,
Leaped thirty feet square and fair,
And came down on his own.

He went up like a block
With the shock,
And when he was there
In the air,
Kissed his hand
To the land;
When he dropped
My heart stopped,
For the first logs had caught him
And crushed him;
When he rose in his place
There was blood on his face.

There were some girls, Baptiste,
Picking berries on the hillside,
Where the river curls, Baptiste,
You know—on the still side
One was down by the water,
She saw Isaàc
Fall back.

She did not scream, Baptiste,
She launched her canoe;
It did seem, Baptiste,
That she wanted to die too,
For before you could think
The birch cracked like a shell
In that rush of hell,
And I saw them both sink—

Baptiste!—
He had two girls,
One is Virginie,
What God calls the other
Is not known to me.

—*by* Duncan Campbell Scott

1. Which of the following statements **best** describes what happens in the poem?
   A. Loggers led a dangerous life.
   B. A man and a woman drown on the river.
   C. The speaker addresses someone named "Baptiste."
   D. A logjam becomes unstuck, but kills a logger and a woman.

2. The repetition of sounds in the words "jammed," "dammed," "rammed," and "crammed," (verse 2) emphasizes
   A. the speaker's frustration at not getting the logs free for three days
   B. the sound the logs were making on the river
   C. how tightly the logs were stuck on the river
   D. the internal rhyme

3. The speaker states that as Isaàc Dufour "floated along" he "tossed us a song." The lightness of the verb "tossed" together with the simple rhyme of "along" with "song" contrast with the
   A. horrible sound of the logs grinding behind him
   B. tragedy of his drowning an instant later
   C. silence of the woman in the canoe
   D. cheers of the men on the shore

4. Which of the following words **best** describes the girl?
   A. Hysterical
   B. Careless
   C. Afraid
   D. Brave

5. That the girl's birch canoe "cracked like a shell" implies
   A. the ease with which shells tend to crack
   B. the ease with which the powerful logs snapped her canoe
   C. that the girl should not have followed Dufour into the water
   D. that the girl did not know how to paddle in those conditions

6. Who is the narrator of the poem?
   A. One of the loggers
   B. Isaàc Dufour
   C. The father
   D. Virginie

7. The **most likely** reason the speaker does not name the second girl is that she
   - **A.** is the one who drowned
   - **B.** did not even know how to swim
   - **C.** was the braver of the two sisters
   - **D.** never told him her name before she went out in her canoe

Read the following passage to answer questions 8 to 11.

SCHOOLS USE DAILY GYM CLASS IN BATTLE WITH CHILD OBESITY

Schools across the country are fighting the epidemic of childhood obesity by scheduling a daily gym class, even if it means doing exercises in a regular classroom.

No longer willing to wait for direction from provincial education ministries, a handful of school administrators have found time in their packed curriculums for an organized period of running, skipping or playing ball five days a week.

Fewer than 200 schools across the country have accomplished the scheduling feat, but the national physical education association that keeps track says it has already received 1,000 applications for its 2004 Quality Daily Physical Education awards.

It took teachers at Wilson Middle School in Lethbridge, Alta., 30 tries before they came up with a daily schedule that includes one period of gym for each of their 600 students in Grades 6, 7 and 8.

5 One day a week the school has four phys. ed. classes going at the same time — two in the gym, one on the school stage and another in a smaller fitness room.

"We had to do something," says Rod Dueck, the assistant vice-principal and part-time gym teacher. "They go home and sit on the couch and play Xbox and snack on chips. It's an epidemic."

Last year, Statistics Canada reported that 37% of Canadian children aged 2 through 11 are overweight, with half of that number considered obese.

The new daily gym classes at the Lethbridge school emphasize participation rather than competition, focusing on games such as tag or capture the flag instead of basketball to ensure everyone is running around.

Fourteen-year-old Brittany Toth admits her classmates sometimes grumble about the daily putting on and taking-off of sneakers and sweat pants, but most have started viewing gym as the best part of the school day. Another result is that the boys and girls are no longer separated during gym class. "That makes it even more fun," Brittany says. "We have to try harder."

10 Mr. Dueck, a life-long athlete who grew his muscles doing chores on the family farm, says he has learned to dream up ways to encourage the awkward, shy members of his classes to get off the sidelines and participate. Lethbridge's three public middle schools abbreviated their competitive sport seasons so more students would come out after school and play soccer and volleyball without fear of getting cut from the team. Upwards of 150 students are turning up after school for sports.

Continued

"At this age, it's devastating for a kid to not make a team," said Mr. Dueck. "You end up cutting kids in middle school when their bodies are growing, and by the time they get to high school, they could have developed into great athletes, but they never got the chance."

The southern Alberta school stopped selling soft drinks, chocolates and fried foods in its cafeteria in September, months in advance of this week's announcement by Coca-Cola and Pepsi pledging to withdraw carbonated beverages from elementary and middle schools across the country before the next school year.

Education ministers in Alberta, British Columbia and Quebec have pondered requiring daily gym classes as a solution to the obesity problem, but none has announced any policy changes so far. A B.C. proposal to make students in Grades 11 and 12 take at least one gym course a year was dropped out of fear it would take time away from academics.

In Ontario, physical education is required only three times a week in Grades 1 through 8. Just one credit in gym is required to graduate high school.

15 But principals such as Mignonne Wood of Lakeview Elementary School in Burnaby, B.C., say physical education can be increased without extending the school day or hiring additional instructors if teachers and administrators are willing to be creative with their schedules.

On Mondays, to ensure everyone has some time in the gym, the students warm up in their classrooms and walk in the hallways to cool down after exercising for 20 minutes.

The suburban school began offering daily gym this year, even though the 250-student, kindergarten through Grade 7 campus has no physical education specialists on staff. Classroom teachers lead the students in daily exercises and games. Officials at Burnaby's school board want all schools in the district to follow suit.

—*by* Heather Sokoloff

8. The reason that schools are trying to fit in more physical education classes is that

A. students need to try harder and become more competitive in life

B. students are not active enough and are becoming more obese

C. too many students go home and play video games

D. the schools need to make better use of space

9. According to Mr. Dueck, one negative result of cutting middle school children from sports teams is that it

A. fosters obesity in youth

B. teaches them that they have poor athletic skills

C. forces them to deal with rejection at too young of an age

D. takes away an opportunity for them to become good athletes

10. What does the use of the words "only" and "just" in paragraph 14 tell you about the article?

A. Many people have been interviewed for the article.

B. The system in Ontario is not very good.

C. There is no bias.

D. There is bias.

11. Lakeview Elementary was able to offer daily gym classes by

A. having principals and vice-principals teach the gym classes

B. adding more teachers to the staff

C. making the school day longer

D. changing the schedule

Read the following passage to answer questions 12 to 18.

WHEN TO HER LUTE CORINNA SINGS

When to her lute[3] Corinna sings,
Her voice revives the leaden strings,
And doth[4] in highest notes appear,
As any challenged echo clear;
But when she doth of mourning speak,
Even with her sighs the strings do break.

And as her lute doth live or die,
Led by her passion, so must I,
For when of pleasure she doth sing,
My thoughts enjoy a sudden spring,
But if she doth of sorrow speak,
Even from my heart the strings do break.

—*by* Thomas Campion

12. Which of the following statements gives the **main** idea of the poem?

A. A singer's audience can be challenging.

B. Music can stir deep emotions in people.

C. Life and death are like sorrowful songs.

D. Instruments can easily fall into disrepair.

---

[3] *lute*—a musical instrument like a guitar, but with a pear-shaped body and often a long neck

[4] *doth*—does; in Campion's day, the verb *do*, when used as an auxiliary, or helping, verb, had these different forms: I *do*, thou *dost*, she *doth*, I *did*, thou *didst*, she *did*; thus, Campion would write *she doth sing*

13. The phrase "Her voice revives the leaden strings" refers to how

A. beautifully Corinna plays the lute

B. the lute strings are on the verge of dying

C. beautiful the lute looks once it is revived

D. the strings echo Corinna's voice when she sings

14. The line "And as her lute does live or die" contains an example of the poetic technique of

A. metaphor

B. hyperbole

C. oxymoron

D. personification

15. When the speaker states that his thoughts "enjoy a sudden spring," he **most likely** means that

A. his thoughts spring up

B. his mind comes to life

C. he feels as if he is drinking from a spring

D. he feels as if his mind is bouncing like a spring

16. Between the first stanza and the second stanza, a shift occurs from

A. the speaker's description of the singing to its effect on his own heart

B. the speaker's description of Corinna's heart to her lute strings

C. Corinna's description of her singing to her speaking

D. a second-person narrator to a first-person narrator

17. According to the speaker, when Corinna sings, she sings about pleasure. When she speaks, she speaks about

A. unhappiness

B. her lute

C. sorrow

D. music

18. The poet has written this poem using

A. rhyming couplets

B. blank verse

C. free verse

D. quatrains

Read the following passage to answer questions 19 to 24.

WHERE THE REIDS LIVED

I never plan art gallery visits; they just happen one day as I am walking past. To paraphrase Forrest Gump's mother: "An art gallery is like a box of chocolates. You never know what you're going to get." There is no need for me to know in advance all I will see. And so it was when I went in about a year ago, when the sign said: "The Group of Seven in Western Canada."

I am greeted by Lawren Harris's Mountain Forms – the image sharp, clean, cold, tall, angular. Where was he standing, I wonder, when he saw the Rockies that way? I have lived near Jasper, Alta. I have seen them as he did.

Frederick Varley is shown in a tiny room with a beautiful stained glass window. I am interested to see a portrait in the grouping, and more interested to learn that the model and the artist were said to be an item. I am pleased and surprised to find, in the next room, that two of the Seven painted abstract pieces. Oh, but I am enjoying myself!

Arthur Lismer's Cathedral Mountain, when I find it, is large and strong. I do not see Cathedral Mountain as he obviously did. Still, it evokes for me visits to nearby Lake Louise when the poppies are in bloom and the lake is so clear and green it can not possibly be real.

5 Harris, J.E.H. MacDonald, A.Y. Jackson. And then, suddenly, there it is. I knew it existed but I had never seen it "live." Doc Snyder's House, L.L. FitzGerald. I can feel the G force as the time machine hurls me back 49 years. It wasn't Doc Snyder's house then – it was mine. I was 10. There is the bedroom window I climbed out to gain access to the porch roof, from where I hoped to see into FitzGerald's yard. I did not go unnoticed, and a lecture ensued about the dangers of climbing out of upstairs windows, not to mention respecting people's privacy. Mother was not amused.

There is the fence, much taller than I was, that I scrutinized for knotholes through which I might see what a real artist looked like. How mysterious and forbidden the FitzGerald garden had seemed.

There were hardwood floors in Doc Snyder's house, my house, and a huge hot air register in the middle of the main floor – between the dining room and the living room. I would stand on it on cold Winnipeg winter mornings, and feel the warm draft up my billowing, flannel nightgown. I could smell the wet wool mittens shrinking on the grid where we placed them to dry after sessions of tobogganing down the banks of the Assiniboine River or skating on it. How tall the house looks against the barren trees and cold Manitoba sky.

There is the edge of Patsy's house next door. It had been wonderful to find that there was a girl just my age! The street had a different name then. It was Oakdale Place and not Deer Lodge Place. There was no identifying plaque on the lawn of Doc Snyder's House. It was simply where the Reids lived.

A lot had changed between 1931, when FitzGerald looked out of his side window one cold winter day and decided to paint his neighbour's house, and 1953, when a family with five kids moved in. A lot has changed since then. The 10-year-old whose fondest wish, besides catching a glimpse of FitzGerald at work, was to learn how to stop on ice skates, is long gone. And where, I wonder, is Patsy?

10 The low murmur of voices in the next gallery activates the switch on the time machine and I am back, not sure how long I have been away. I am standing in the Nova Scotia Art Gallery. There are more paintings, Maud Lewis and others, but I don't want to see them today. I will come again, though, the next time the gallery beckons.

—*by* Mary Bowen

19. The fact that the writer does not see Cathedral Mountain or her old house as the artist does tells you that she

A. has a different point of view

B. does not appreciate paintings

C. is unable to understand the art

D. has matured and is now more critical

20. As a young girl, the writer thought the artist next door was

A. intimidating

B. intriguing

C. talented

D. aloof

21. The description of the house in paragraph 7 contains many examples of

A. foreshadowing

B. stereotypes

C. viewpoints

D. imagery

22. The **predominant** tone of this passage is

A. amused

B. nostalgic

C. sympathetic

D. melodramatic

23. Which of the following statements provides the purpose of the metaphor of the time machine?

A. It shows how quickly the writer's mind moves to different times and places in her life.

B. It explains how she is able to recall the details of her old house.

C. It demonstrates the significance and importance of the past.

D. It creates a contrast between the different places.

24. Which of the following words **best** describes the writer's style?

A. Antiquated

B. Elevated

C. Emotive

D. Formal

Refer to "When to Her Lute Corinna Sings" and "Where the Reids Lived" to answer questions 25 and 26.

25. Which of the following statements presents an idea that is common to both passages?

A. Art is intimidating.

B. Art has the ability to take people away.

C. The artist is more important than the viewer or listener.

D. The viewer or listener must pay close attention to be able to appreciate a piece.

26. A feeling that is shared by both the speaker in "When to Her Lute Corinna Sings" and the writer in "Where the Reids Lived" is

A. jealousy

B. jubilation

C. depression

D. enjoyment

ANSWERS AND SOLUTIONS—READING AND LITERATURE STUDIES PRACTICE QUESTIONS

1. A	**13. C**	**25. A**	**37. C**	**49. B**
2. B	**14. D**	**26. B**	**38. C**	**50. A**
3. C	**15. C**	**27. C**	**39. D**	**51. B**
4. D	**16. A**	**28. D**	**40. B**	**52. B**
5. C	**17. D**	**29. C**	**41. A**	**53. B**
6. D	**18. A**	**30. D**	**42. C**	**54. A**
7. C	**19. D**	**31. A**	**43. A**	**55. C**
8. A	**20. B**	**32. D**	**44. A**	**56. B**
9. B	**21. B**	**33. A**	**45. C**	**57. A**
10. B	**22. B**	**34. A**	**46. B**	**58. A**
11. C	**23. D**	**35. B**	**47. C**	
12. B	**24. A**	**36. D**	**48. A**	

1. A

Of the alternatives, *personification* is the only one that accurately describes the human qualities given to a "breathing" mountain at sunset. Personifying this mountain does support the main idea of the essay that the natural world is vibrant and alive.
One could reasonably argue that a "breathing" mountain is an image, but in the context of this essay, the mountain does not characterize the unity of native people, and therefore is not a satisfactory response.
Since a metaphor is a comparison that does not use *like* or *as*, and alliteration describes words with similar consonant sounds, both of these are incorrect answers.

2. B

Since the paragraph just preceding this one describes "the Indian way of seeing," the gathering darkness permits him to "see" the natural world the same way his ancestors did by gaining insights into their symbiotic relationship with nature. The gathering darkness "erases the tension of life in the city," and does "[remind] him of the simple pleasures of a walk upon the land"; however, neither of these alternatives alludes to his reconnection with his people's traditions, and thus are weaker responses.

3. C

Tone goes beyond the definition of ideas, indicating instead what the writer is feeling about them. The three phrases here beginning with "this is" indicate the writer's feelings of confidence rather than arrogance, sentimentality, or criticism because they underscore the strength of the convictions that he is beginning to understand through his communion with the "purple world" as night falls.

4. D

Cosmopolitan shares the same root meaning as *cosmos*, suggesting that someone who is cosmopolitan understands the importance of all cultures and peoples living together in harmony. While this view may seem enlightened, in the context of this essay it suggests the cosmopolitan person has become too sophisticated in his or her familiarity with the ways of people from living in cities and has lost touch with the important, though simpler, lessons that nature teaches. Because *vulgar* refers to common, and now generally obscene, language, and *foreign* refers to people outside of a culture, neither of these is close in meaning to *cosmopolitan* and must be dismissed.

5. C

It is possible that the land the writer describes in this essay could be explored while remaining unspoiled; therefore, "unspoiled" is the more satisfactory definition of *untrammeled* in this context. *Picturesque* and *powerful* are both excellent words to describe nature, but here they do not express enough of the idea that nature has been unspoiled by human contact, and therefore are weaker responses than *unspoiled.*

6. D

The phrase "But it's a start" is a positive one, allowing you to rule out disillusionment and depression on the basis of their negative cast. Selecting the correct answer from the two remaining can be successfully accomplished by considering the context of the paragraph that just precedes this short sentence. Since the writer speaks of the "seven days" that are devoted to changing people's attitudes toward the "finite resources" of nature, only alternative D expresses this idea.

7. C

No one could live without the material goods of food, clothing, and shelter, but in the context of this essay, these things become a trap by preventing people from maintaining a "spiritual connection" with the environment. This alternative provides the greatest contrast with "material trappings."

8. A

Generally, the more specific answer is the most successful response, ruling out the broad references to "ancient messages" and "a complex concept." However, the scope of the alternative does need to match that of the stem, so even though the "unity between peoples" is more specific than "all things," it is nevertheless still an incorrect response. Alternative A is the most successful choice because its reference to the interconnectivity of "all things" echoes the "honor of one thing is the honor of all" in the stem.

9. B

Each of the pairs of words in the alternatives contains an adjective that modifies a noun. Of these, the only one that seems to be contradictory is the second, because the mundane repetitiveness implied by "redundancy" is usually not associated with the distinctiveness of "elegance."

10. B

Since the writer expresses positive attitudes toward his culture's spiritual heritage on the land, you can eliminate "shrewd and aggressive" and "egotistical and sophisticated," leaving you with "honest and practical" and "perceptive and sincere." While the writer is honest in his assessment of his relationship with nature and his cultural traditions, he does not offer much practical advice about how to save the environment. Instead, his sincere attempts at changing his attitudes toward nature based on his perceptions leave you with "perceptive and sincere" as the correct choice.

11. C

Instead of reading the entire passage again to find the primary purpose, you can save time by focussing on the introduction and conclusion of the essay. In the last paragraph, Wagamese says "You learn to accept the responsibility that comes with being a part of creation." Of the alternatives on this list, the only one referring to personal responsibility in the natural world is alternative C.

12. B

The primary purpose of the essay is to argue for individual responsibility in people's relationships with nature. The only alternative that expresses this idea is alternative B, with its reference to the "one heartbeat" that all living things share. A "walk upon the land" "amid the rough and tangle of pristine creation" could lead to an acknowledgment of the rocks' stories, but they do not express the essay's theme of humanity's symbiotic relationship with nature and are therefore failed responses to the question.

13. C

"Opportunity to succeed" might be a reasonable answer to this question, especially considering her mother's comment, "Your day's going to come," after she shows her the circus poster. However, since the story contains more descriptions of the poster's effect on her imagination, the circus does represent an "enchantment that is missing from her life." The only reference to her escaping from the arguments she hears is when Tom interrupts an argument and asks her to leave with him, so this option can be eliminated. The final choice can be ruled out because Jenny does not express a desire to see the circus with her brother, Tom. She is only excited to share the news of its arrival with him.

14. D

Here the strongest answer is "thoughtfulness," because Tom thinks of how excited Jenny will be when he sees the poster in the street. His off-handed shrug might show his condescension to her, but he makes this gesture after giving her the poster, so this selection can be safely ruled out. He does not display curiosity or tolerance in this situation, and so both of these options can be dismissed as well.

15. C

Jenny is ecstatic because of the circus's arrival in town, allowing you to eliminate the two choices that have negative meanings, "hysterical" and "anxious." Of the two that remain, "happy" is a weaker answer than "thrilled" because it does not express the intensity of her excitement.

16. A

Tom is not being defeated in this narrative. Although he does feel surprised by Jenny's enthusiasm, he gives no indication of feeling shocked, and he is certainly not envious. He does think, however, that he should have known that his eleven-year-old sister would have been overly impressed by a small-town circus and perhaps should not have brought the torn poster home for her. Therefore, the best answer from this list is "questioning his own judgment."

17. D

Since "white eagerness" is similar to "soaring impetus," this choice can be ruled out. Similarly, the "filmy tissues" can also be eliminated because, in the context of the paragraph, the phrase refers to her hopes for the future. The strongest competing response, "sudden dilation," refers most directly to the shrinking, or "dilation," of her circus dream. This contrast is not as strong as "furtive poise" because the stem asks for the most effective contrast with "white eagerness." Since "white eagerness" describes her uncontained enthusiasm for the circus, the sharpest contrast of this behaviour is described by her furtive, or secretive, poise as she quickly leaves the kitchen before being caught by her mother.

18. A

The phrase "stab and rack" expresses feelings of pain. These feelings are contrasted with the excitement she feels about the circus. The only selection of the four that refers to pain in relation to happiness is "pain as a partner to joy."

19. D

In the passage, the narrator states "she wanted the excitement and the soaring, even though it might stab and rack her, rather than the barren satisfaction of believing that in life there was nothing better, nothing more vivid or dramatic, than her own stableyard." Although "the town," "the pasture," and "her classroom" are plausible answers, the narrative refers to her stableyard, making this the correct selection.

20. B

Her brother's criticism of both parents makes Jenny feel proud of him so this can be eliminated as a correct response.
On the other hand, the story does indicate that her "father is made to feel guilty about the family's poverty" and that her parents appear to care more about their problems than for Jenny and her brother, but neither of these reasons are what make Jenny angry. Instead, she feels "furious" because she disagrees with her mother's assessment of her as "gawky" and a "know-nothing."

21. B

Since Jenny's mother is criticizing her father about their poverty on the farm, "critical of their children" can be ruled out. She may feel "desperate for companionship" and "frustrated with doing her husband's chores," but because the narrative does not state this explicitly, these would be weak responses to this question about her mother's feelings. What you can safely infer from her comments is that she feels "despair about their children."

22. B

While scolding Jenny, downplaying the circus's appeal, and consoling her all reflect Tom's maturity to some extent,
his willingness to speak up at the dinner table most clearly reveals his maturity because he understands something about the adult world that his parents occupy.
He understands that his parents' quarrel is about issues that run deeper than Jenny's attendance at the circus.

23. D

Immediately following her expression of impatience, the narrator states, "If only they would just keep quiet and leave her alone—join her, if they liked, to see the circus." Although she does wish to be alone, "escape her family" does not express why she wants to be alone as well as "savour the excitement within herself." The other choices do not refer to her desire to be alone.

24. A

The least successful of the choices offered here are those that do not directly refer to the dilation, or expansion, of life that she feels with the excitement of the circus. Therefore, alternatives B and D can be eliminated. The other option does allude to her new feelings, but the context of her trying to explain them to adults who would not understand weakens this answer. The closest expression of her feelings of excitement is offered in the first choice in the "new world" that gave "soaring impetus to her imagination."

25. A

All four of the choices allude to the importance of the circus for Jenny, but she is not really tempted to go and does not face a confrontation with the circus, so these options can be quickly dismissed. Of the two alternatives that remain, "impact upon" refers most clearly to the force that the circus has on her imagination, and so this is the most successful response.

26. B

A simile is a comparison that uses *like* or *as*. Here, the qualities of the bubble are described as "fragile," which means the correct answer expresses this fragility. Of the four alternatives, the only one that alludes to this fragility is "delicate."

27. C

The first alternative refers too narrowly to the moment when Jenny tells her father about the circus. The second alternative also refers too narrowly to Tom's interrupting their parents' quarrel at the dinner table. Likewise, alternative D refers only to the advice Tom gives Jenny about returning to help with dishes. Only the expression of Jenny's pride in alternative C refers most closely to the scope of Tom's influence on her.

28. D

The first paragraph of the essay, which consists of one very long sentence, describes the frogs' awakening from hibernation.

29. C

While it is true that the writer wants the reader to appreciate the value of the frogs, the better answer is nevertheless alternative C because it gives more detail regarding why the reader should appreciate the frogs that Horwood celebrates in this essay. As he writes, "this is perhaps the most ancient music in the world, changed little if at all from the music of amphibians who were singing long before the first bird flew…"

30. D

In the given phrase, the word "apocalypse" emphasizes that whole populations of frogs have been wiped out.

31. A

The attribution of human characteristics to non-human entities is called personification. In the given phrase, the writer gives the month of April the ability to breathe.

32. D

The writer's decision against introducing the tadpoles of the large frogs into his pond is best expressed through the Darwinian model of survival of the fittest. The bullfrogs are likely to eat the smaller frogs, newts, and snakes that already live in his pond.

33. A

The fourth paragraph focuses on past recognition of faulty science.

34. A

The writer states that the frogs are most vulnerable in terms of their egg laying: "Being egg layers, they can reproduce rapidly if nothing stops them, but that's just where they are now most vulnerable. Their eggs can be destroyed by polluted water, by acid rain, or by excessive doses of ultraviolet B pouring down from a sky drastically altered by human insanity."

35. B

The most notable of the similarities the writer describes as existing between frogs and humans is potential extinction. Both humans and frogs are described as potentially nearing extinction as a result of environmental damage, the majority of which has been caused by humans.

36. D

The narrator does not begin the paragraph by using a factual tone or revealing a vital fact, but instead presents an experience that she assumes most people have shared, thus making Alternative D the strongest answer from this list.

37. C

Although the sentence does have an informal tone because of the children's speech, you cannot take the further step of connecting the brevity of the paragraph with this tone, and therefore must rule this out as a correct choice. Similarly, although the paragraph contains dialogue, you cannot infer that this dialogue is the main reason for the paragraph being this brief, since other dialogue in this essay is placed in longer paragraphs. The final choice might seem reasonable because a contrast between the children and parents is set up, at least partly, because of the single sentence paragraph. However, this answer is weaker than emphasizing the children's suspense, because it does not state specifically the quality that is being contrasted between them. The space on the page separating the one paragraph from the other helps to emphasize the suspense the children are experiencing, which makes the third choice the strongest response.

38. C

Parents is a plural form of the noun *parent* and *reply* is a verb, indicating what the parents are doing. No apostrophe is needed. For the apostrophe to be correct, *reply* would have be a noun that the parents both possess. "The parents' reply with big happy smiles" is the only answer with an error in punctuation.

39. D

The parents do express confusion about trip preparations, but are nevertheless committed to the family's vacation; however, these choices are weaker than alternative D because this choice adds the further level of information about the writer's understanding of the confusion and commitment that are involved with the vacation. The writer does not express a desire to remain at home with the pets.

40. B

If the main purpose of a narrative passage was to showcase the writer's abilities with sentence structure or grammatical effectiveness, then the narrative itself would likely become weak. You can safely rule out these two choices as the main purpose of paragraph 6. A writer could reasonably spend a paragraph describing the setting, but since the focus is on the humorous interactions between the parents in the front seat and the kids in the back, alternative B is the best response.

41. A

Alternative A is grammatically correct. The second comma in Alternative B is an example of a comma splice, in which one comma joins together two otherwise complete sentences. Alternative D features a misplaced second comma that does not separate two distinct clauses. Finally, the third choice represents a run-on sentence since it does not have the appropriate punctuation or conjunction where they are required.

42. C

Since the writer describes each event in the family holiday in the order in which it occurs, the correct answer is "chronological order." This technique draws the reader along with presumably recognizable moments in the family holiday, helping the writer make her argument about the ultimately regrettable experience of these holidays. The other selections here are commonly used to organize arguments by describing events according to their location, making arguments that juxtapose with others, and asserting conditions by beginning or ending with the most significant. However, none of these techniques are recognizable in this piece.

43. A

Although the writer is addressing an adult audience, she is trying to appeal to childhood memories of family vacations. She uses what is called a "rhetorical question," or a question that is stated more for effect than to elicit an answer. Each of the other selections does describe some aspect of the family trip that the reader hopefully could relate to, but none of them use such an effective writing technique as is exemplified in alternative A.

44. A

The apartment house is symbolic of the world. Many different kinds of people and personalities live under one roof in an apartment house, just as there are all kinds of people living on one planet. One person's actions affect other people.

45. C

The ceiling/floor imagery seems more closely related to the end of the poem, where a former acquaintance calls out to the apartment dweller as he walks his dog near the ally where "some people congregate in shame." The contrast between those who succeed and those who fail is clearly evident.

46. B

Although the speaker suspects there have been some suspicious occurrences, and what he hears in the hallway supports that suspicion, he is reluctant to peek outside to acknowledge it or try to intercede to prevent it.

47. C

The "apartment house sense" refers to the act of minding one's own business or using one's common sense in a potentially risky environment of living among strangers.

48. A

It can be inferred that the "strange goin's on" occur on an ongoing basis. If the elevator man, who stops at all the floors in the apartment building, has seen too much and been frightened, he would probably leave the job. The image of an elevator that no longer functions also evokes the image of isolated apartment "floors," which suggest that different parts of society have lost their connections with one another and become isolated.

49. B

The song criticizes the isolation and fear that comes with living in an area of concentrated population. Constant violence, fear, and an unwillingness to get involved only serve to further isolate people.

50. A

Although the speaker knows something is going on, he feels it is wiser to stay inside his apartment and not get involved. The poem suggests that this attitude is the cause of many problems.

51. B

The speaker, who wants to remain anonymous, does not want to involve himself in the lives or problems of others. It can be inferred that he lives in fear.

52. B

The indisputable rule that if the rent is not paid, the tenant will be evicted represents the guidelines for survival in the inner city—it is critical to stay out of trouble, even if it means knowing that another person is being treated unfairly.

53. B

The speaker lives in the building, and his comments about clothes "messing up the lobby floor" and the elevator man not working "no more" suggest that he notices things as he walks through the lobby to the elevator, which no longer has an attendant. His fears about getting involved suggest he is a tenant more concerned about his own survival then about helping anyone else or addressing any of the problems.

54. A

This proverb refers to the fact that there is more than one way of looking at the same thing. It also points out that as one man rises, another falters.

55. C

The fact that there is violence in the building, strange occurrences, and people hanging out "in shame" in the alleys at night suggest that this is perhaps a slum or at least a less-than-affluent part of town.

56. B

The people are probably doing something they should not be doing. The shame may be from their perspective or it could be the speaker's own judgement of their activities.

57. A

The phrase "going's on" is sometimes used to refer to things—or incidents—that are occurring (going on), usually with a negative connotation; that is, questionable or suspect incidents are sometimes referred to as "going's on."

58. A

The term "hard feelings" refers to anger or hurt. The speaker is referring to people who have been angered by society.

ANSWERS AND SOLUTIONS—READING AND LITERATURE STUDIES UNIT TEST

1. D	7. A	13. A	19. A	25. B
2. C	8. B	14. D	20. B	26. D
3. B	9. D	15. B	21. D	
4. D	10. D	16. A	22. B	
5. B	11. D	17. C	23. A	
6. A	12. B	18. A	24. C	

1. D

The best response fully describes what happens: a logjam becomes unstuck but kills a logger and a woman. The other responses are true but limited.

2. C

The repetition of sounds emphasizes that the logs are tightly stuck. The words not only rhyme, they have similar connotations. The repetition of meaning and sound emphasizes that the logs were stuck tight.

3. B

The lightness of Dufour's song emphasizes his skill and daring and his courage in the face of danger. When the whole jam roars free he cannot make it to the shore, so without hesitation he leaps forward, riding a log out ahead of the rush. His coolness and his confident boasting (he "tossed us a song") as he kept his balance ("floated along") on a bucking log contrast with the tragedy of his drowning an instant later as he is thrown into the water and crushed.

4. D

The girl dared to paddle straight into the crush of logs. It is not clear whether she meant to try to save Dufour or if she meant to follow him no matter what (line 64 suggests the second possibility). Either way, *brave* is the best word to describe her.

5. B

The quick, sharp sound of the word "cracked" emphasizes the ease with which the heavy logs snap her canoe.

6. A

In lines 11 to 21, "we" free the logs. In line 29, "I" and ten other loggers scramble ashore as the logs move. It must be one of the loggers who is breaking the news to Baptiste.

7. A

Of course the man knows the names of both sisters. But at the beginning of the poem, after naming Virginie, he breaks off without naming her sister because Baptiste guesses and is about to rush away. At the end, Baptiste does rush off, and the narrator is left to repeat his words. Only now he ends dramatically: "What God calls the other/Is not known to me." He is not ignorant of the name she went by before her death. Her name is held back to emphasize the drama and the tragedy.

8. B

The title of the article explains that schools use gym classes to battle obesity. Schools can require students to attend more physical education classes, which will make them more active.

9. D

In the quotation in paragraph 11, Dueck explains that cutting kids from teams is devastating because they are not given the chance to become great athletes.

10. D

The use of these words emphasize that the writer thinks the physical education requirements are not strong enough. Notice the difference between "There are three classes a week" and "There are ONLY three classes a week." Bias is when a writer influences the reader to have the same opinion has her or him. Bias can be weak, moderate or strong. When there is bias present, you can say the article is biased or the writer is biased.

11. D

The school was able to offer daily gym classes by changing the schedule (see paragraph 15).

12. B

Corinna's music stirs deep emotions in the poet: "And as her lute doth live or die, / Led by her passion, so must I" (lines 7–8). The idea can be extended to music and people in general.

13. A

Corinna's singing and playing ("When to her lute Corinna sings") give life to the lute strings. The strings are leaden without her playing. In other words, she plays beautifully.

14. D

Corinna's lute "lives and dies." This is an example of *personification*, or the attribution of human characteristics to inanimate objects.

15. B

Since the poem is already full of images of life and death, the best response is to say that his mind comes to life like the world coming to life in spring. Spring's new life follows winter's death.

16. A

Although the second stanza opens with a reference to the lute, as did the first stanza, the line that follows contains the clue. The pronoun "I" at the end of the line indicates that the speaker has shifted his thoughts from their focus on Corinna's singing to a new focus on the effect that Corinna has on him (lines 8–10).

17. C

When Corinna speaks, she speaks of sorrow: "But if she does of sorrow speak" (line 11).

18. A

The rhyme scheme is *aabbcc*, and so on. Each pair of lines rhymes. The poem is written in *rhyming couplets*.

19. A

The writer states she does not see Cathedral Mountain as being large and strong the way the artist did. She has different memories, associations, and experiences with both Cathedral Mountain and the house, so you can say she has a different point of view (also referred to as viewpoint—how you see things).

20. B

The writer describes how she wanted to catch a glimpse of the artist's yard and how she wanted to see "what a real artist looked like." She was intrigued by him.

21. D

Imagery is an appeal to the senses—sight, hearing, touch, taste, and smell—to create a vivid description. The writer uses many sensory descriptions in this paragraph, such as "feel the warm draft" and "smell the wet wool mittens."

22. B

Tone is a writer's attitude toward his or her subject (what he or she is writing about). *Nostalgia* is a sentimental look at the past. This most accurately describes the tone of this piece.

23. A

A metaphor takes the ideas around one object and transfers them to another and compares the two. The writer compares the feeling of suddenly being in the past when she looks at the painting of her house to being in a time machine. It serves to show how quickly her mind can move to a different time in her life.

24. C

Style refers to the manner of writing or the way a person writes. In this piece, the writer works to capture and convey her feelings and memories; thus, her style is emotive.

25. B

Both the speaker in the poem and the writer in the personal essay are transported by the art: the speaker's feelings follow Corinna's lute, and the writer's imagination is taken back to her childhood.

26. D

The speaker in the poem clearly enjoys the music and says, "My thoughts enjoy a sudden spring." In the same way, the writer obviously enjoys the paintings and says, "Oh, but I am enjoying myself!"

NOTES

Class Focus
Writing

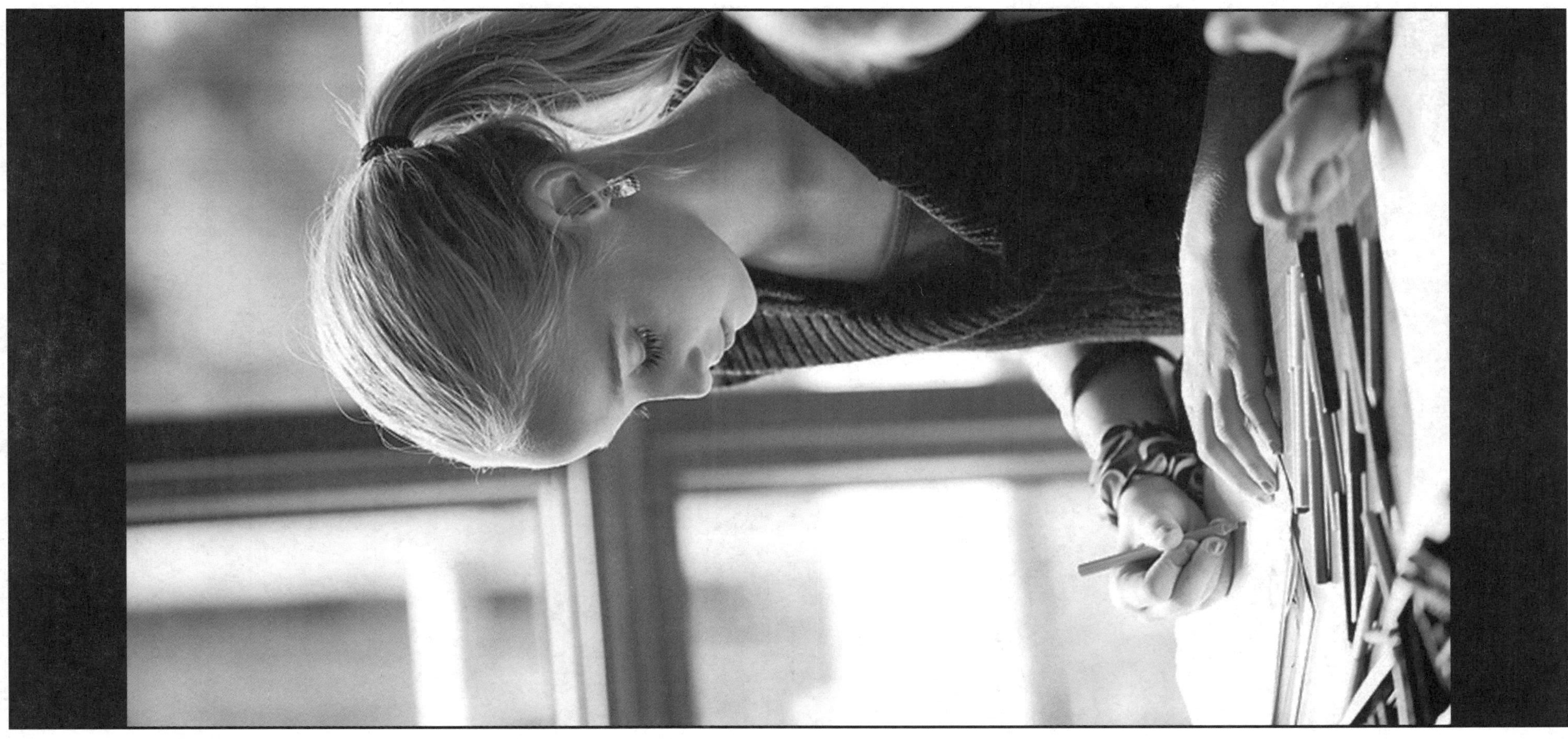

TABLE OF CORRELATIONS			
General Expectation	**Specific Expectation**	**Practice Questions**	**Unit Test**
Students are expected to:			
10W1.0 generate, gather, and organize ideas and information to write for an intended purpose and audience. (Developing and Organizing Content)	10W1.1 identify the topic, purpose, and audience for a variety of writing tasks. (Identifying Topic, Purpose, and Audience)	Writing Prompt	Writing Prompt
	10W1.2 generate, expand, explore, and focus ideas for potential writing tasks, using a variety of strategies and print, electronic, and other resources, as appropriate (Generating and Developing Ideas)	Writing Prompt	Writing Prompt
	10W1.3 locate and select information to appropriately support ideas for writing, using a variety of strategies and print, electronic, and other resources, as appropriate (Research)	Writing Prompt	Writing Prompt
	10W1.4 identify, sort, and order main ideas and supporting details for writing tasks, using a variety of strategies and organizational patterns suited to the content and the purpose for writing (Organizing Ideas)	Writing Prompt	Writing Prompt
	10W1.5 determine whether the ideas and information gathered are relevant to the topic, accurate, and complete and appropriately meet the requirements of the writing task (Reviewing Content)	Writing Prompt	Writing Prompt

10W2.0	draft and revise their writing, using a variety of literary, informational, and graphic forms and stylistic elements appropriate for the purpose and audience (Using Knowledge of Form and Style)	10W2.1	write for different purposes and audiences using a variety of literary, graphic, and informational forms (Form)	Writing Prompt	Writing Prompt
		10W2.2	establish a distinctive voice in their writing, modifying language and tone skillfully to suit the form, audience, and purpose for writing (Voice)	Writing Prompt	Writing Prompt
		10W2.3	use appropriate descriptive and evocative words, phrases, and expressions to make their writing clear, vivid, and interesting for their intended audience (Diction)	Writing Prompt	Writing Prompt
		10W2.4	write complete sentences that communicate their meaning clearly and accurately, varying sentence type, structure, and length to suit different purposes and making smooth and logical transitions between ideas (Sentence Craft and Fluency)	Writing Prompt	Writing Prompt
		10W2.5	explain how their own beliefs, values, and experiences are revealed in their writing (Critical Literacy)	Writing Prompt	Writing Prompt
		10W2.6	revise drafts to improve the content, organization, clarity, and style of their written work, using a variety of teacher-modelled strategies (Revision)	Writing Prompt	Writing Prompt
		10W2.7	produce revised drafts of texts, including increasingly complex texts, written to meet criteria identified by the teacher, based on the curriculum expectations (Producing Drafts)	Writing Prompt	Writing Prompt

10W3.0	use editing, proofreading, and publishing skills and strategies, and knowledge of language conventions, to correct errors, refine expression, and present their work effectively (Applying Knowledge of Conventions)	10W3.1	use knowledge of spelling rules and patterns, a variety of resources, and appropriate strategies to recognize and correct their own and others' spelling errors (Spelling)	Writing Prompt	Writing Prompt
		10W3.2	Build vocabulary for writing by confirming word meaning(s) and reviewing and refining word choice, using a variety of resources and strategies, as appropriate for the purpose (Vocabulary)	Writing Prompt	Writing Prompt
		10W3.3	use punctuation correctly and appropriately to communicate their intended meaning (Punctuation)	Writing Prompt	Writing Prompt
		10W3.4	use grammar conventions correctly and appropriately to communicate their intended meaning clearly and fluently (Grammar)	Writing Prompt	Writing Prompt
		10W3.5	proofread and correct their writing, using guidelines developed with the teacher and peers (Proofreading)	Writing Prompt	Writing Prompt
		10W3.6	use a variety of presentation features, including print and script, fonts, graphics, and layout, to improve the clarity and coherence of their work and to heighten its appeal for their audience (Publishing)	Writing Prompt	Writing Prompt
		10W3.7	produce pieces of published work to meet criteria identified by the teacher, based on the curriculum expectations (Producing Finished Works)	Writing Prompt	Writing Prompt

DEVELOPING AND ORGANIZING CONTENT

Imagine you are going on a road trip. How would you prepare for it? Without a map, planning out a route to your destination, or even without choosing where you want to go, your trip would probably not be very enjoyable. Preparation and organization is important in every area of life, and writing is no exception. Planning before you write is very important. Developing your purpose for writing, your topic, and how you will organize your content will ensure that your writing will be clear. It will also make the writing process much easier.

No matter what type of composition you are writing, being organized is key to clear communication that has a logical pattern or sequence. It is important to identify your key or main ideas and distinguish them from supporting details. There are different methods of grouping ideas, both during the planning stage and during the drafting stage of your writing. Effective visual organizers and advice on how to best organize are included in this section of your *KEY*. Organizing your information throughout the writing process will save you time and will improve the quality of your writing.

ON 10W1.1 identify the topic, purpose, and audience for a variety of writing tasks

Writing with Purpose

By Grade 10, you are becoming a more experienced writer. You have already accomplished a wide variety of writing tasks. Every writing task, from a short paragraph to a research report, shares the same first steps:

- determining a reason or purpose for writing
- choosing a topic
- considering the prospective audience for your finished product

The process of successful writing is like preparing for and going on a journey. If you plan and follow the steps in the writing process, you will reach your destination. Before starting to write, it is wise to sit back and think about your topic, purpose, and audience.

Choosing a Topic

Choosing a topic can be difficult if you are not sure where to begin or if you are having trouble choosing between topics you are interested in. Assigned topics and topics you choose yourself may offer different challenges when you start organizing your work.

Assigned Topics: Often, a topic or a list of acceptable topics will be provided by your teacher. You may be asked to write a research paper, a story, a poem, a movie or book review, a business letter, or other creative texts.

Self-Chosen Topics: If you decide to choose your own topic, some of the following guidelines may help you arrive at a decision.

- Think of issue-related topics. These are topics that generate a range of opinions, such as when teenagers should be eligible to drive, what world leaders should do about global warming, and so on.
- Think about topics of personal interest to you. When you are passionate about Canadian hockey, the harmful effects of cyber-bullying, or future trends in transportation, you are more motivated to research and explore the topic thoroughly.

- Brainstorm and eliminate. Quickly think of and list six topics. Do a quick Internet search to see how much information is available online—this usually means information about those topics will likely be available at the library as well. Some topics may immediately lead you to a brick wall because resources on the topic do not seem to be available. Cross these topics off your list. You probably do not have time to spend hours hunting for related information.
- Think of topics that would be of interest to your target audience. Since your audience often consists of your peers, you can probably think of topics that would interest your classmates. These topics are more likely to motivate you, too, because you probably share many of the same interests as your classmates.
- Break down a broad topic to a manageable size. If your topic is too broad, you will need to sort through too much information. Narrowing your topic before you begin will make your writing task less frustrating and easier to handle.

Deciding on Your Purpose for Writing

Good writers usually have a specific purpose for writing a given text. Your purpose in writing an assignment can act as a way to focus and stay on topic. Generally, there are five purposes for writing:

To inform (to interpret in detail, to make clear): This form of writing is concerned with the "what" of a situation.

- Announcements, news broadcasts, catalogues, labels, and documentaries are all examples of communication that informs.

To explain (to interpret, to make clear): This form of writing is concerned with the "why" or "how" of a situation. It is also known as *explanatory writing* because readers are given explanations and not just informed about an event.

- Charts, recipes, brochures, invitations, and textbooks are examples of communication that explains.

To entertain: This form of writing is meant to be light and entertaining. It may be humorous, but it can encompass many different kinds of fiction.

- Action, science fiction, and romance novels are examples of communication that entertains.

To impress (to affect deeply): This form of writing aims to make readers feel strongly about a topic.

- Editorials, complaint letters, and self-help books are examples of communication that impresses.

To convince (to persuade by argument): This form of writing aims to change the reader's beliefs; the writer will state a belief and then appeal to the reader's feelings.

- Advertisements, editorials, and debates are examples of communication that convinces.

Choosing an Audience

Another factor that affects a writer's purpose is his or her audience. Before writing a composition, writers must decide who their audience is and how they want their audience to react. For example, if you are writing an assignment for your teacher, you should write the report in a formal manner, keeping in mind that your audience is your teacher and that correct grammar, spelling, punctuation, and formal style are usually required. If you are writing a friendly letter to a friend, the manner can be less formal, and conventional rules are less important.

The following list is not exhaustive, but it includes a range of potential audiences for your writing:

- peers/classmates
- teacher
- prospective employer
- general public
- children
- parents
- pen pal
- politician
- celebrity
- role model

ON 10W1.2 generate, expand, explore and focus ideas for potential writing tasks, using a variety of strategies and print, electronic and other resources, as appropriate

Generating and Developing Ideas

There are many different ideas to write about. Some can be borrowed from your personal experience, while others can come from your imagination or knowledge. Here are some examples of techniques that writers use to generate ideas:

Brainstorming: Write down all the ideas you have, no matter how trivial or silly they seem. Then choose the idea that is most compatible with your purpose and that you find the most interesting. Brainstorming is a technique that is often productive when you are in a group situation and a variety of ideas are brought up.

Webbing: Also known as mapping or clustering, this technique involves using a diagram to sort out ideas. Place the general topic in a circle in the middle of a page. As you think of more specific details for the topic, place them on the page around the general topic. This technique allows you to create sub-details and expand on each specific detail.

Free writing: Many interesting ideas can come from simply spending some time writing on a topic without spending too much time planning out what you want to write about. With this technique, rules about spelling, capitalization, punctuation, and grammar are not very important. The focus of free writing is to stimulate thinking in order to generate ideas.

Lists: Choose the general topic of your writing and brainstorm ideas about that topic. For each idea, create further ideas. Once you have a lot of ideas, you can arrange the list in order from least important to most important detail.

Organizing information helps you at several stages in the writing process. Staying organized while you are forming ideas at the developing stage of a writing assignment helps you understand what you want to write about. It also gives you ideas of the information you can use in your assignment. You can keep tabs on what information you want to use and what you might eventually like to leave out.

Once your ideas are developed, organizing your information helps your reader understand your ideas more precisely. Being organized in your writing helps you create clearly-formed ideas and helps you get those ideas across to your reader. Use the methods that work the best for you. Time spent organizing before you sit down to write will save you a lot of time in the long run and will ensure that you create the best writing possible.

ON 10W1.3 locate and select information to appropriately support ideas for writing, using a variety of strategies and print, electronic, and other resources as appropriate

Research

After you decide on a topic, you are ready to find ideas and information related to it. These ideas and information will be basic to the substance, or main body, of your writing. Following through with some or all of the steps and strategies below will help you keep your research manageable, find reliable resources, and acknowledge the experts and writers who provided you with your information.

Create a Research Plan

A checklist-style plan can help you stay focused and on track, as shown in the following example:

1. Topic chosen: ______________________
2. Assignment expectations: ______________________
3. KWL chart created
4. Webbing for preliminary ideas

Example:

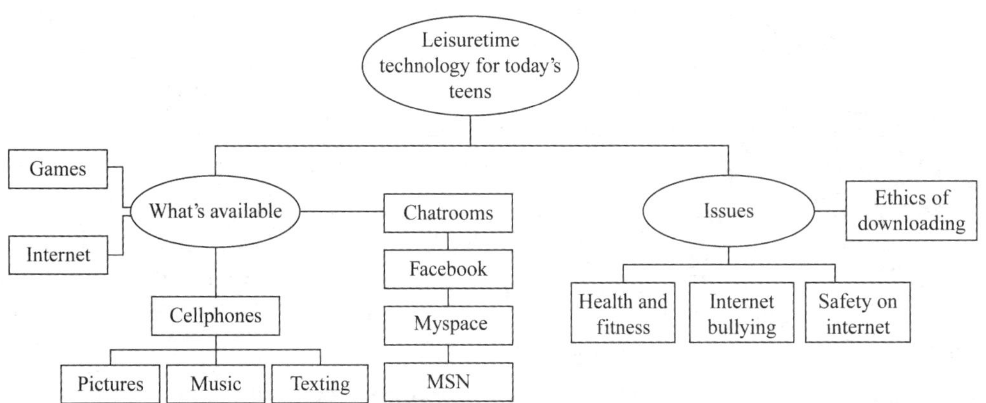

5. Topic restated as a question
6. Preview of available information in the form of a quick list of readily available resources, people you could interview, etc.
7. Preliminary research conclusion—does my topic need to be adjusted so that it fits available resources?
8. Further questions related to the topic: ______________________
   ____
9. Data collected and point-form notes completed
10. Source information recorded for bibliography
11. Information organized and outline drafted
12. Rough draft of paper completed
13. Proof-reading and editing of paper
14. Good copy of paper completed
15. Bibliography added
16. Title page and table of contents added.

Sticking to these steps will ensure that your writing will be the best that it can be on the day the assignment is due.

Online Searches

Online searches involve using keywords and phrases related to your topic. Be as specific as possible when searching. For example, the keywords "Provincial election in Ontario" will yield more specific results than just using the keywords "Provincial election." Sometimes you have to try a few different keywords or phrases before you find sites that match what you are trying to research. When you find an article related to your topic, watch for hyperlinks to other related articles or websites.

The sites that are listed first in an online search are determined in different ways depending on which search engine you are using. Some search engines index sites by number of hits or by number of links to a site. Sometimes, the owners of websites will pay to be ranked on the first page of a search. Usually the websites listed on the first page of your search results will be the most relevant, but this is not always the case. Play around with key words and phrases. Often, if you see the same sites more than once, those sites are likely to be relevant. Any information gathered from an Internet source should be verified and come from a reliable, credible site or source.

Information from the Internet is like any other kind of published information, so you must make sure to cite the information in your bibliography if you use any material from an online source.

Interviews

Interviews with experts or community members can also yield excellent information. Interviews are especially useful if you are reporting on something that is very current. Chances are there will not be much information on a very new topic or event going on in your area. In this situation, an interview might be the best resource for getting up-to-date information.

Checking Reliability

How do you decide whether or not to believe what you read? Can you tell fact from opinion? How do you decide whether or not you can trust the writer?

Factual statements are clear, accurate, and verifiable. Much of what you read has not been tested, but you usually accept it because it appears to be true or others whom you trust say that it is true. Magazines, books, newspapers, websites, bulletin boards, and blogs, for example, should not be trusted until the writer's knowledge and experience on the subject has been verified. Faulty conclusions are often made because the evidence relied on may be based either on incorrect observations or observations that are prejudiced, wishful, or imaginative.

In order determine how credible a piece of writing is, try examining it from the following angles:

Writer's viewpoint: Who is the writer? What does he or she stand to gain or lose? An article about politics may be very biased if it is written, for example, by the leader of a political party.

Text structure: Is the information presented well? Are the arguments easy to understand, logical, and supported by reasonable evidence? Sloppy work may indicate that the work is not credible.

Writer's word choice: Do the writer's words express ideas and convey facts, or are they meant to inflame readers' emotions? Does the tone of the writer seem balanced or angry?

Final Tips on Reliability and Accuracy

- Compare facts using various resources and watch for differences or contradictions.
- Consider the publishing date: is the information current?
- Consider the expertise and reputation of the source.
- Watch for biases. Is the information objective or does it favour/criticize a particular group?
- Double-check Internet sources: is there proof of the writer's expertise? Is the site reliable overall? How recent is the information on the website? Is the website educational or commercial in nature?

Double-checking accuracy is an important part of publishing your work. Make sure your information is valid before doing a final print of your assignment.

This section of your KEY illustrates how different aspects of reading and writing contribute to publishing your work. How your final product of writing looks is important to your reader being able to understand your writing easily. A clean, organized, accurate, and attractive final product will make it as easy as possible for your reader to interpret your writing and find it appealing. Publishing your work usually occurs near the end of the writing process, so it also gives you an opportunity to think about what you have written and how you want that writing to look once it is on the page.

ON 10W1.4 identify, sort, and order main ideas and supporting details for writing tasks, using a variety of strategies and organizational patterns suited to the content and the purpose for writing

Organizing Ideas during the Planning Stage

When you write according to an organized plan, your writing tends to flow more logically and coherently. Organizing your writing first also saves you time. Use the planning strategy that works best for the topic and purpose of your writing piece.

Specialized Text Features

Certain kinds of texts, such as newspapers, have design features that are related to their purpose. Newspapers are designed for rapid reading for people on the go. Large newspapers come in sections so readers can quickly find the topics that they are more interested in first. The front page will present a listing, similar to a table of contents, of the main sections and daily features, such as the entertainment section, classifieds, and letters to the editor. It also shows an overview of the weather and the newsworthy stories of the day. As you examine the structure of the news articles, you will see how the stories themselves are presented in a design or format that makes the key facts from the news quickly accessible to the readers.

ON 10W2.1 write for different purposes and audiences using a variety of literary, graphic, and informational forms

Writing with Purpose

Your topic, purpose for writing, and audience can all play a part in determining the form that you will choose for your writing piece. For example, a cover letter to a prospective employer for a summer job would suggest a business letter form. In the situation provided by the topic or implied by the purpose and audience, you should consider what will work best for an appropriate writing form:

- essay
- research report
- ballad-form poem
- editorial
- news story
- multimedia presentation
- formal invitation

Once you have a topic or a purpose for writing, you can choose the best form according to what you want to say, how you could best say it, and who your audience will be.

The following chart displays some writing forms and the motivation you might have for using them.

Personal Letter	Letter to the Editor
• to a friend who has moved • to thank a relative for a gift • to a parent from camp	• to express your viewpoint on a community issue • to comment on a news item • to express public appreciation for something
Review	**Poem**
• a book you have read • a movie you have watched • an event you have attended	• to express feelings • to describe something • to celebrate a special occasion • to express a descriptive passage in a short story
Report	**Narrative**
• to share research • to explore an assigned topic • to hand in to a social studies or science teacher	• to relate a personal experience • to create a short story • to write a journal entry
Comic Strip	**Trading Cards**
• to depict scenes from a story for young children • to portray an issue • to summarize chapters in a novel	• to describe mythological figures • to describe characters in a novel • to make mini bios of inspirational people

Following are some methods you could use to apply your knowledge of form to some specific writing projects.

Writing Persuasive Compositions

If you are writing a persuasive composition, the opening paragraph requires close attention. The introductory paragraph is crucial to keeping your reader's attention. Persuasive writing appeals to a reader's emotional faculties. The logic you use must be stated clearly to ensure your reader will understand. You must use examples that are drawn from an emotional source in order to fully convince your reader of the plausibility of your position.

Both logical arguments and emotional appeals are useful to persuade your reader, but try to create a good balance between the two.

Type of Appeal	Examples
Emotional	1. Gives personal anecdotes 2. Asks questions 3. Appeals to readers' emotions 4. Uses emotional words
Logical	1. Provides facts 2. Provides reasons 3. Recognizes opposing arguments

Suppose you are writing a persuasive argument for the topic of school uniforms. The first decision to make when writing a persuasive argument is to choose a position to take. Once you have chosen your position, you can start to research your position to find existing arguments and information to help you. Suppose your position is that "greater use of school uniforms is a way to protect students and promote learning." Rhetorical devices can help support your argument in a persuasive way.

Rhetorical Devices

Provide your audience with statistics and researched information:

Example

> Research has shown that schools that require student uniforms have better attendance rates, higher academic achievement, and less fighting.

Appeal to your reader's emotions or ethical beliefs:

Example

> Teachers have been frustrated in the past because their classes are regularly disrupted by students looking at themselves in a mirror, painting their fingernails, combing their hair, or comparing designer labels. Parents who are without money to waste often watch in dismay and helplessness as their children are bullied for wearing "uncool" clothes.

Relate a personal anecdote to bring your audience closer to your position. Rather than sharing statistics or numbers, a personal story can make an audience feel the emotional impact that your issue can have:

Example

> When I went to school, we had to wear uniforms. I remember a time when a student misbehaved on the bus going home: a passenger (who recognized the uniform as belonging to our school) reported the incident to our principal. The principal was very quick to reprimand the culprit, who was identified by his bright red hair and freckled face!

Give examples of cases where your argument can be supported:

Example

> An individual does not lose his personality when wearing a uniform. Uniforms are commonplace to people in many walks of life, such as flight attendants, bus or train drivers, postal workers, restaurant employees, military personnel, members of school sports teams, and choirs or bands. These people are able to wear uniforms without any loss of personality or personal freedoms.

Clarifying and Defending Your Position

Being clear in defending your position means making sure your reader knows what you are trying to say. Get a classmate or friend to read over a text you have written that is opinion-based. Do they understand what you are trying to say after reading it through only one time? That is a good sign that your ideas and opinions are clear. To clarify and defend your position, use precise and relevant evidence including facts, expert opinions, quotations, expressions of commonly accepted beliefs, and logical reasoning.

As you prepare your arguments, ask people their views and record them. Additionally, you could research the findings of someone like Dr. David Brunsma from the University of Alabama, who has written numerous books and articles on the subject of school uniforms; you might use the Internet to look up court cases and appeals involving school boards that have a school uniform policy; WHEN (World Home Education Network) also has statements on its website regarding school uniforms. The more supported facts you can find to support your argument, the better your persuasion will be.

Addressing your Audience

As you prepare your composition, you must be prepared to address concerns from both sides of your argument. While remembering that your position is that the "greater use of school uniforms is a way to protect students and promote learning," you can argue

- the safety of Canadian students is fundamentally more important than any loss of freedom of expression that might occur by introducing school uniforms
- it is an infringement on citizens' clearly established constitutional rights to tell students what to wear to school
- school uniforms are not nearly as important as a good school atmosphere, clear rules and expectations, and parental involvement in student learning

Creative Methods of Relating Information

Many teachers will allow you freedom of creative choice when it comes to selecting a writing form. If you are studying a unit on children's literature, for instance, you could write a fairy tale and publish it as a children's book, utilizing the information about children's literature that you learned from class to create this story.

For example, instead of researching and preparing a list of Greek mythological figures, you could look in books or perform an Internet search to find information, such as the short descriptions provided here.

Example

Greek Mythological Figures

Achilles was the half-mortal son of the sea-goddess, Thetis. Because Thetis held her infant son by the heel when she dipped him in the river of immortality, he was immune to mortal attacks, except through his undipped heel. Hence, one's fatal flaw or weakness is sometimes known as one's "Achilles heel."

Atlas was a Titan of immense physical strength who carried the sky upon his shoulders. The Titans were an ancient race of giants.

Medusa was a terrifying Gorgon sister whose hairdo was a squirming, writhing mass of hissing snakes.

Narcissus was a boy who fell in love with his own reflection in a stream, gazing at it so long that he grew roots and grew into a flower on the bank.

After you have gathered your information on Greek mythological figures, you could use it to create a set of trading cards of mythological figures. Drawing pictures of the figures on the cards to accompany the text information could be not only more enjoyable for you as a student, but could make the descriptive information easier to remember. Always try to choose the best form to serve your purpose and engage your audience, even if your audience is only yourself!

To make your information more distinctive, you could rewrite a traditional fairy tale, modernizing the story and illustrating your children's picture book yourself. You could then present your published (good copy) children's book to a class of younger students. Always try to choose the best form to serve your purpose and engage your audience, even if your audience is only yourself!

ON 10W2.2 establish a distinctive voice in their writing, modifying language and tone skillfully to suit the form, audience, and purpose for writing

A Writer's Voice

What is a writer's voice? Generally, a writer's voice can be described as how the writing sounds, or its overall effect on the writer's audience. The writer's voice is a unique blend of careful word choices that express what the writer means, as well as the writer's attitude toward their topic. Voice becomes an important part of the writer's writing style, combining word choices, phrasing, and word arrangement in distinctive sentence pattern. Even punctuation plays a part. As you discover your own writer's voice in different writing assignments, remember that big words are not nearly as important as the way those words are put together. Voice should be deliberate, appropriate, and consistently adapted to your form, audience, and purpose for writing.

Voice and Form

In a book report, for example, your form should include some sort of evaluation of the book's merits, supported by evidence. However, your voice would vary according to the form. For example, an interview would probably use a voice that imitates the speaking style of at least one character. A letter could have a polite and formal voice because you would be addressing your comments and questions to an adult.

Voice and Audience

You should adjust the level of formality to match your intended audience. Your readers could be adults, peers, or children. Another part of voice that could change would be the technical language you use. You want to use technical language that suits the level of expertise of the audience. For example, a research report might require a voice that explains difficult words or technical terms. You would probably have to assume that your audience is uninformed and lacks background information. A sports article for the school newspaper, on the other hand, might be in a more familiar voice, with contractions, exaggerations, possibly some slang, or jokes you know your readers will understand.

Voice and Purpose

To an extent, your purpose for writing will determine the voice of your writing.

If you are sharing or relating a personal experience, your voice would probably be written in first person and would include specific details along with personal thoughts, feelings, and reactions.

If your purpose is to inform, your voice would most likely be written in third person objective. You would want a more detached, unemotional voice. Adding humour might sound out of place or might detract from the information you are presenting.

If your purpose is to entertain or inform, your voice might vary. If you were writing an article for a school newspaper section, for example, your voice might change according to the type of article you are writing. For an article on the front page, your voice should be precise, clear, and objective, while an article in the sports section could depict a writer's voice that includes lively, age-appropriate description, exaggeration, humor, and even slang.

ON 10W2.3 use appropriate descriptive and evocative words, phrases and expressions to make their writing clear, vivid, and interesting for their intended audience

Word Choice

Diction is word choice. It is important that your ideas are expressed simply and accurately so that your reader can easily understand them. The *denotation* of a word is the dictionary definition. By using words that mean what you want them to mean, you can express your ideas clearly. The *connotation* of a word refers to all the associations the word takes on through everyday speech and a particular culture.

Perhaps the most basic element of writing style is diction, or word choice. Diction is word choice, and using the right word properly and at the right time makes your meaning clear. The choice can affect the meaning, effectiveness, and tone of your writing.

When you are speaking, your tone can be more readily attained from your body language, facial expressions, and intonation. However, when you are writing, your choice of words indicates your tone or attitude.

ON 10W2.4 *write complete sentences that communicate their meaning clearly and accurately, varying sentence type, structure and length to suit different purposes and making smooth and logical transitions between ideas*

Writing Sentences

An understanding of sentence construction makes it easier to write and punctuate clear sentences. No matter how long or short it is, a complete sentence requires a subject, the minimum length of which is a noun, and a predicate. The minimum length of a predicate is a single verb.

Example

Subject	+	Predicate
Dogs		bark
Dogs		bark under the trees
Wild, fierce dogs		bark every night

You can develop your skills as a writer and communicator by creating clear, correct, but varied sentence patterns. Variety can make your writing style unique and interesting to readers. Near the end of this section, you will find extra strategies used by good writers to refine and improve their sentences.

Sentence Variety

Sentence Types

There are four main types of sentences:

1. **Declarative** (statement): I recognize that man.
2. **Interrogative** (question): Are you sure that you recognize him?
3. **Imperative** (command): Hand me those binoculars.
4. **Exclamatory** (exclamation): Of course I recognize him!

Sentence Structures

Sentence patterns follow variations of four basic structures, determined by the number and type of clauses in the sentence. Here is a quick review of clauses:

A clause is a group of words containing a subject and verb (predicate).

He was an expert rider. He had ridden horses all his life.

Main clause: A clause that stands alone and makes sense as a complete sentence.

He was an expert rider.

Subordinate clause (also called relative or dependent clause): A clause that does not make complete sense on its own but does make sense when combined with a main clause.

Because he was an expert rider, he placed second in the Olympic trials.

Sentence structures, therefore, can be categorized as follows:

Simple

An independent clause (a sentence) containing one subject and one verb is called a simple sentence.

- *The boy stood on the garden wall.*

Sentence order can be altered for variety or to emphasize one part of the sentence. The emphasized part usually comes first.

- *On the garden wall stood the boy.*

Compound

Two independent clauses (or sentences) joined by a coordinating conjunction are called a compound sentence.

- *The boy stood on the garden wall, but no one noticed him.*

With a small alteration, the sentence order can be changed.

- *No one noticed the boy as he stood on the garden wall.*

However, the sentence is now complex rather than compound.

Complex

Two clauses joined by a subordinating conjunction are called a complex sentence. One clause must be independent, and the other clause must be dependent (subordinate).

- *Although the boy stood on the garden wall*, no one noticed him.
- No one noticed the boy, *although he stood on the garden wall.*
- *While the firefighters were distracted by brush fires*, three houses burned to the ground.
- Three houses burned to the ground *while the firefighters were distracted by brush fires.*
- An actress *who has won three Oscars* will be present tonight.

Although this last example can be written in a different order, you may choose to reserve this for more formal writing.

Example

Present tonight will be an actress *who has won three Oscars.*

Compound-Complex

A compound-complex sentence contains at least two independent clauses and one dependent clause.

- While I slept, *the sun rose*, and *the birds began to sing.*
- Although she didn't win a medal, *Janine competed at the Olympics,* and *she has never forgotten the wonderful experience.*

TRANSITIONS

It is important to establish and maintain coherence in your writing through the effective use of transitions. *Coherence* simply refers to writing that is clear, easily followed, and does not confuse the reader. *Transitions* are words and phrases that "connect" your ideas in logical ways so they do not seem scrambled or appear as random lists.

Transitional devices are words and phrases like *because*, *also*, *in addition*, *nevertheless*, and *as a result*. These words show the relationship between ideas in the following example:

> ***In addition**, the witness has already admitted to lying. **Therefore**, you must consider whether or not any of her evidence can be believed. **On the other hand**, other witnesses have confirmed some of her statements.*

Careful writers use transitional devices to make the relationships between the parts of an essay clear. Transitional devices can be used to show a sequence or to begin a paragraph by showing how the ideas in the paragraph are related to the ideas in the preceding paragraph.

> *As you consider the evidence, you will have to keep in mind the fact that the witness has admitted to lying on three occasions. **First… Next… And finally…***
>
> ***On the other hand***, her evidence about the escape vehicle has been confirmed by**…**
> ***Therefore***, you will have to decide how much weight to give to her statements about**…**
>
> *To conclude, it seems that we can agree**…***

Some convenient and frequently used transitions are listed in the following table.

Purpose	Transition Words and Phrases
To show differences	on the other hand in contrast in opposition to this instead unlike however in comparison but yet
To show similarities	just as important not very different from this in much the same manner similarly hence alike also likewise
To show preferences	in preference to this preferred by more people however nevertheless

To indicate time	at the same time a few days prior following the completion of next soon in subsequent months
To indicate more	in addition to that to add to on top of this furthermore therefore moreover it is also true that in the same way another example of this is as well
To indicate time, place, and order	afterward later earlier elsewhere farther on earlier first second third
To indicate reasons	therefore thus as a result
To clarify	for instance for example

In a play, transition is provided through scene changes. In a novel, you often see a new chapter beginning with a transition. Sometimes the chapter begins with a transitional phrase, like "Soon," "By Friday," or "As the plane descended into the Halifax Airport…" A short story writer may use a transitional technique, like short paragraphs, to indicate a change in the plot or setting.

If you can follow the writing without feeling confused, then the transitional devices, no matter how subtle, are effective.

APPLYING KNOWLEDGE OF CONVENTIONS

Conventions are essential for reading and writing. Grammar allows you to use your vocabulary properly. Correct grammar allows you to communicate your ideas clearly. It may seem as though you can be successful at grammar by simply following its rules and guidelines. Following the rules of grammar is important, but it is just important to learn grammar through reading. The more observant you are about the grammar you read in any text, the better you will understand it when the time comes for you to write.

This section will also show you how to use vocabulary properly by using correct grammar.

ON 10W3.1 *use knowledge of spelling rules and patterns, a variety of resources, and appropriate strategies to recognize and correct their own and others' spelling errors*

Spelling

Spelling is one of the most essential parts of vocabulary and grammar. By Grade 10, you have been introduced to the most common English spelling patterns, learned basic spelling rules, and have been taught to use spelling resources like dictionaries and the spell-check feature on a computer. Draw upon that knowledge to spell words correctly as you use them in your writing. Keep personal lists for correct spelling, such as

- words misspelled in writing assignments
- science terms
- math terms
- social studies words

Aim to spell the words that you use correctly, and not only when you are doing school assignments. Correct spelling shows that you are a good communicator. The following section will provide some spelling review.

Basic Spelling Rules

ei or *ie*

If the sound is a long *e*, put *i* before *e* except after *c*.
If the sound is a long *a* (as in weigh), reverse this order.

Example

long *e* – niece, thief, piece, perceive, receipt, receive
long *a* – weight, vein, sleigh, veil, neighbour
exceptions: height, science, either, their, weird

Doubling the Consonant

If the word is one syllable with one vowel and one final consonant, double the final consonant before an ending (except when the word ends in *x*).

Example

shop + *-ed* = shopped
wet + *-est* = wettest
sun + *-y* = sunny
tar + *-ed* = tarred
wax + *-ed* = waxed

In words of more than one syllable, follow this rule if the final syllable is stressed.

Example

begin + *-ing* = beginning
occur + *-ed* = occurred
permit + *-ing* = permitting

e + Ending with a Vowel

If the base word ends in a silent *e*, drop the *e* before adding an ending that begins with a vowel.

Example

excite + *-able* = excitable
love + *-ing* = loving

Exceptions are words that end in *ce* or *ge*; then the *e* stays.

Example

courage + *-ous* = courageous
change + *-able* = changeable
notice + *-able* = noticeable

Changing *y* to *i*

When the base word ends in *y*, change the *y* to *i* before adding endings.

Example

baby + *-es* = babies
carry + *-es* = carries
try + *-ed* = tried

Forming Noun Plurals

Generally you add *-s* to a noun to make it plural. However, there are a few exceptions that you need to learn.

a. If the noun ends in *s*, *ss*, *ch*, *sh*, *x*, or *z*, you add *–es*.
For example, *glasses*, *bushes*, *foxes*.

b. If the noun ends in *y* with a consonant in front, you change the *y* to *i* and add *–es*.
For example, *baby* to *babies*, *sky* to *skies*.

c. Some nouns ending in *f* are changed to *v* before adding *–es*.
For example, *leaf* to *leaves*, *dwarf* to *dwarves*.

d. If the noun ends in *o* with a consonant in front of the *o*, you add *-es* unless the noun is a musical term.
For example, *potato* to *potatoes*, *tomato* to *tomatoes*, but *piano* to *pianos* (no *-es*).

Some words need a different word in the plural form. These plurals are called *irregular*.

mouse = mice
tooth = teeth

Some words stay the same.

sheep = sheep
deer = deer
fish = fish

ROOTS, AFFIXES, SYLLABLES, AND SPELLING

Root: most basic part of a word

Example

root word *act*=related words *reaction*, *transaction*

Affix: "added on word part"

Example

prefix: added on to beginning of word=*pro*active, *re*action
suffix: added on to end of word=practic*al*, beaut*ify*

The spelling of a root may change when an affix is added.

Example

excite*ment*	no change
excit*ing*	silent *e* dropped

Syllable: word part containing a single vowel sound

Example

beau / ti / fy	3 syllables
con / trast	2 syllables

Spelling Tips for Common Prefixes

–*ad* sometimes changes to *a*: amend, arise, ascend
–*ex* sometimes changes to *e*: emission, elastic
–*in* sometimes changes to

il before root words beginning with *l*: illegal, illogical
im before root words beginning with *m* or *p*: immovable, immeasurable
ir before root words beginning with *r*: irresponsible

Spelling Rules for Adding Suffixes

1. Drop the *e*

Example

imagine=imaginable
excite=exciting

2. Keep the *e*

Example

excite=excitement
notice=noticeable

3. Double the final consonant (usually when it is preceded by a short vowel)

Example

admit=admitted
sag=sagged

4. Do not double the final consonant

Example

defeat = defeated
regret = regretful
invert = inverting

5. Change the *y* to *i*

Example

friendly = friendliness
carry = carried

6. Do not change the *y* to *i*

Example

enjoy = enjoying
cry = crying

Using syllables to break a word into natural "parts" helps you to spell more correctly.

Syllable rules for diving words into parts:

- after a prefix dis/
- between double consonants ap / point
- before a suffix /ment

Example

dis / ap / point / ment

Syllables and Inflection

Pay attention to the pronunciation of the word *present* in the following two sentences.

Example

Ron is nervous to *present* his speech on Friday.
The correct pronunciation is prē-sent′

What *present* are you buying for your best friend?
The correct pronunciation is prĕ-sent

The word *present* sounds different in each sentence, but both words are spelled the same. Another word for different pronunciation is *inflection*.

Frequently Misspelled Words

Certain words in the English language are frequently misspelled, even by people who think of themselves as good spellers. Some of these are listed below. Try to master them now because the older you become, the harder it will be to change faulty spelling patterns.

Here is a list of some commonly misspelled words. The tricky parts of these words have been underlined for you.

across	conscience	experience	immediate	possession	rhythm
argument	definitely	foreign	lightning	really	schedule
calendar	discipline	government	mischievous	relevant	separate
column	embarrass	grateful	neighbour	restaurant	until
committed	equipment	height	occasionally	rhyme	weird

Being Strategic About Spelling

The following five step strategy may have been shared with you when you were an elementary student. Your vocabulary may have become more complex since then, but the five steps still work. Try them on a new word that you would like to master. Take charge of your own spelling!

In your writing, it is important to always use proper spelling, plurals, verb tenses, consonant doubling, and contractions. There are many strategies to help writers spell new words and ones they find difficult, such as words with double letters, silent letters, or vowels that are pronounced differently than expected. One spelling strategy is called "Look-Think-Cover-Write-Check." It has five steps.

1. LOOK: Look very closely at the word. Say each letter aloud, and then read the complete word aloud. Can you make the word easier by breaking the word up into smaller parts or syllables?

Example

knowledge: *know+ledge*

2. THINK: Are there any parts of the word that may cause problems (double letters, silent letters, tricky letter combinations, and so on)? If so, study this step carefully.

knowledge: Silent: *k*

Tricky letter combination: *ow*

Consonant blend: *dg*

3. COVER: Cover the word. Picture it in your mind.

knowledge

4. WRITE: Look at the word again, and then write it down without looking back at it.

5. CHECK: Check your spelling to see if you are correct. Do not worry if you made a mistake! Look at the problem area and try again.

ON 10W3.2 build vocabulary for writing by confirming word meanings(s) and reviewing and refining word choice, using a variety of resources and strategies, as appropriate for the purpose

Vocabulary

Expanding your vocabulary has everything to do with using it. The more you use words you learn, the better they will stick in your head and become a part of your everyday speech and writing. Like your reading vocabulary, your writing vocabulary should be a consistently growing body of words that you are incorporating into your writing with increasing confidence.

You should only use words you understand yourself in your writing. If you are looking for a more precise word, check a thesaurus.

The words in a thesaurus are arranged in alphabetical order. Here is an example of an entry for the word *bright*.

> **Bright**: Adj (adjectives/synonyms) 1. sunny, fair, mild, balmy; brilliant, vivid, resplendent 2. smart, brainy, brilliant, clever, gifted, talented, sharp, keen
>
> (antonyms) 1. dull, flat, dingy, cloudy, faded, leaden, dim, pale, weak, faint 2. slow-witted, dim, slow, thick-headed, bland, desensitized

Do you need a synonym or an antonym? Do you want the literal/denotative meaning ("sunny") or a more connotative (associated) meaning like "brainy?" A thesaurus helps you add variety to your writing. Avoid choosing words simply because they sound more elaborate. A simple word may be your best word choice for the situation. If you are using technical terms or "content" words in something like a research report, do not underestimate the dictionary as a useful reference.

Dictionaries are always a good place to start when you are looking for the meaning of a specialized term. Look for the meaning associated with the specific subject or content area.

A **computer thesaurus** is a very useful tool when writing. However, be careful not to overuse this tool as it will make your writing feel artificial. You must also completely understand the definition of the words that you are using as replacements, as the subtle differences in meaning for the synonyms listed, when you use the computer thesaurus, must be taken into consideration.

How can a thesaurus help you to choose specific vocabulary? Read the following paragraph created by a student writer. Notice the underlined vocabulary:

> Jeremy <u>thought carefully about</u> his <u>great</u> idea. It could work! If he <u>planned</u> his disappearance <u>carefully</u>, the wedding would <u>continue</u> as planned, because his sister, the bride, would be too <u>busy</u> to notice his absence, and Jeremy would be well along the path to the river on his bike before anyone missed him. Of course, he needed to <u>return</u> before the reception buffet <u>started;</u> Mom would be <u>looking</u> for him in the food line and would be on the phone to the RCMP if she didn't <u>see</u> him heaping up his plate. A perfect July afternoon shouldn't be wasted at a garden wedding reception when the fish were biting and the river was beckoning!

Here is the same paragraph after the student used a thesaurus to find more interesting and specific words to replace the underlined ones:

> Jeremy <u>pondered</u> his <u>magnificent</u> idea. It could work! If he <u>staged</u> his disappearance <u>craftily</u>, the wedding would <u>proceed</u> as planned, because his sister, the bride, would be too <u>preoccupied</u> to notice his absence, and Jeremy would be well along the path to the river on his bike before anyone missed him. Of course, he needed to <u>reappear</u> before the reception buffet <u>commenced;</u> Mom would be <u>checking</u> for him in the food line and would be on the phone to the RCMP if she didn't <u>spot</u> him heaping up his plate. A perfect July afternoon shouldn't be wasted at a garden wedding reception when the fish were biting and the river was beckoning!

Building Vocabulary

The following list describes different ways to build your vocabulary:

- extensive and varied personal reading
- personal lists of new words and phrases from texts you read
- lists of subject-related words and their definitions
- using new words in conversation
- word games
- classroom word walls

Classroom word walls are interactive and usually involve a weekly or monthly addition to the wall. Each student posts up words they have learned and want to share with the class. Even if word walls are not part of your classroom environment, you can create a mini word wall of your own in the back of your writing or English binder. Jotting words down from different sources in one easy-to-find location may encourage you to actually use the words in your writing.

Using New Vocabulary

It is a good idea to keep personal vocabulary lists at the backs of binders or in separate vocabulary binders. If you learn a new word in any content area, try to remember to add the word and its definition to your list. If the word is an adjective, for instance, also record its other forms.

Example

frugal (adjective), meaning "reluctant to spend"
frugality (noun form), meaning "a reluctance to spend"

The best way to increase your vocabulary is to start using new words as often as you can after you learn them, in both speaking and writing. This helps you to "internalize" both the words and their meanings.

ON 10W3.3 use punctuation correctly and appropriately to communicate their intended meaning

Punctuation

Imagine if punctuation did not exist. Reading anything would be extremely tiring. Punctuation ensures that the meanings of the words you have chosen are understood clearly. You can choose your words carefully, but if your punctuation is incorrect, your meaning can be lost or confused. It is a good idea to use the following section to review what you know about punctuation and what you might be unsure about. The following pages chart most of the basic punctuation needed for writing clearly.

End Punctuation	A sentence will always end with a period, a question mark, or an exclamation mark.
Period	The period is used at the end of most sentences and after fragments that are deliberately used as sentences. *I walked to the end of the world. And stared.*
Question Mark	Use a question mark when your sentence asks a question. *Are you ready for dinner?*
Exclamation Mark	When you want to register a strong emotion, such as surprise, you might want to use an exclamation mark. *I am so ready for dinner!*

Apostrophe	**Apostrophe with Possessives** Most possessives are formed by adding an apostrophe and an *–s*. a *girl's* smile one *country's* history The possessive of a noun ending in an *s* sound is formed by adding an apostrophe and an *–s*. the *boss's* car *Charles's, Alex's* The possessive of a plural is formed by adding an apostrophe after the *–s* of the plural. five *girls'* smiles three *countries'* histories **Apostrophe with Contractions** Letters are omitted from common words or phrases, such as *cannot* and *does not*, to become the contractions *can't* and *doesn't*. An apostrophe replaces the missing letters.
Comma	**Commas with Introductory Phrases** Some introductory phrases have been previously mentioned. Other kinds of introductory phrases are also followed by a comma. *During the long summer afternoon, we were able to catch up on our work.* *Knowing he was beaten, he conceded defeat.* *Near a small clump of trees, we made our camp.* *As he was running out of money, he cabled home for more.* *In addition, we will need rope and flashlights.* **The Serial Comma** Use a comma after all the items in a series. *Bring food, extra clothing, a first-aid kit, and matches.* *A dictionary, a thesaurus, and a writing guide may be used for the test.* **Commas to Set Off Appositives** An appositive, a noun or a word or phrase used as noun, is set off by commas. *Our team, the Hornets, is in first place.* *His cousins, the Sinclairs, were all present at the reunion.* *Everyone in Toronto, the home of the Maple Leafs hockey team, is watching the Stanley Cup playoffs.* **Commas with Adjectives** When more than one adjective appears in front of a noun, commas are sometimes necessary. *fierce, tough dogs* but *three fierce, tough dogs* and *three fierce, tough old dogs* and *three fierce old sheep dogs*

<table>
<tr><td></td><td>
Do not put a comma between adjectives that build on each other to modify a noun. Each adjective modifies the noun and adjective group that follows it.
four vile yellow plastic figurines
her beautiful old Georgian townhouse
Cumulative adjectives have a certain order; they cannot be switched around.
Incorrect: vile four plastic yellow figurines
Incorrect: beautiful her Georgian old townhouse
Comma to Separate Clauses
When you link two longer independent clauses with a coordinating conjunction such as and or but, you should use a comma before the conjunction.
We completed our tour of the museum by lunchtime, and then we ate lunch in the patio courtyard.
We enjoyed having our lunch outside, but our picnic came to a sudden stop because of rain.
Other Uses of Commas
Setting off a transitional word, phrase, or clause at the beginning of a sentence
On my birthday, I expect many presents.
Separating direct speech from the rest of the sentence
"I need some new shoes," Paul told his mother.
Before a quotation
Hamlet's famous speech, "To be or not to be / That is the question" is an example of a soliloquy.
Separating the date and the year
January 22, 2008
Separating the city and province
Sudbury, Ontario
Separating the parts of an address
2011 Beech Street, Toronto, Ontario
</td></tr>
<tr><td>Semicolon</td><td>
Use to connect independent clauses rather than creating two sentences, especially when the sentences (independent clauses) are short and related.
two sentences: Lightning flashed. Thunder shook the valley.
compound sentence/two independent clauses: Lightning flashed, and thunder shook the valley.
semicolon: Lightning flashed; thunder shook the valley.
A semicolon should be used after each item in a series when the items already include commas.
The men endured a long, hot march; flies, dust, and brackish water; and a raging, howling sandstorm.
</td></tr>
</table>

<table>
<tr>
<td>Colon</td>
<td>
Colons can be used in the following situations:
Before a list
As we made the cake, we added the following ingredients: flour, eggs, sugar, and milk.
Before an example that enriches a point or idea that you want to make
I feel that the following point needs to be made: most people do their best at their job.
After the introductory salutation in a formal letter
Dear Mr. Evans:
Dear Sir:
Between numbers to tell time
7:08 A.M.
11:15 P.M.
When used in a sentence, a colon must follow an independent clause.
It introduces a list, an explanation, or an appositive (a word or phrase that restates a noun).
You should bring the following items: a sleeping bag, a change of clothes, and matches.
There is only one honest thing to do: admit you made a mistake and apologize.
His character was summed up in his name: Grad Grind.
The list may be set up in point form. The same rule applies.
The introductory course will cover three topics:
1. algebra
2. geometry
3. trigonometry
If a list does not follow an independent clause (a complete sentence), no colon is used.
You must bring a sleeping bag, a change of clothes, and matches.
The introductory course will cover
1. algebra
2. geometry
3. trigonometry
Helpful Hint: A simple way of checking colon use is to cover up all the words after the colon. Can the first part of the sentence now stand alone as a sentence? If not, then do not use the colon.
Incorrect: You must bring: a sleeping bag, a change of clothes, and matches.
Correct: You must bring the following items: a sleeping bag, a change of clothes, and matches.
</td>
</tr>
</table>

<table>
<tr>
<td>Quotation Marks</td>
<td>
Use quotation marks at the beginning and end of all words in a direct quotation (someone's exact words). Watch for the use of quotation marks before and after a speech tag. Also notice the use of the comma after the speech tag (Alfred said) as in the first example.

Alfred said, "We are ready."
"I'm finished the job," said Alfred. "We can go now."
"When we are ready," said Alfred, "we will go."

Also notice that the closing quotation mark is placed after a comma or a period.

Closing quotation marks are also used with exclamation marks and question marks. When these punctuation marks belong to the sentence, they are placed outside the closing quotation marks.

Didn't you hear him say, "I'm in trouble"?

If the question mark belongs to the quotation, it is placed inside the quotation marks.

He said sadly, "Why is it always me?"

The same rules apply to end punctuation used for other purposes. Periods and commas belong inside the quotation marks. Exclamation and quotation marks belong either outside or inside the quotation marks, depending on whether they belong to the sentence as a whole or to the words inside the quotation marks.

You could say that her acting was "over the top."
I can't believe that's your "best effort"!

Indirect quotations or quotations that do not repeat exact words never require quotation marks.

Alfred asked if we were ready.
Alfred said that he had finished the job and that we could go.

Quotation marks are also used set off the titles of short stories and poems.

Marjorie Pickthall wrote "Stars."

Quotation marks indicate that a word is being used in an unusual sense.

"Housekeeping" on the space station is challenging.

Quotation marks can also show that a word is used ironically. When a word is used ironically, it has a meaning opposite to its literal meaning.

It seems that your "help" has put this project three weeks behind.

Quotation marks are used to quote the exact words from a source.

From an individual

"It is not the mountain we conquer, but ourselves." [Sir Edmund Hillary, the first person to reach the Summit of Mount Everest in 1953]

From a published source in which the quote will not exceed four typed lines of text

It was reported in The Guardian of January 22, 2008, that an "investment banker ... may face jail after posing as a university under graduate in order to help a student cheat his way through his final year economic exams."

Note that while the exact original words have been quoted, ellipses (…) have been used to show that some wording at that point has been omitted.
</td>
</tr>
</table>

OTHER PUNCTUATION

Brackets and Parentheses

Brackets [ ] and parentheses ( ) are similar but have slightly different uses.

- Brackets [ ] enclose words that are inserted into a direct quotation but are not part of the original quotation.

Examples

So that, my friends, [laughter] is the punch line!
"Once I found the stolen goods, I arrested [the accused] immediately," explained the officer.

- Parentheses ( ) are used to include "extra" information that does not change the overall meaning of a sentence.

Examples

At that moment, in walked (you guessed it) my Mom.
Many brave American sailors died at Pearl Harbor (December 7, 1941).

Dashes

The em dash (—) is the width of the capital letter "M" (if you use a computer but your software does not provide an em dash, use two hyphens with no space between them). The dash can be very effective punctuation—but because it is so noticeable and forceful, it is easy to overuse! Do not fall into the habit of always substituting dashes for semicolons, colons, commas, and parentheses. Here are some examples of the use of dashes:

- To show a sudden break in thought or tone

Example

I want to tell you first—so shut the door quickly.

- To separate an interrupting word or words from the rest of the sentence

Example

Marley shrugged into her uniform—lab coat, goggles, and rubber gloves—before entering the lab.

- To set off an appositive phrase clearly

Example

Sam Gunther—the newly elected mayor—stepped up to the podium.

Hyphens

Hyphens are shorter than dashes and are used differently.

- To join the parts of some compound words

Example

good-bye sister-in-law great-aunt

If in doubt, check a dictionary. The hyphen has been dropped from most compound words.

	• To separate parts of a compound modifier *Example* half-hearted attempt self-centered athlete • In compound numbers from twenty-one to ninety-nine *Example* My uncle turns forty-three next Saturday. • To divide words at margins *Example* In Mexico, we bought pon- chos at the market. • After some prefixes *Example* half-sister **Italics and Underlining** When using a computer word processor, use italics to indicate the title of a novel, long play, television series, album title, etc. If you are handwriting, underline to indicate the italics. *Example* After I finish watching *Friends* I will read the next act of *Romeo and Juliet.* Italics (or underlining) can also be used to indicate emphasis or sarcasm. *Examples* I *really* enjoyed the movie version of *The Lord of the Rings*. How can you behave *that* badly at your grandmother's house?

Punctuation plays an important role in meaning. Even if the words you use are clear and well-chosen, punctuation can determine how your sentence is understood. Always double check to make sure that your punctuation is correct or if it could be improved on.

ON 10W3.4 use grammar conventions correctly and appropriately to communicate their intended meaning clearly and fluently

Grammar

Like correct punctuation, grammar conventions allow you to communicate your ideas clearly. Grammar conventions revolve around the eight parts of speech.

Parts of Speech

Nouns

- are people, places, or things
- may be concrete or abstract nouns

  boy, city, building (concrete)
  peace, thoughtfulness (abstract)
- Capitalize proper nouns, which are the names of specific persons, places, or things.

  Simon, Toronto, CN Tower

Pronouns

- Take the place of nouns

Simon is on the phone; *he* would like to speak with *you*.

Adjectives

- Modify, or describe, nouns and pronouns

  the *tall* boy, the *crowded* city, the *gold* building
- The articles *a*, *an*, and *the* are considered adjectives.

Verbs

- Usually name actions such as *laugh*, *sleep*, *think*
- Most English verbs are regular; that is, their past tense and past participle forms end in *-ed*. There are about three hundred irregular verbs.
- Transitive verbs have a direct object. They do something to the object.

  In the sentence, "The ball struck the batter," *batter* is the direct object of *struck*.
- Intransitive verbs do not have direct objects. The verbs *lie* (to tell a *lie*) and *arrive* are intransitive. You cannot *arrive* anything or *lie* anything.

  I hope I arrive on time.
- Most verbs are transitive or intransitive depending on how they are used.

  transitive: He produced a sheaf of papers.
  intransitive: When irrigated, the wasteland produced abundantly.
- Linking verbs like *be, taste*, *look*, and *sound* describe states of being. Other linking verbs such as *turn*, *become*, and *grow* describe changes in state. Remember that linking verbs are usually followed by nouns or adjectives; that is, nominals or adjectivals.

  She *is* a *lawyer*.
  This *milk* tastes *sour*.

Adverbs

- Modify, or describe, a verb, an adjective, or another adverb

  She ran *quickly*. (*quickly* describes how she ran)
  His *extremely* brilliant argument was presented yesterday. (*extremely* modifies the adjective *brilliant*)
  They worked *very* hard. (*very* modifies the adverb *hard*)

Prepositions

- Words placed in front of nouns and pronouns for a cause *by* them

Conjunctions

- Join words, phrases, clauses, and sentences
- Coordinating conjunctions such as *and*, *so*, and *or* join equal parts

  You must lead *or* follow
  Chopping firewood *and* painting trim are next.
  We went to the wedding ceremony *and* we went to the reception.
- Correlative conjunctions like *either, or* and *neither, nor* join equal parts

  You must *either* lead *or* follow.
  Either you must chop firewood *or* you must paint the trim.
  Parker likes *neither* skiing *nor* snowboarding.
- Subordinating conjunctions like *whenever* and *however* join unequal parts

  Whenever I hear that song, I want to laugh.
  You must be careful *whenever* you cross the street.
  However you arrange it, be sure that you are back by Tuesday.

Interjections

- Express some form of strong emotion

  Ouch! That hurts.
  Oh, I don't know.

You can use your understanding of grammar to place the correct form of a word in a sentence and to combine phrases and clauses in a variety of sentence patterns.

Examples of Complete and Correct Sentence Patterns

1. Simple sentence: one subject (noun/pronoun) and one predicate (verb)

   O.C. Marsh discovered the brontosaurus.
2. Simple sentence with a prepositional phrase.

   [Like a prehistoric monster,] the gentle brontosaurus lumbered slowly [across the clearing.]
3. Compound sentence: at least two simple sentences.

   [The brontosaurus lumbered slowly], yet [he was surprisingly agile].
4. Complex sentence: main clause and at least one relative/subordinate/dependent clause. A main clause is a simple sentence.

   relative adjective clause
   The brontosaurus [which you study in school] was really a dinosaur discovered earlier, called an Apatosaurus.

   relative adverb clause
   The gigantic brontosaurus swayed slightly [as it lumbered slowly across the clearing]

5. Compound–Complex sentence: at least two main clauses and at least one relative clause.

adverb prep. phrase — main clause — adverb phrase

[In the cartoon], [Fred Flintstone drives his brontosaurus] [like a bulldozer] and

main clause — relative adverb clause

[he also downs a few brontosaurus burgers] [while he is bowling with Barney.]

Most correct sentences will be a variation of these basic sentence patterns. However, the variations offer many creative possibilities to you as a writer.

Common Sentence Errors

The most frequent sentence errors involve incomplete sentences, known as sentence fragments, and run-on or comma splice sentences. These errors are easy to make but easy to fix in most cases.

Complete Sentences

A sentence is a group of words that expresses a complete thought. Each group of words should make sense by itself. Which of the following sentences expresses a complete thought?

A. While Sonia was hurrying to the station.
B. Kevin finished the test early.

If you guessed that the second sentence expresses a complete thought, you are correct. A complete sentence has both a *subject* and a *predicate.* The subject of a sentence tells *what* it is that you are talking about—the person, place, or thing. The predicate tells something *about* the subject. Every complete sentence must have a subject and a predicate.

In the second example, "Kevin" is the subject of the sentence, and "finished the test early" is the predicate. In the first example, you are left wondering what happened while Sonia was hurrying to the station. It is not a complete sentence because it is not a complete thought. While writing, make sure you write in complete sentences. By maintaining solid sentence structure, you will be able to express your ideas more clearly.

This fragment could be easily corrected in at least two ways:

1. Create a simple sentence
   Sonia was hurrying to the station.
2. Use the fragment as a relative clause
   While Sonia was hurrying to the station, she slipped on some ice.

Run-on Sentences and Comma Splices

When writing, avoid run-on sentences. Run-on sentences generally occur when two or more complete sentences are joined together without the proper punctuation. Run-on sentences do not have to be long to be wrong. Consider the following example:

Bobby loves to draw cartoon strips he is a talented artist.

This is an incorrect sentence because the statements "Bobby loves to draw cartoon strips" and "he is a talented artist" can both stand alone as complete sentences. They are both independent clauses. They cannot run together into one sentence without somehow separating them. There are several ways to fix these types of sentences.

1. You could separate the two clauses into two sentences:
   Bobby loves to draw cartoon strips. He is a talented artist.
2. You could use a semicolon to properly punctuate the two clauses:
   Bobby loves to draw cartoon strips; he is a talented artist.

3. You could use a coordinating conjunction (and, but, or, for, yet, nor, so) to properly separate the two clauses:

   Bobby is a talented artist and he loves to draw cartoon strips.

4. You could use a subordinating conjunction (*after*, *although*, *before*, *unless*, *as because*, *even though*, *if*, *since*, *until*, *when*, *while*) to properly separate the two clauses:

   Since Bobby is a talented artist, he loves to draw cartoon strips.

5. You could use a semicolon and transitional word or phrase (*however*, *on the other hand*, *therefore*, *otherwise*) to properly separate the two clauses:

   Bobby is a talented artist; therefore, he loves to draw cartoon strips.

A comma splice is similar to a run-on except that the writer has used commas where there should be full stops, like periods, or at least semicolons.

Incorrect: *Bobby loves to draw cartoon strips, he is a talented artist.*
Correct: See above examples

Incorrect: We were in the city for a whole day, we shopped in every mall, I could hardly walk when we boarded the subway.
Correct: *We were in the city for a whole day;* *we shopped in every mall, so I could hardly walk when we boarded the subway.*

Comma splices can be corrected using the same strategies used to correct run-on sentences.

Verb Agreement

When you are writing, it is important to check that all your verbs agree in number (singular and plural) and tense (past, present, future). Agreement can sometimes be confusing, so take care when you are editing your writing.

Agreement in Number

If the subject is singular, the verb must be singular.

The *box* full of Christmas decorations *is* already open. (The box is open).

Agreement in Tense

Make sure that the tenses (time relationships) are properly expressed.

Correct: After she *moved* to Ottawa, she *discovered* that she *liked* the rain. (past tense for all three verbs)
Incorrect: After she moved to Ottawa, she discovered she likes the rain. (The word *like* is in the present tense, while *moved* and *discovered* are in the past tense.)

Remember to check the time relationships between all verbs in your sentences and paragraphs.

Pronoun Agreement

Pronouns are words that are used to replace nouns so that you do not have sentences sounding like this:

Jerry wondered whether Jerry had lost Jerry's iPod at the park.

Fortunately, you can replace nouns like *Jerry* with personal pronouns (*I*, *me*, *you*, *he*, *she*, *it*) and their related forms, so the sentence would read this way: *Jerry wondered whether he had lost his iPod at the park.*

Pronouns must agree with their antecedents. The antecedent is the noun represented by the pronoun.

Examples

1. *Julia* noticed that *she* had accidentally picked up the wrong *camera*, so *she* gave *it* to the tour leader.

    Julia is the antecedent of the pronoun *she*, and camera is the antecedent of the pronoun *it*.

2. The contest was disappointing for *Hong*, *who* had counted on winning.

    Hong is the antecedent of the pronoun *who*.

3. The *man* in the tower was flashing a signal to proceed when *he* suddenly disappeared from the tower window.

    Man is the antecedent of the pronoun *he*.

Use a plural pronoun with a plural antecedent, and singular with singular.

1. When the highway *policemen* arrived at the scene of the collision, *they* immediately put roadblocks in place.
2. When the highway *policeman* arrived at the scene of the collision, *he* immediately put roadblocks in place.

Use the same gender as the antecedent.

1. As *he* stepped into the mineshaft, *Marshall* listened for sounds below.
2. *Marian* suddenly remembered *she* had to babysit after school.

It is *not* acceptable to use the pronoun *they* when the gender is not specified.

Incorrect: If *anyone* knew the answer, *they* would share it.
Correct: If *anyone* knew the answer, *he* or *she* would share it.

When one singular and one plural antecedent are joined by *or* or *nor*, the pronoun should agree with the nearest antecedent.

1. Either you or your *friends* should leave *their* phone numbers.
2. Neither the friends nor *John* left *his* phone number.

ON 10W3.5 proofread and correct their writing, using guidelines developed with the teacher and peers

Proofreading

When you have finished writing the content of a piece of written work (including revising and rewriting), you should proofread and edit it for correct grammar, punctuation, capitalization, and spelling. Though you may have spent a great deal of time organizing and writing your ideas down, your reader's ability to understand and enjoy them will suffer if the final document contains basic errors and inconsistencies.

Grammar

Verb Tense
Subject/Verb Agreement
Complete Sentences
Comparative and Superlative Forms of Adjectives and Adverbs
Subordinate Clauses and Coordinating Conjunctions
Modifier Placement
Correct Word Usage

Verb Tense

The tense of a verb tells the reader when the action happens. The most common verb tenses you will use in your writing are the past tense (before), the present tense (now), and the future tense (later).

Here is an example of the three tenses of the verb *to work*.

Past Tense	Present Tense	Future Tense
He worked.	He works.	He will work.

When planning a story, think about when your story will take place: the past, the present, the future, or some combination of these timeframes. You may decide to begin your story in the present but include flashback sequences. Make sure that when you are writing in the present, your verbs reflect the present tense. When you use a flashback sequence, make sure that the verbs are written in the past tense. Whatever you decide, make sure that you use consistent verb tenses in your narrative writing.

Consistent: Her uncle often *came* to visit her. One day he *asked* her…
Inconsistent: Her uncle often *comes* to visit her. One day he *asked* her…

Subject/Verb Agreement

Most of the difficulties in subject-verb agreement are caused by difficulties in recognizing singular and plural subjects.

When subjects are joined by *or* or *nor*, the verb agrees with the nearest subject.

Either Miller *or* Smith *is* guilty.
Neither Miller *nor* Smith *wants* to confess.
Neither the speaker *nor* the listeners *are* aware of the irony.

When one part of the verb is singular and the other plural, write the sentence so the plural part is nearest the verb.

Weak: Neither *band members* nor the *conductor* is satisfied.
Better: Neither the *conductor* nor the *band members* are satisfied.

Nothing that comes between a singular subject and its verb can make that subject plural. Students should not make the verb agree with the nearest noun.

Our school *basketball team*, the Gerbils, *is* victorious again.
The *prime minister*, accompanied by several cabinet ministers, *arrives* at the airport shortly.
Either *Miller* or *Jones*—both are suspects—*is* guilty.
The *contestant* with the most votes *is* now on stage.
One of the girls *sings* better.
The ringleader who was at the head of the rebellious miners *is* sorry.

Indefinite pronouns such as *each*, *each one*, *either*, *neither*, *everyone*, *everybody*, *anybody*, *anyone*, *nobody*, *somebody*, *someone*, and *no one* are singular.

Each of the contestants *wins* a prize.
Everybody near the river *is* in danger.
No one who wants to be successful in the exams *is* likely to be late.

Collective nouns are singular unless there is a reason to consider them as plurals.

The *group works* well.
The *company is* bankrupt.
The *jury is* deliberating *its* verdict.
The *jury are* arguing among themselves.

Using the correct pronoun is often a problem because the form of a pronoun varies depending on how the pronoun is used.

Use *I*, *you*, *he/she/it*, *we*, *you*, *they*, and *who* as the subject of a sentence or clause and for the complement of a linking verb.

You have been chosen.
We will be the last of the contestants.
Who is going to be next?
It is *she* who will be chosen.

Use *me, you, him/her/it, us, you, them,* and *whom* as direct or indirect objects of verbs or as the object of a preposition.

Give it to *me*.
Hit the ball to *them*.
Ask *them* the time.
The child next to *him* laughed suddenly.

Use *my*, *your*, *him/her/its*, *our*, *their*, and *whose* as adjectives.

my car
your umbrella
its fur

Use *mine, yours, his/hers/its, ours, theirs,* and *whose* as a subject of a sentence or as the complement of a linking verb.

Yours is the one on the left.
This is *mine*.
Theirs is next.

The possessive pronouns *my*, *your*, *his*, *hers*, *its*, *our*, *yours*, *theirs*, and *whose* **never** use an apostrophe to show possession.

Complete Sentences

As a general rule, all sentences should be complete sentences.

Correct: *He went ahead with his plan, even though it was faulty.*
Incorrect: *He went ahead with his plan. Even though it was faulty.*

Occasionally, an incomplete sentence is used deliberately for effect. Fragments that are used deliberately are sometimes called *minor sentences*.

Correct: *Is anyone in favour of dictatorship? No? Well, of course not.*

Dialogue and reported speech are exceptions to the rule about fragments.

"Ready yet?"
"Not yet."
"Well then—!"

The opposite error is the "sentence" that is really two sentences. Either punctuation between sentences is omitted or a comma is used to join two sentences.

Run-on: *We went to Toronto we decided to visit the zoo.*
Comma splice: *We went to Toronto, we decided to visit the zoo.*

These errors can be fixed by correcting the punctuation or by rewriting the sentence.

We went to Toronto. We decided to visit the zoo.
We went to Toronto. Then we decided to visit the zoo.
After we went to Toronto, we decided to visit the zoo.
We went to Toronto, and then we decided to visit the zoo.

Comparative and Superlative Forms of Adjectives and Adverbs

Comparatives and superlatives are special forms of adjectives and adverbs. They are used to compare things. When you compare *two things*, use the comparative form.

Example

A car is much *more expensive* than a lollipop.
Five plus five is *greater* than four plus four.

When you compare *more than two things*, use the superlative form.

Example

That was the *best* movie I have ever seen.
I wanted to buy the *largest* dog in the window.

The following chart provides some examples that compare the base form of an adjective or adverb with the comparative and superlative forms of the same word.

Base	Comparative	Superlative
fast	*faster*	*fastest*
good	*better*	*best*
wide	*wider*	*widest*
bad	*worse*	*worst*
quickly	*more quickly*	*most quickly*
harmful	*more harmful*	*most harmful*

Subordinate Clauses and Coordinating Conjunctions

A clause is a group of words containing a subject and a predicate. A subordinate clause is a group of words that cannot stand alone as a sentence. Using subordinate clauses allows you to create interesting sentences by combining ideas.

Example

My sister, *who is a doctor*, has four children.
While I clean my room, I like to listen to music.

The clauses *who is a doctor* and *while I clean my room* cannot stand alone as sentences and are therefore called subordinate clauses. Subordinate clauses add information to a sentence but are not complete ideas on their own.

Coordinating conjunctions are words used to join two clauses together. Some examples of coordinating conjunctions are *for, and, not, but, or, yet,* and *so*. These simple words can be used to join ideas and create complex sentences.

Example

Wendy loved to read books *but* did not enjoy magazines.
John heard the weather report *and* hurried home.
The sun was shining brightly, *yet* the air was still cold.

Modifier Placement

As a general rule, a modifier (usually an adjective or an adverb) should be placed as closely as possible to the word being modified.

Vague: Entering the room, the door was shut by mother.

Clear: [Entering the room], mother shut the door.

Vague: At six years of age, my parents started me in piano.

Clear: [At six years of age], I started taking piano lessons.

Correct Word Usage

The following words are frequently confused:

lie/lay

Correct: Father would *lie* down for a ten minute nap after lunch. *(recline)*
Correct: We were asked to *lay* our uniforms neatly on the shelf. *(put or place)*
Incorrect: Father would *lay* down for a ten-minute nap after lunch.

accept/except

Correct: Jeremy will *accept* the reward on behalf of his brother. *(receive)*
Correct: Everyone in the family *except* Nolan came down with the flu. *(With the exception of)*

borrow/lend

Correct: May I *borrow* your baseball glove? *(borrow "from")*
Incorrect: May I *loan* your baseball glove?

Correct: Could you *lend* me your text? *(lend "to")*
Incorrect: Could you *borrow* me your text?

to/too/two

Correct: We need *to* decide whether *two* pies will be *too* much.

their/there/they're

Correct: The students will take *their* final exam on Friday morning. *(possession)*
Correct: We decided *there* were enough people present to take a vote.
Correct: The Smith family lived *there* for thirteen years.
Correct: If *they're* arriving Tuesday, someone should meet them at the airport. *(contraction of "they are")*

its/it's

Correct: Although the cat injured *its* left front paw, it's recovering nicely. *(Its: possessive pronoun; no apostrophe needed)*
Correct: *It's* time you went to school. *(it's: contraction of "it is")*

lose/loose

Correct: Try not to *lose* your backpack.
Correct: Our mechanic discovered that the engine problem was caused by a *loose* bolt.

Hint: You "lose" the extra "o" when you write "lose" instead of "loose."

can/may

Correct: Most children *can* print their own name by the age of five. *(are able to)*
Correct: You *may* eat your lunch outside today. *(are allowed to)*
Incorrect: You *can* eat your lunch outside today.

in/into

Correct: Sara needs the key to get *into* her house.
Correct: All the information is located *in* your portfolio. *(within)*
Incorrect: Sara needs the key to get *in* her house.

whose/who's

Correct: I don't know *whose* wallet is missing. *(belonging to whom)*
Correct: *Who's* willing to help pick up this litter? *(contraction of "who is")*

good/well

Correct: It seemed like a *good* idea.
Correct: Terri didn't feel *well* after her game.
Incorrect: Terri didn't feel *good* after her game.

different from/different than

Correct: Lettuce is *different from* cabbage.
Incorrect: Lettuce is *different than* cabbage.

The expression "different than" is **always incorrect** English.

could have/could of
would have/would of
should have/should of

Using *of* with these verbs is **always incorrect**. The word *have* is the correct choice.

Correct: I *could have* spelled that word correctly.
Correct: I *would have* spelled it correctly if I had paid closer attention.
Correct: You *should have* warned me that this test counted.

Capitalization

Although there are many special rules for capitalization, the following rules are the most important to practice for now.

- Capitalize the first words of sentences, including sentences used in quotations.
- Capitalize proper nouns, including any specific person, place, or thing.
  - For instance, capitalize *Suzie Walker*, *Happyville School*, *Pasadena*, *December*, *Christmas Day*, *Doctor Newman*, and *Artemis Fowl*. However, do not capitalize common nouns, such as *the girl*, *a school*, *our city*, *a month*, *the day*, *the doctor*, or *a book*.
- Always capitalize the word *I*.
- Capitalize some abbreviations.
  - For example, *R.S.V.P.*, an abbreviation for a French phrase that means "please respond," and *Ave.*, an abbreviation for *Avenue*, both require capital letters, as do titles, such as *Mr.*, *Mrs.*, *Dr.*, and so on.

- Capitalization can sometimes be useful when you are trying to emphasize a certain word or create an emotional response.
  - For example, "*WOW! I could not believe my eyes. My brother was flying!*"
- Capitalize the main words in a title, such as *The Cat in the Hat* or *My Summer in Mexico.*

Proofreading Checklist

The following proofreading checklist may help you make sure that your revised draft is ready for publishing or handing in. Always save your working draft on the computer in case you have to make changes after proofreading. Proofread both silently and aloud, if possible.

- Check for smooth flow of ideas, with all of your revision made to the draft
- Sentences: varied lengths, beginnings, types, no run-ons or fragments
- Punctuation: all end marks, commas, quotation marks, etc.
- Capitalization
- Spelling: use spellcheck, dictionary
- Check for agreement: subject/verb/pronoun/antecedent
- Check with your "personal alert" list from your writing binder: (1) your most frequent usage errors; for example, run-ons or verb agreement; (2) your most frequent punctuation and capitalization errors; (3) words you have misspelled this year
- Print or write your final, edited copy

Peer Conferences

Peer Conferences can be helpful both at the revision and the proofreading stages of your writing. At a peer conference, always read your work out loud. For this reason, peer conferences work very well in a partner situation.

Tips for Reader

1. Show your punctuation through pauses.
2. Don't rush your reading.
3. Be open to suggestions.
4. Jot notes for changes on your draft.
5. Clarify your partner's comments with questions as needed.
6. Thank your partner.
7. Appreciate that your peer is trying to help you improve your writing.

Tips for Listener

1. Listen carefully and pay attention to your reader's ideas.
2. Make sure to tell the reader what they have done well.
3. Be specific in criticism: "That sentence is confusing," "You need a stronger verb there"
4. Try to be constructive: "What if you switched those two ideas to make the argument more clear?"
5. Remember that you are only trying to help. The writer may choose not to follow some of your suggestions.

Figures of Speech

Figures of speech make your writing interesting. A well-chosen figure of speech helps your reader better visualize the setting, object, or action.

A **simile** compares unlike objects or ideas using the words *like* or *as*.
Example

The train was as fast as a speeding bullet.

A **metaphor** compares unlike objects or ideas without using the words *like* or *as*.
Example

She flew around the corner with great speed.

Personification attributes human qualities or characteristics to inanimate objects
Example

The trees waved their branches in the wind.

Idioms are expressions that should not be taken literally.
Example

She was walking on air when she heard the good news.

Appropriate Modifiers

Adjectives modify nouns by telling what "kind" of person, place, or thing they are.
Example

Wild geese, *high-flying* geese, *honking* geese, *southbound* geese, *excited* geese (what kind);
those geese, *that* goose, *my* geese, *six* geese, *some* geese, *your* goose (limit the description further)

Adverbs modify verbs or other modifiers by telling when, where, how, or how much.
Example

The wild geese flew *south* (where) *yesterday* (when).
The wild geese flew *noisily* and *swiftly* (how) *in a 'V' shape* (how).

Modifiers can also be phrases that do the work of a single adverb.
Example

The geese flew *toward the south.*
With loud honking and flapping of wings, the geese flew south.

Active and Passive Voice

Active voice is stronger and more direct than passive voice, and it usually makes your writing more effective. A sentence is written in the active voice when the subject clearly *does* the action; a sentence written in the passive voice when the subject of the sentence *receives* the action. Look at these examples to help you understand how much stronger and direct the active voice is.

Active Voice	My dad packed the car for the trip.
Passive Voice	The car was packed for the trip by my dad.
Active Voice	Sue ate her birthday cake.
Passive Voice	The birthday cake was eaten by Sue.

In the active voice, the subject of each sentence is placed before the object. You can see that active language conveys the same ideas in fewer words.

All of the information that is presented in this section has been included so you can develop vocabulary and grammar skills. Remember that both careful reading and writing will help you better understand how proper grammar works and how to expand your vocabulary. The rules and guidelines you have learned in this section of your KEY offer tools that are meant to be used when you are reading and writing. After you have finished reading something, take another look at the text for grammar and vocabulary. Note how sentences are made, which words are being used, and how they are used. Remember that your vocabulary and grammar will improve through knowing and following rules and guidelines. Reading and being curious and observant in your reading will help improve your vocabulary and grammar as well.

PUBLISHING YOUR WORK

ON 10W3.6 use a variety of presentation features, including print and script, fonts, graphics, and layout, to improve the clarity and coherence of their written work and to heighten its appeal for their audience

How your work looks is important. The final stage of writing usually involves printing out your assignment, but publishing your work involves several stages of planning during your work. Some of the important expectations this year include organization of your ideas, adequate development of information and ideas, the appropriate use of form and style, and the appropriate use of conventions.

The following section of your KEY addresses formats for publishing your work and offers methods of publishing and formatting your assignments.

ON 10W3.7 produce pieces of published work to meet criteria identified by the teacher, based on the curriculum expectations

Organization of Ideas

In Grade 10, you will use your writing and creative skills to produce assignments that meet criteria from your teacher. Since teachers usually give assignments to help you meet the expectations of the curriculum, it is important that you consistently try to follow teacher guidelines. If you are asked to write a business letter, for instance, follow the business letter guidelines provided in the classroom. If the teacher has assigned an essay, the criteria would probably involve some of the following criteria:

Essay Structure

- **Introduction**
  - This is the first paragraph or two of an essay.
  - It is the point at which the reader is made aware of the writer's intentions for the piece of writing.
  - The introduction provides information on the topic and allows the reader to figure out what kind of essay it is.
- **Body**
  - This is the bulk of the essay where most information is provided.
- **Conclusion**
  - The end of the essay, usually one or two paragraphs in length, where the writer wraps up the argument or otherwise ties together the content of the essay for the reader.
- **Thesis**
  - This is the main idea of the essay that ties the whole piece together. It is like the theme in a short story.
- **Transitions**
  - These are words that allow the reader to slide smoothly from one idea to the next or from one paragraph to the next.

If the essay is persuasive, the teacher might also require an outline to show that your points of argument are organized effectively. Effective organization includes a clear introduction, well-supported arguments, and a conclusion that meaningfully restates your main idea.

SHAPING YOUR IDEAS

Once you have collected ideas and information about your topic, organized these ideas in groups, and written your thesis sentence, it is time to focus more specifically on the structure of your essay. A good method of structuring your essay is to shape your ideas into hierarchies. Establishing a hierarchy means deciding which ideas are more general and which more specific. The following example shows you how an outline for an essay can be structured.

Example

Thesis Sentence

I. First argument
- **A.** First section of the first argument
  - **1.** First example or illustration
    - **a.** First fact or detail
    - **b.** Second fact or detail
  - **2.** Second example or illustration
- **B.** Second section of the first argument

II. Second argument
- **A.** First section of the second argument
  - **1.** First example or illustration
    - **a.** First fact or detail
    - **b.** Second fact or detail
  - **2.** Second example or illustration
- **B.** Second section of the second argument

You may have been asked to provide at least three arguments to support your thesis, so you would proceed to complete your outline following the pattern shown in "I. First argument."

Creating an outline before you begin to write the essay gives you the advantage of mapping out the terrain you plan to cover. With an outline, you are more likely to stay on topic. You should allow yourself some flexibility to change the outline as you begin to write. While writing, you may discover that one section of the argument proceeds more naturally to a different aspect than what is in your outline. Shifting parts of the essay around is a common practice, especially when revising the first draft. As you are writing, try to stay flexible enough to alter the course of your argument if necessary. Use your outline as a guide, not a fixed format.

ADEQUATE DEVELOPMENT OF INFORMATION AND IDEAS

Development refers to improving and shaping your ideas while you work on an assignment. Development includes such things as examples, illustrations, definitions, descriptions, facts, statistics, anecdotes, quotations, etc. The following elements of writing will help you develop ideas and help you to decide what kind of information you want to include in your writing.

Narration and Description

Narration involves telling the sequence of events of what happened; description involves telling what a person, place, or thing looks like. Both narration and description should be used sparingly, since they do not advance arguments on their own. Instead, these techniques can be used to briefly support the case you are making. You may be tempted to use narration and description in too great detail, especially if your assignment asks for a word count and you are not sure if you have enough to say. It is better to extend one of the arguments you are making instead. When used carefully, narration and description make an essay more engaging for a reader because they offer concrete examples to support abstract arguments.

Facts and Statistics

Facts are objective pieces of information; statistics are collections of facts that are organized into numerical data. When quoting facts or statistics in your essay, remember the importance of the source from which you draw your quotation. Usually, a conversation overheard on the street would not provide an authoritative source of information that you could use in an assignment. If you are quoting statistics, you need to use credible, unbiased sources. For example, statistics from a university researcher regarding the link between cigarette smoking and lung cancer would be more credible that those provided by a cigarette manufacturer.

Definitions

Defining a key term is an excellent way to begin an essay or to solidify an argument in the middle of one. Definitions do not have to come from a dictionary, although this is a very good source. Other reliable books, such as textbooks, manuals, and encyclopaedias, offer definitions that could be useful for supporting your argument. Often definitions from other authoritative books are more specialized.

Unless your argument requires a definition, it should not take up too much room in the body of your paper. If you intend to use a definition, make sure that you are defining the word correctly. You will need to cite the source of your definition, whether it is from a dictionary, a textbook, or a web-site.

Providing a definition shows the way in which *you* plan to use the term for your argument, although there may be several other ways it is used in everyday speech.

Be sure to develop your ideas and information, but always stay relevant to your topic or subtopic. Teachers can tell when a student is padding their paper. Padding your paper means adding non-essential or unrelated information to make your assignment appear longer. Longer is not necessarily better!

Appropriate Use of Form and Style

Your teacher will provide you with specific expectations in the writing assignments, such as

- **Form**: short stories, sonnets, businesses letters, news stories, editorials, etc., follow fairly specific form guidelines. For example, short stories follow the expectations of a plot graph or outline (setting, conflict, rising action, turning point, outcome), and sonnets are 14 line poems with specific rhyme schemes and rhythm patterns.
- **Style**: formal writing style is expected in business letters and editorials. You might be allowed to write a short story in a humorous, informal style of language in which the main character uses teenage slang.

Manuscript Requirements

When you are ready to write your final copy of an essay, report, or research paper, you need to find out from your teacher the correct format and any other specific instructions. There are many different formats for presenting your work, and your teacher may have certain requirements. The following example demonstrates some expectations for a manuscript that would include a bibliography.

Title Page

Title

Your Name

Course name
Teacher's name
Date submitted

Pagination: refers to the numbering of your pages. Your title page should not be numbered, so begin with your first page of text. Be consistent with where you place your page numbers—top right-hand corner or bottom center.

Spacing and Margins: your work should be double-spaced and have margins set for one inch at the top, bottom, and sides of your text. Either indent five spaces for each new paragraph or leave an extra line above the new paragraph with no indentation.

Integration of Source and Support Material

- When you include short quotations, work them into your writing with as little disruption to the flow of your writing as possible.

Example

> Walt Disney was one of film's most imaginative creators, who built his empire on a "little mouse named Mickey."

- Larger quotations should be indented an extra inch, and page numbers (for fiction or essays) or line numbers (for poetry) should be given.

Example

In an essay discussing Shakespeare's use of light images in Romeo and Juliet, you might write the following example:

> Light images seem to collect whenever Juliet's name is mentioned.
>
> But, soft! What light through yonder window breaks?
> It is the east, and Juliet is the sun.
> Arise, fair sun, and kill the envious moon,
> Who is already sick and pale with grief,
> That thou her maid art far move fair than she.
>
> (Shakespeare Romeo & Juliet 2.2.2-6)

Romeo's well known speech upon seeing Juliet at her window uses the extended metaphor of light and dark.

- Whenever you use quotations, charts, diagrams, maps, or ideas that are not your own, you must use citations or footnotes. You might want to use reference books to decide how to document your sources, as there are many different formats. For example, the University of Chicago's style for documenting sources is one of the most versatile and comprehensive styles available. It covers how to document every type of publication, such as books, public documents, interviews, the Internet, reference materials, and unpublished materials.
- At the end of your work, remember to create a bibliography on a separate sheet of paper on which you list all of the sources you have used, arranged in alphabetical order according to the writer's surname.

The following example displays proper format for a bibliography.

BIBLIOGRAPHY

"Arctic Lemmings," *The American Encyclopedia* 3rd ed. 2007. (encyclopedia article)

Chartrand, Emily, *Myths About Lemmings,* New York, Avenue Publishers, 2001. (book)

Doherty, Paul and Phillips, John and Rollester, David, *Lemmings in the Wild*, Chicago, University of Chicago Press, 2002. (book by more than one author)

Gallager, Stuart, *Lemmings in the Arctic*, Special report prepared at the request of the Alaskan Department of Conservation, August 15, 1998. (department document)

"Lemmings Unlimited," 2001 photo gallery, http://www.lemmingsunlimited.org/2001.html (the Internet)

Rogers, Neil, *All About Lemmings*, Arctica, March 2002.

Appropriate Use of Conventions

During the revision and editing stages of the writing process, teachers expect you to make your writing as correct as possible with respect to sentences, punctuation, capitalization, grammar, and spelling. Different writing forms have different format rules or conventions. For example, consider the envelope for a business letter.

How to Address an Envelope

Return Address

The return address includes the name and address of the person mailing the letter. If, for some reason, the post office is unable to deliver the letter, it can be returned to the person who sent it.

You should always write your name and address on the top, left corner of the envelope. The return address consists of your name, street address, city, province, and postal code.

Example

JENNIFER ROSS
56 FERRET LANE
WINDSOR ON X1A 1J8

Mailing Address

The mailing address consists of the name and address of the individual to whom you are mailing the letter. This address should be placed in the centre of the envelope and should be identical to the inside address on the letter.

Example

MR. SAM SMITH
GENERAL DIRECTOR
WIDGETS INTERNATIONAL
1101 YONGE STREET
TORONTO ON M1B 2B2

JENNIFER ROSS
56 FERRET LANE
WINDSOR ON X1A 1J8

STAMP

MR. SAM SMITH
GENERAL DIRECTOR
WIDGETS INTERNATIONAL
1101 YONGE STREET
TORONTO ON M1B 2B2

The following details are based on standards set by Canada Post. Keep these details in mind when you are writing an address on an envelope for your business letter.

- Addresses should be typed or written in upper case or block letters.
- Format all lines of the address with a uniform left margin.
- Do not use punctuation marks unless they are part of a place name (St. John's).
- The postal code should always appear on the same line as the municipality and province name and should be separated from the province by two spaces.
- The two-letter symbol for the province name should be used wherever possible (see examples preceding).

The return address should be formatted in the same way as the main address.

PUBLISHING WITH A COMPUTER

If you use Microsoft Word, there are a number of program features that enable writers to improve the clarity and coherence of their written work and to engage their audience. Become familiar with all of the features of Word or whatever word processing program you use. Be curious and play around with some of the different features. The better you are at navigating Word, the quicker and easier it will be to publish clear and attractive assignments.

PRESENTATION FEATURES

1. Print and Script refers to your font. It can provide a more effective presentation for a note or memo inserted into a story or if your writing assignment is a friendly letter.
2. Fonts should be selected for the effect you wish to present. Make sure to check with your teacher about fonts. Sometimes your teacher may prefer one font for an assignment. Think about the type of font you want to use and experiment with different fonts, italics, and boldface. Following are examples of fonts:

   - **Arial Black** and **Britannic Bold** are clear and easy to read
   - Castellar is an open font you could use for titles

   You can achieve the effect of emphasis simply by altering the size of the font you are using. You may want headings or titles to have a larger font size than the rest of your text. Check with your teacher to see if he or she has any preferences as to font size. *Italic* font is useful for typing the titles of published works in your text. Novel and film titles are examples of works that should be italicized in a writing assignment about literature or in a book report.

1. Graphics are an effective method of clarifying information in your document. By hand or with a computer, you can create flow charts, pie charts, diagrams, graphs, or use pictures from clip art or from your own pictures to enhance an assignment.
2. Remember to clarify the graphics as well, using labels, captions, and titles as needed.
3. *Layout* refers to the overall appearance of your written document and inclusions like graphics. The following presentation features can be used to make your published work look appealing and professional using your computer:

- **Alignment:** You can choose left, centre, right, or justified alignment for any document.

Example

Left aligned	Centre aligned	Right aligned

- **Justification**: makes your lines line up along a straight edge for left and right margins. ("Ragged" means you align only the left margin.)
- **Bullet**: Use the bullet feature to clarify points or lists.
- **Emphasis Features**: You can make information stand out from the text by using features like bolding, colour, font size, text boxes, and text pull-outs created with colour and size features. Text pull-outs are catchy quotes "pulled" from your magazine or newspaper article, enlarged, and printed below the article title, perhaps in a contrasting colour.
- **Paragraphs**: You have a choice to indent one tab space or use "block form," which requires no indentation. Instead, leave a double space between paragraphs. This is a fairly standard layout format for a business letter, for instance.
- **Columns**: Use the Microsoft Word column feature to create professional-looking layouts for newspaper and magazine articles.
- **Headers and Footers**: special lines at the top and bottom of pages. This feature is useful for numbering pages or for providing footnotes for quotes.

1. Colour for graphics or backgrounds is a presentation feature that requires some advance planning. Coloured text should be used with restraint. You could use colours on the title page or to label something on a chart or picture. For most assignments, however, you will want to stick to black text.
2. Balance of white space, text, and graphics means that you would not crowd the pictures on your title page, but would arrange them so that your finished product looks clean, organized, and attractive.

Before working on a school assignment, try playing around with Word using some text that you can afford to make mistakes with. You can try out different fonts, insert graphics, and manipulate the text in as many different ways as you can find. This will acquaint you with all of the different features that are available to you using Word.

ON 10W4.1 describe a variety of strategies they used before, during, and after writing; explain which ones they found most helpful; and identify appropriate steps they can take to improve as writers

Evaluating Your Progress

Metacognition consists of two processes occurring at the same time: monitoring your progress as you learn, and changing and adapting your strategies if necessary. In writing, this involves identifying what strategies you found most helpful before, during, and after writing and what steps you can take to improve as a writer. After you have finished a writing project, think back to how you developed your ideas for writing, the research you did, and how you sorted and organized it. This will help you to identify the strategies you used. Next time you do similar writing, use the strategies that worked best for you and reconsider the others.

For example, a Grade 10 student came up with the following examples of strategies he used during the first half of the year. It looked like this:

My Writing Strategies

Before Writing

- Went online to find information about topics when I could, like the natural disaster topic after we read the short story "The Worst Day Ever."
- Jotted down books, TV shows, and music titles related to topic
- Talked with mom about topic choice
- Wrote down purpose, audience
- Made a web plan or outline

During Writing

- Spread out notes and outlines by computer
- Tried to follow outlines
- Checked with assignment criteria
- Tried to write correctly
- Tried to use good transitions
- Tried to include things teacher was emphasizing, like different sentence openers, "said is dead" replacements, etc.

After Writing

- Labelled my revisions to make sure I was intentionally including teacher suggestions
- Read drafts aloud from computer screen while revising and editing
- Paid attention to my peer partner so we could help each other improve

Next, the student explained the strategy he found the most helpful. The strategy he chose was the idea of labelling revisions to require thinking specifically about what he was changing and why. Since the students were sharing their metacognition activities with the teacher, he submitted the following paragraph:

Example

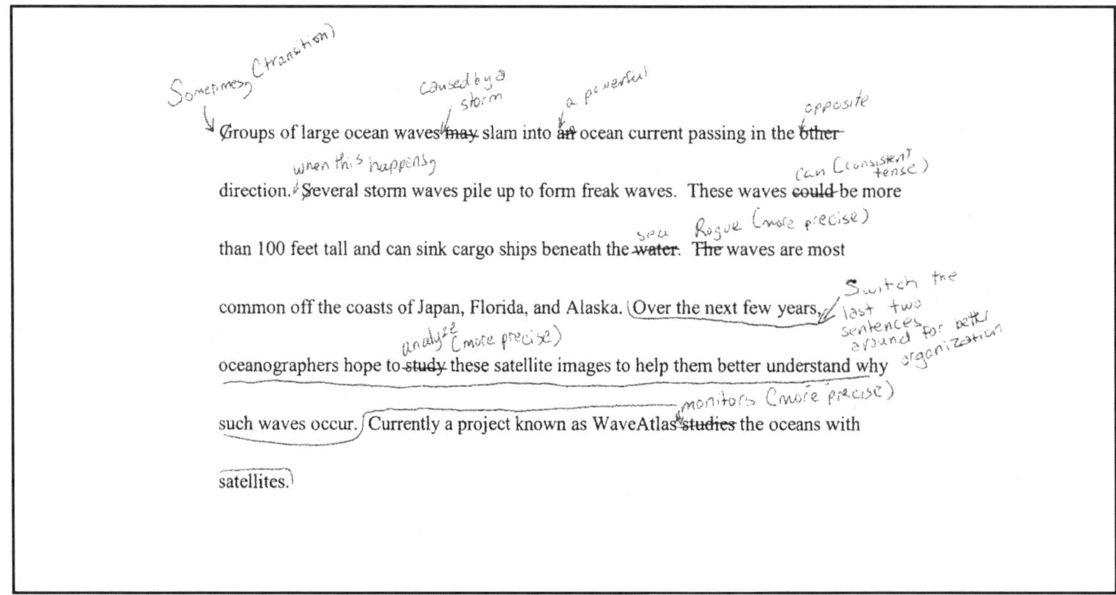

Groups of large ocean waves ~~may~~ slam into ~~an~~ ocean current passing in the ~~other~~ direction. Several storm waves pile up to form freak waves. These waves ~~could~~ be more than 100 feet tall and can sink cargo ships beneath the ~~water~~. ~~The~~ waves are most common off the coasts of Japan, Florida, and Alaska. Over the next few years, oceanographers hope to ~~study~~ these satellite images to help them better understand why such waves occur. Currently a project known as WaveAtlas ~~studies~~ the oceans with satellites.

Under the paragraph, the student added the following note to the teacher:

Example

> Ms. Harmon: Thanks for making us stop to think about our growth as writers. It is helping me improve. I just wanted to add that there should not be many errors in the paragraph because I really tried to be careful and to write correctly. That did make the revision easier.
>
> Your Student,
> Lyall
>
> P.S. I tried to use the points you listed on the board when I was revising, like improving organization/using transitions and making ideas consistent, clear, and making details precise.

Finally, the student identified several steps he could take to improve as a writer. His list included the following ideas:

1. Keep a writing log, with sections: Spelling Errors, Writing Errors, Story Ideas
2. Start a list of words I want to use in my writing
3. Look online for sites where I can share some of my writing

After collecting the class's reflections, Ms. Harmon gave the students two 4×6 cards to tape inside their writing logs. The cards contained reminders to help the students think about each piece of writing.

This Piece

- What is best?
- What could I improve?
- What stage was smoothest?
- What ideas could I use for new writing?

Learning from this Piece

- Have I learned any new techniques?
- Did I try something new?
- Have I eliminated personal errors that I have commonly made in the past, like sentence fragments?

Writer's Reflection

Reflecting on your writing is something you probably have to do in class. The following example shows you an example of answers a fictional student has written in response to metacognition questions from his or her class. You may have to answer questions similar to these in class about your own writing and language skills. See if you can answer the following questions yourself.

Example

Before Grade 10, what did you know or understand to be your strengths as a writer? Has this changed?

I always thought that my greatest strength was writing humour. It was because I found it easy to remember the punch line of a good joke, and I could always seem to make my friends laugh. Sometimes at the wrong time, like in the middle of your class on sentence fragments! When you asked us in September to think hard about our strengths and to think of ways to branch out from those strengths, I realized that one reason I can describe things in a humorous way is that I am a people watcher. I am always watching what people do, how they react, and what they say in certain situations.

I used that strength to branch out when I wrote my one act play on peer pressure. With realistic sounding dialogue and characters based on what I had really seen around me, I think I was able to get some serious points across using humour. During your comments after my group presented my play, you said our dialogue was convincing and real.

What did you learn about yourself as a writer as a result of the group writing experience?

You mean the short story project. The truth is, I wasn't too happy at first. I actually like writing independent stories from my own head, so it was annoying to have to stop and pay attention to the other two guys in my group. One hated writing, period, and the other didn't want to write anything but fantasy, which I have never read. We wasted a bit of time in the beginning, but when you started posting deadlines on the board, we had to think of something. We had just learned about parodies, so we decided to write a modernized parody of a well-known fairy tale. The partner who hated writing didn't mind working from a basic plot we all knew – "Little Red Riding Hood." He even started to contribute a few ideas. My other partner added some twists, I added some ideas for humour, and we all liked the result because it turned out like a bit of a fantasy. What I learned about myself as a writer was that

- I am more creative than I realized
- Sometimes other points of view can improve writing
- I can motivate a peer who thinks writing is an unpleasant chore

How do you determine whether the peer feedback you receive is valid or not?

I pay the closest attention to revision ideas. I figure if my ideas are boring or confusing to any reader, especially a peer, I need to fix that. Sometimes it's just the organization that is confusing, so I make it more chronological or use better transitions. When a peer suggests different spelling or punctuation, I look at it, but not as hard, unless the peer is a classmate I know to be a strong speller, or one who makes very few errors in his or her own writing. Even when I don't agree with the peer feedback, it does force me to take another look at my writing before publishing the final draft.

How you learn matters. Keeping track of what has affected your language skills is important. How easy was it to answer the three questions in the example? Could you think of any other questions that might be good to ask about your learning? Metacognition means thinking about your learning while you are learning. The more you ask yourself questions like the ones in the given example, the more aware of your learning you will become.

ON 10W4.2 identify a variety of skills they have in listening, speaking, reading, viewing, and representing and explain how the skills help them write more effectively

Interconnected Skills

Learning to be a good writer does not happen in isolation. What you hear, speak, and see influences what you write. Many of the skills you practise every day help you develop as a writer. In fact, everything you do and experience can become part of your writing experience if you take time to reflect on it. To start thinking about how language skills are connected, consider the following questions.

- What do you know about different media texts that might help when you are writing? (Media texts are found in newspapers and magazines as well as in advertising, posters, and leaflets.)
- In what way do you think that the reading you do helps you as a writer? Can you give an example?
- What do you listen to that might help you as a writer (e.g., radio talk shows, conversations between adults sharing their opinions/views on arts and culture or the environment)?
- Have you ever seen a picture or a movie that made you think of a story? Or, have you ever written a story based on something you saw?

The following chart shows how different communication skills overlap and interconnect to help you write more effectively.

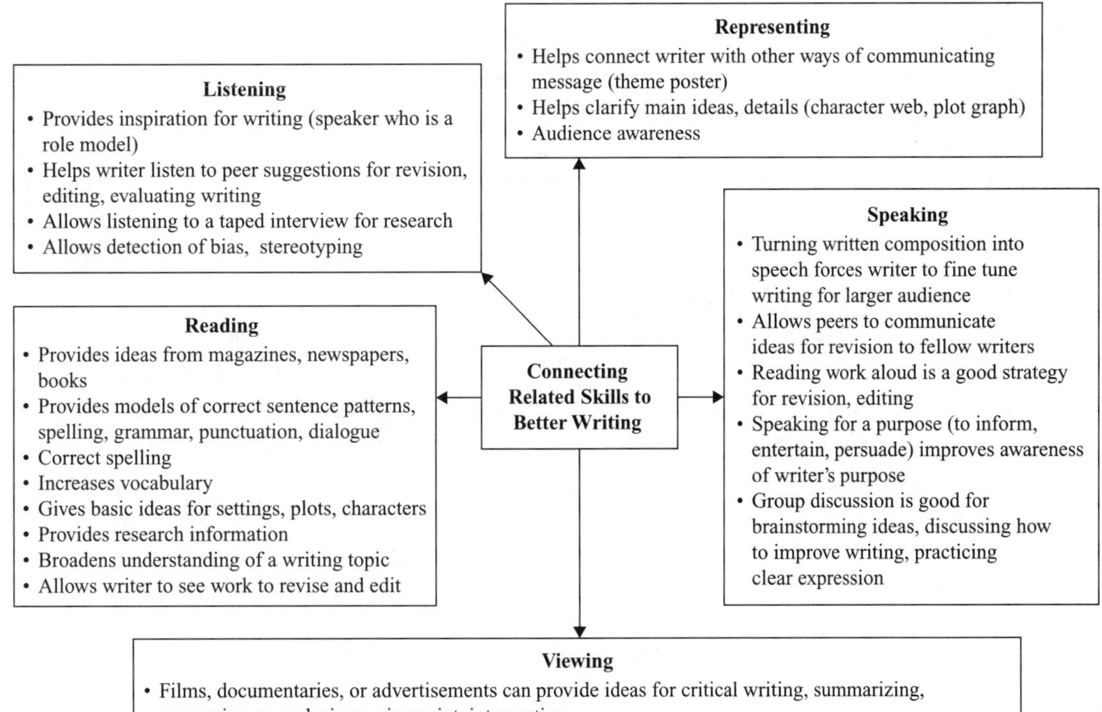

Read the following fictional experience of Timothy, a Grade 10 student, which shows how using interconnected skills helped Timothy to write more effectively. As you read, think about how your own experiences in Language Arts can be improved upon by using a variety of skills.

Example of Interconnected Skills and Writing Improvement

Listening

Timothy is sitting with his friends in a Grade 10 Assembly. He doesn't know what to expect as his English teacher, Mr. Kennedy, introduces the guest speaker:

"Ladies and gentlemen, our guest today was once a teacher like myself. Like me, he too wracked his brains on a daily basis, trying to think of ways to encourage his students to write, to get them excited about writing. He came up with the idea of writing a novel for them. The novel, *Stand Your Ground*, was set in the school where he worked. The setting was his community. Many of the characters had the same names as his students. That novel came out in 1993. It was a big hit, especially with the students who found their names in the book.

Since 1993, our guest has given up his teaching career to become a full time writer of at least 45 novels, with more on the way. He has won more than 30 awards, including the Ontario Library Association Silver Birch Award, three times. The selection panel was made up of over 750,000 young people like yourselves, country-wide, who voted for Mr. Eric Walters. It is my honour to present him to you today. Eric Walters is a man who loves a great story, and who knows how to turn young people into fans of his books."

As the writer approaches the podium, Timothy starts to pay attention, especially when Mr. Walters launches into the dramatic reading of a chapter from his novel called *Shattered.* The chapter is about a 15-year-old boy, Ian, starting to work as a volunteer in a soup kitchen as part of a social studies project. After a near mugging, in which Ian is saved by a homeless man, Ian later spots the man at the soup kitchen. It turns out he is a retired member of the Canadian Armed Forces whose last tour had involved peacekeeping duties in Rwanda.

Mr. Walters also reads a foreword from the novel, composed by Canadian General Romeo Dallaire, Force Commander for the United Nations Mission to Rwanda. The rest of the presentation is a blur. Mr. Walters calls a couple of students up who have prepared some interview questions. He is both entertaining and serious, and he talks about writing and about researching historical events in Canada to get ideas for writing. All Timothy can think about is getting his hands on that first novel. Timothy is not from Rwanda, but his parents did come to Canada from Zaire before it was renamed Congo. He was too young to remember, but he wants to find out about why his parents ended up in a refugee camp for a year before they emigrated.

Reading and Viewing

Timothy signs out the novel *Shattered* from the school library. The librarian suggests that he might also like to watch the movie *Hotel Rwanda*, which is about a courageous hotel manager who saved some people from being caught in a tribal massacre during the Rwandan crisis. Timothy rents the movie after he finishes the book.

Writing

The teacher, Mr. Kennedy, has encouraged his students to try writing some form of historical fiction using suggestions from Eric Walters. Timothy decides to create five journal entries written by a fictional character, Akunda, who lives with his parents in a refugee camp in Congo, from where they are hoping to emigrate to Canada.

Speaking

Timothy tapes his journal entries to play for his writing group. He uses his older brother to be the voice of Akunda, and he reads the part of the narrator. As a writer, Timothy is supposed to use the group's suggestions to help him revise his writing.

Reflection

Mr. Kennedy poses the following two questions to his student writers, which they are to answer and attach to the final draft of their writing before handing it in. You can read Timothy's answers to both questions:

How did listening to the taped reading of your writing help you to revise it?

One of my peer listeners suggested that I write two more entries to show the contrast when Akunda started his new life in Canada. He said the journal ended too abruptly. I thought that was a good idea, so I added those to my assignment. They also thought I could make the African entries a bit more realistic if I used actual places, so I looked up a map of the Congo on the Internet when I went home and changed a couple of location names.

What did you discover from reading Young Adult fiction that you could apply to your own story?

After Mr. Walters spoke to us a month ago, I read his novel, *Shattered.* I tried to make my character, Akunda, seem as real as Ian seemed to me when I read the book. I also did some research on the Congo and talked to my parents about their experiences to make the journal entries as authentic as I could. I went on Eric Walters' website for more ideas. What I learned from that one novel was

- use real places and events
- make your main character have the same worries and concerns as young people all over the world—with dreams of a better life, a successful future, and solid friendships

The great thing about all your language skills being connected is that you can tailor your learning to how you learn best. If you learn better by talking to others or by speaking out loud about your ideas, do that. Your writing will improve if your ideas come to you more easily through verbal communication. Or maybe you need to write out what you think before you prepare a formal essay. Some people learn better by reading and some learn better by listening to others speak or by watching others demonstrate something visually.

It is important to remember that related skills in listening, speaking, reading, viewing, and representing contribute to improving your proficiency as a writer. The more you are able to recognize these connections, the better your writing will become.

ON 10W4.3 select a variety of examples of different types of writing that they think reflect significant advances in their growth and competence as writers and explain the reasons for their choice

PORTFOLIOS

A portfolio is a collection of your writing pieces, usually representing a time period of at least one school year. Keeping your writing together allows you to

- see your growth as a writer
- review topics and writing forms you have tried
- evaluate your writing skills
- set writing goals for improving or refining your skills

A portfolio may also contain a writer's log or journal, personal spelling list, personal vocabulary lists, personal error record, or reflections about your writing. In this section, you will find some examples of ways you could use your portfolio as a resource to help you improve your writing skills.

In the following example, a student compares a first draft to a final draft, both of which he has found in his writing portfolio. Look at the first draft of a paragraph on rogue waves that appears earlier in this section. Next, read the revised final draft from the student's portfolio. By comparing the two drafts, the student was able to not only pinpoint the improvements she made, but also to explain what she learned from the redrafting process.

Example

Revised Final Draft of Rogue Waves Paragraph

Sometimes, groups of large ocean waves caused by a storm slam into a powerful ocean current passing in the opposite direction.
When this happens, several storm waves pile up to form rogue waves. These waves can be more than 100 feet high and can bury cargo ships beneath the sea. Rogue waves are most common off the coasts of Japan, Florida, and Alaska. Currently, a project known as WaveAtlas monitors the oceans with satellites. Over the next few years, oceanographers hope to analyse these satellite images to help them better understand why freak waves, or "rogue waves" as they are known to scientists, occur so that scientific warnings can prevent unnecessary tragedies at sea.

Improvements Made

- Used better transitions
- Used more precise and consistent vocabulary
- Used consistent verb tenses throughout paragraph
- Created a more logical order in last section of paragraph
- Added a safety reason for scientific studies to round out paragraph

What I Learned from the Redrafting Process

- Read out loud to make sure writing flows smoothly
- When you use consistent verb tenses throughout a piece of writing the ideas are clearer to the reader
- Your writing can sound better if you take the time to think about changes for improvement
- It is more satisfying to hand in redrafted work because you are sure that it is clear and says what you want it to

In the following example from a fictional student's writing portfolio, the student had been given the following point-form information from a local television news broadcast during a week of bitter cold in the city.

- Only some of the 1200 available overnight shelters are being used.
- City Council fears homeless people are not using the shelters.
- The hotline number is 416-SHELTER.
- Citizens urged to cooperate to prevent homeless people from freezing.
- The city spokesperson is Ellen McCall.

The assignment involved writing a poem and a news report based on the information the student was given. He was asked to include a reflection with his writing, comparing the processes used for each form and identifying challenges he had to overcome.

Included here are the student's two writing pieces, followed by the reflection that accompanied the pieces in the portfolio.

DEEP FREEZE INCREASES RISK TO HOMELESS

Fears Grow for Unsheltered

Toronto Sun City Desk

Toronto – While most of us struggle with getting the car to start and risking a fender-bender on the way to work, the homeless of our city struggle with survival in the frigid temperatures that have gripped the region this past week.

Ellen McCall, spokesperson for city shelter co-ordination, reports that the 1200 beds prepared for weather emergencies are not being filled nightly.

While no one is being turned away from shelter facilities, it is feared that some people needing shelter may not be finding it for a variety of reasons, including voluntary choices to spend the night in makeshift temporary shelters outside.

Bus drivers and police have been cautioned to be on the alert for anyone needing assistance or shelter.

Commuters and other citizens are asked to report possible shelter-related emergencies to the shelter hotline at 416-SHELTER (743-5837). All calls will be treated as urgent.

So far, there have been no reported deaths due to freezing. However, each period of severe cold in the past has generated at least one fatality in the city. It is hoped that 2008 will remain fatality-free

—*by* E. Meyer

BALLAD OF A COLD MAN

The winds, they chill me to the bone,
A man who calls Toronto home,
My cardboard walls are way too thin
I wish I could go home again.

Chorus

Home again, yes home again,
I wish I could go home again,
To Mother's stew without the pain,
I wish I could go home again.

The streets they mock me with their ice,
The cops assume I act with vice,
My cardboard walls no shelter give,
Must move if I expect to live.

Chorus

How did I reach this point so low?
How did my dreams descend below?
The ice outside, that's not so bad,
It's ice within, that makes me sad.

And so if winter's got you down,
And risky drivers make you frown,
Just pause while at that traffic light,
And say a prayer for someone's plight.

I, too, was once a man like you,
The 401 my trial too,
But life can change and paths can turn,
So don't complain, be still, and learn.

—*by* E. Meyer

MY CHALLENGES FOR THIS WRITING ASSIGNMENT

The news story was not too difficult to write because of the notes we had from class on the inverted pyramid format for news reporting. Most of the key facts were provided in the points listed on the board, so I tried to be as factual as possible. To create the by-line and dateline correctly, I checked a newspaper at home and tried to make it look similar with my computer, using special fonts and the column feature. I sometimes made spelling mistakes on words like "frigid," so I used spellcheck and also had my older sister proofread my draft for spelling. I remembered that newspaper reporting should always be correct English, so I used sentence patterns I could use with confidence and did not try anything fancy.

I was able to be more creative with the poem. I chose the ballad form because of the repetitive rhyme scheme and chorus, which I thought I could imitate, and because I think the misfortunes of the homeless make a sad story that seems to have no end, just like a sad ballad that goes on and on. I struggled with the line in the chorus, "To Mother's stew without the pain," because I didn't really like the effect of that wording, but I could not seem to come up with a better line that would express the emotional pain against something comforting like a mother's cooking. My favourite line was the figurative language in "It's ice within, that makes me sad." Other than that, I think my biggest challenge was expressing the ideas I had according to the poetic form I had chosen.

—*by* E. Meyer

Metacognition and Making Revisions

In this third example from a fictional student's writing portfolio, the student was asked to revise a descriptive paragraph by creating a variety of sentence beginnings using different openers, such as adjectives, prepositional phrases, and past participles, to replace the overused pattern of *the* plus a noun (subject). The original draft and the revised paragraph are reproduced below. A student reflection follows the two paragraphs, in which the student comments on the effect of the revision on the writing. Both drafts and the reflection would be kept in the student's portfolio. Take a look at the revisions, make a note of what has changed, and see if you prefer the revisions. What might you change about the original paragraph?

First Draft of Descriptive Paragraph

The room where I feel most relaxed is my bedroom. Mother and I painted it in my favourite color scheme, pale green and navy blue. The wide south window looks out over our sweeping back lawn with its massive weeping willow, where I once played as a child. I would play house, pretend it was a robbers' hideout, or even read a book under the umbrella of its cool shade on a hot July afternoon. The window is framed in white, with a softly draped sheer navy valance across its top. I like to sit by that window in my white wicker armchair during a thunderstorm, watching lightning stab the sky in jagged tears as angry raindrops pound against the glass. I feel cozy and secure. This is my own special place.

Paragraph with Revisions

<u>Painted</u> in my favourite color scheme of pale green and navy blue, the room where I feel most relaxed is my bedroom. *(Began sentence with a past participle)* The wide south window looks out over our sweeping back lawn with its massive weeping willow where I once played as a child. <u>Under the umbrella of its cool shade</u> I would play house, pretend it was a robbers' hideout, or even read a book on a hot July afternoon. *(Began sentence with two prepositional phrases)* The window is framed in white, with a softly draped, sheer navy valance across its top. <u>In my white wicker armchair</u>, I like to sit by that window during a thunderstorm, watching lightning stab the navy sky with jagged tears as angry raindrops pound against the glass. *(Began with a prepositional phrase)* <u>Cozy and secure</u>, I burrow deeper into my chair. *(Began with two adjectives)* This is my own special place.

Student Reflection on Revisions

I thought my original draft was quite good, probably because I enjoy describing things and my room is a special place that I was able to share through precise description. When you taught us about sentence beginnings, I could see right away from your examples that this was a good way of adding variety to writing. It is hard to believe that we fall into the habit of repeating the same sentence pattern, even while using lots of effective descriptive phrases. Here is how I thought the revisions improved my writing with this paragraph:

1. Placing the participle "Painted" at the beginning of the first sentence helped the reader to immediately see the color scheme, which is probably the most striking feature of the room.
2. The prepositional phrases in this sentence ("Under the umbrella of its cool shade") provided a good transition and link with the "weeping willow" that I had introduced in the preceding sentence.
3. This prepositional phrase ("In my white wicker armchair") provided a change from the more predictable beginning of the sentence just before it ("The window is…").
4. These two adjectives ("Cozy and secure") describe the atmosphere of my room, as well as how I felt there during the storm. By moving them to the beginning of the sentence, I was able to give the adjectives a more important status and to stress the mood in the room.

I liked the freedom to move words and phrasing around to add variety to my paragraph, without eliminating vocabulary that I had carefully chosen for the description. I thought the overall effect was much improved!

The applications of metacognition in this section are only examples. You can apply the language skills you have learned in many different ways. Reading aloud, reading with others, discussion, writing, and reworking texts are all useful. As you try different methods, you will begin to see which ones are the most effective for your learning style. The more information you can process and understand, the better able you will be to interact with and interpret the world.

Taking time to focus on metacognition will improve your skills in language arts. There is not one correct method for metacognition. It is best to use a variety of methods in order to determine how you learn best. Reflecting on how you learn should be an ongoing process. Metacognition is something that you can use throughout your life, in school, work, and other areas of your life. Examining how and why you do certain things gives you insight on how you can change and improve. Reflecting on how you read and write also helps you practise your reading and writing skills.

WRITING—PRACTICE QUESTION

Write a narrative or an essay that shows how people can make changes that will improve the society in which they live. You may write about yourself or other people, real or fictional.

WRITING—UNIT TEST

Write a narrative or essay that shows how one of your experiences has shaped or altered your life. You may write about yourself or other people, real or fictional.

ANSWERS AND SOLUTIONS—WRITING PRACTICE QUESTION

THE ACHIEVEMENT CHART FOR LANGUAGE

You are probably familiar with the Achievement Chart shown below. Each example of writing in this section is given an achievement level based on the Achievement Chart. There is a short explanation about why the example achieves a particular level. Try to use these examples of writing to improve your writing and to understand what is needed to receive a high level.

Categories	50–59% (Level 1)	60–69% (Level 2)	70–79% (Level 3)	80–100% (Level 4)
Knowledge and Understanding – Subject-specific content acquired in each course (knowledge), and the comprehension of its meaning and significance (understanding)				
	The student:			
Knowledge of content *(e.g., forms of text; strategies used when listening and speaking, reading, writing, and viewing and representing; elements of style; literary terminology, concepts, and theories; language conventions)*	demonstrates limited knowledge of content	demonstrates some knowledge of content	demonstrates considerable knowledge of content	demonstrates thorough knowledge of content
Understanding of content *(e.g., concepts; ideas; opinions; relationships among facts, ideas, concepts, themes)*	demonstrates limited understanding of content	demonstrates some understanding of content	demonstrates considerable understanding of content	demonstrates thorough understanding of content
Thinking – The use of critical and creative thinking skills and/or processes				
	The student:			
Use of planning skills *(e.g., generating ideas, gathering information, focusing research, organizing information)*	use planning skills with limited effectiveness	uses planning skills with some effectiveness	uses planning skills with considerable effectiveness	uses planning skills with a high degree of effectiveness
Use of processing skills *(e.g., drawing inferences, interpreting, analysing, synthesizing, evaluating)*	uses processing skills with limited effectiveness	uses processing skills with some effectiveness	uses processing skills with considerable effectiveness	uses processing skills with a high degree of effectiveness

Use of critical/creative thinking processes *(e.g., oral discourse, research, critical analysis, critical literacy, metacognition, creative process)*	uses critical/ creative thinking processes with limited effectiveness	uses critical/ creative thinking processes with some effectiveness	uses critical/ creative thinking processes with considerable effectiveness	uses critical/ creative thinking processes with a high degree of effectiveness
Categories	**50–59% (Level 1)**	**60–69% (Level 2)**	**70–79% (Level 3)**	**80–100% (Level 4)**
Communication – The conveying of meaning through various forms				
	The student:			
Expression and organization of ideas and information *(e.g., clear expression, logical organization)* **in oral, graphic, and written forms, including media forms**	expresses and organizes ideas and information with limited effectiveness	expresses and organizes ideas and information with some effectiveness	expresses and organizes ideas and information with considerable effectiveness	expresses and organizes ideas and information with a high degree of effectiveness
Communication for different audiences and purposes *(e.g., use of appropriate style, voice, point of view)* **in oral, graphic, and written forms, including media forms**	communicates for different audiences and purposes with limited effectiveness	communicates for different audiences and purposes with some effectiveness	communicates for different audiences and purposes with considerable effectiveness	communicates for different audiences and purposes with a high degree of effectiveness
Use of conventions *(e.g., grammar, spelling, punctuation, usage),* **vocabulary, and terminology of the discipline in oral, graphic, and written forms, including media forms**	uses conventions, vocabulary, and terminology of the discipline with limited effectiveness	uses conventions, vocabulary, and terminology of the discipline with some effectiveness	uses conventions, vocabulary, and terminology of the discipline with considerable effectiveness	uses conventions, vocabulary, and terminology of the discipline with a high degree of effectiveness
Application – The use of knowledge and skills to make connections within and between various contexts				
	The student:			
Application of knowledge and skills *(e.g., literacy strategies and processes; literary terminology, concepts, and theories)* **in familiar contexts**	applies knowledge and skills in familiar contexts with limited effectiveness	applies knowledge and skills in familiar contexts with some effectiveness	applies knowledge and skills in familiar contexts with considerable effectiveness	applies knowledge and skills in familiar contexts with a high degree of effectiveness

Transfer of knowledge and skills *(e.g., literacy strategies and processes; literary terminology, concepts, and theories)* **to new contexts**	transfers knowledge and skills to new contexts with limited effectiveness	transfers knowledge and skills to new contexts with some effectiveness	transfers knowledge and skills to new contexts with considerable effectiveness	transfers knowledge and skills to new contexts with a high degree of effectiveness
Categories	**50–59% (Level 1)**	**60–69% (Level 2)**	**70–79% (Level 3)**	**80–100% (Level 4)**
Making connections within and between various contexts *(e.g., between the text and personal knowledge and experience, other texts, and the world outside the school)*	makes connections within and between various contexts with limited effectiveness	makes connections within and between various contexts with some effectiveness	makes connections within and between various contexts with considerable effectiveness	makes connections within and between various contexts with a high degree of effectiveness

SAMPLE STUDENT RESPONSE – LEVEL 3

Volunteering is a very important thing that you can do to help make society better. It can make you a better person because you are learning not to be selfish and it can make others happy because you are doing something for them. People ask for volunteers the whole time like at school when you can join peer support and when they ask for food for the food bank. At home you can volunteer by shoveling your neighbors drive.

Peer support is a good thing to do at school because you get to have lunch meetings and we get to go to go to the old peoples home every month. It is good to visit the old people because some of them do not have familys and they are lonly and they like it when we read to them or tell them what we are doing in school. I like visiting one old lady because she lets me brush her hair and it is white and silky, she also likes it when I tell her about the funny thinks my little brother does. Like picking the neighbors flowers. In peer support you get to help other kids. Like if someone is having problems they can come to someone in peer support and we can help them. Lets say you are being bullyed well you can talk to someone in peer support about that and they will help you by telling a teacher or talking to the bullys.

At school we have food drives and we bring non parishible cans of food for the food bank. We have a big collection of food and it makes like a mountain of cans and jars and packets of food. It is good to give food to people who do not have enuff to eat.

I like to shovel my neighbors drive because they are old and they might get a heart attack if they do it theirselves. When I shovel our drive I just go over to their drive and do their too. This is how I volunteer in the winter at home and it is good to do thing for other people without their asking. I sometimes rake their leaves in the fall.

These are just some of the ways you can volunteer to make changes that will improve the society you live in. There are lots and lots of other ways to volunteer but you have to do what is right for you. You can ask at school or at home or in the community about volunteering to make life better for everyone.

Rationale for Student Exemplar Level 3 Essay

Content

- The student's exploration of the topic in the discussion of how "Volunteering is a very important thing that you can do" and "It can make you a better person because you are learning not to be selfish" is clear and logical.
- The student's purpose to examine, by using many examples, how volunteering "is good to do thing for other people" is evident.
- The ideas presented by the student (e.g., "some of them do not have familys and they are lonly" and "we have food drives and we bring non parishible cans of food") are appropriate and predictable.
- Supporting details (e.g., "when we read to them or tell them what we are doing in school," "We have a big collection of food," and "rake their leaves in the fall") are relevant but general.
- The writing is straightforward (e.g., "like at school when you can join peer support") and generalized (e.g., "Like if someone is having problems") and occasionally arouses the reader's interest using personal examples (e.g., "I like visiting one old lady because she lets me brush her hair").

Organization

- The introduction ("Volunteering is a very important thing that you can do to help make society better. It can make you a better person because you are learning not to be selfish and it can make others happy because you are doing something for them.") is functional and establishes a focus regarding the positive results of volunteering that is generally sustained.

- Details (e.g., "Peer support is a good thing to do at school because you get to have lunch meetings and we get to go to the old peoples home every month" and "they are old and they might get a heart attack if they do it theirselves") are developed in a discernible order although coherence may falter occasionally (e.g., "In peer support you get to help other kids")
- Transitions (e.g., "At school we have food drives" and "These are just some of the ways") tend to be mechanical and are generally used to connect details within sentences (e.g., "she also likes it when") and between paragraphs.
- Closure is related to the focus on the benefits of volunteering and is mechanical and artificial. (e.g., "These are just some of the ways you can volunteer to make changes that will improve the society you live in. There are lots and lots of other ways to volunteer but you have to do what is right for you.")

Sentence Structure

- Sentence structure is generally controlled (e.g., "This is how I volunteer in the winter at home and it is good to do thing for other people without their asking") but lapses (e.g., "Like picking the neighbors flowers") may occasionally impede meaning.
- Sentence type and sentence length are sometimes effective (e.g., "Peer support is a good thing to do at school because you get to have lunch meetings and we get to go to the old peoples home every month") and varied (e.g., "I sometimes rake their leaves in the fall").
- Some variety of sentence beginnings is evident (e.g., "At home you can," "Lets say you are being bullyed," and "When I shovel our drive I just go").

Vocabulary

- Words and expressions (e.g., "it is white and silky," "it makes like a mountain of cans and jars and packets of food," and "they might get a heart attack") are generally used appropriately.
- General words and expressions (e.g., "tell them what we are doing in school," "Like if someone is having problems," and "it is good to do thing for other people without their asking") are used adequately to clarify meaning.
- The tone created by the student (e.g., "Peer support is a good thing to do at school" and "You can ask at school or at home or in the community about volunteering") is discernible but uneven.

Conventions

- The quality of the writing is sustained through general correct use of conventions (e.g., "Like if someone is having problems they can come to someone in peer support and we can help them").
- Errors that are present in mechanics (e.g., "familys," "lonely," "bullyed," "parishible," and "enuff") and usage (e.g., "old peoples home," "I tell her about the funny thinks my little brother does," "Lets say you," "theirselves," and "and do their too") occasionally reduce clarity and sometimes interrupt the flow of the response.

Sample Student Response – Level 3

Volunteering in Society

There are many ways that we can volunteer today that will improve the society in which we live. Volunteering gives us opportunity to do something for others and to give back to the community. At school and at home we can give up some of our free time and volunteer in a way that will help others and make life easier for them. At school we can join peer support which does many things to make life easier for others, and we can also contribute to food drives when asked. At home we can do things around our own neighbourhood such as shoveling a neighbour's drive in the winter, helping with community bottle drive or even participating in the community clean up.

Peer support is a different kind of volunteering. It involves many activities which aim to make life better for the school community. You may be called upon to help a student who is being bullied or who is having problems with understanding math or science or social or L.A. it doesn't matter what you are asked to do, you do your best to make life better for the person seeking help. In our school, once a month, the peer support team go to an old peoples home where we spend some one on one time with an old person. There are many elderly men and women who are lonely and we brighten up their day when we arrive by reading to them or telling them about our school and friends and families. This is also an important time for us to listen as the old folks talk about their families and their memories of the good old days and the things they did when they were young and energetic.

Many times throughout the year food drives are held at school or at church for those who rely on the food bank for their daily nourishment. It is easy to bring cans of soup and packets of spaghetti and paper products like toilet paper as well as other non perishable products but it takes a bit more effort to volunteer to help load the food into people's cars and vans so that it can be taken to the food bank. At Christmas especially there is a great need for food and presents for those who are not rich or unemployed. By volunteering to bring food or help with the loading up of cars, is one way that people can make a change that will improve our society and make life easier for others.

School is not the only place where we can volunteer. We can also offer our talents and time to our own community where we live. Maybe there is an elderly neighbor who has had heart surgery and finds it difficult to shovel the snow from his drive in the winter. It doesn't take much effort to clean the neighbour's drive at the same time as you are shoveling your own. Sometimes communities hold bottle drives to help pay for a sports team or some other function. A Saturday would be well spent giving your time to help collect bottles from your neighbourhood. Usually once a year a community has an area clean up where many people put on rubber gloves and walk around the neighbourhood picking up old newspapers, bottles, Mc Donald's hamburger rappers, and other garbage. If the weather is nice and you do it with friends then the job can be quite fun.

It doesn't matter how you decide to volunteer but volunteering is one way that all people can make a difference to their society and make the world a better place to live in. In the end the decision is our own and we have to do what we think is best for ourselves but sometimes we must also think about others and do something that will make life better for them.

Rationale for Student Exemplar Level 3 Essay

Content

- The student's exploration of the topic in the examination of how volunteering makes life better for people in our society is adept and plausible (e.g., "Volunteering gives us opportunity to do something for others and to give back to the community").
- The student's purpose to examine how three methods of volunteering can assist the community is intentional in that the student gives concrete examples to support the thesis.
- The ideas presented by the student are thoughtful (e.g., "At school we can join peer support which does many things to make life easier for others and we can also contribute to food drives when asked") and sound (e.g., "At home we can do things around our own neighbourhood such as shoveling a neighbour's drive in the winter, helping with community bottle drive or even participating in the community clean up").
- Supporting details (e.g., "reading to them or telling them about our school and friends and families," "cans of soup and packets of spaghetti and paper products like toilet paper," and "an elderly neighbor who has had heart surgery") are relevant and specific.
- The writing is considered (e.g., "Peer support is a different kind of volunteering. It involves many activities which aim to make life better for the school community") and elaborated (e.g., "food drives are held at school or at church for those who rely on the food bank for their daily nourishment") and draws the reader's interest by discussing throughout the response the many ways volunteering can help society.

Organization

- The introduction ("There are many ways that we can volunteer today that will improve the society in which we live") is purposeful and clearly establishes a focus ("At school and at home we can give up some of our free time and volunteer in a way that will help others and make life easier for them") that is capably sustained throughout the discussion about volunteering.
- Details are developed in paragraphs in a sensible order, evident in the manner in which the student discusses "Peer support," "food drives," and how "we can also offer our talents and time to our own community," and coherence is generally maintained.
- Transitions (e.g., "At school," "This is also an important time," and "Sometimes communities hold") clearly connect details within sentences and between paragraphs.
- Closure (e.g., "It doesn't matter how you decide to volunteer but volunteering is one way that all people can make a difference to their society and make the world a better place to live in" and "we must also think about others and do something that will make life better for them") is appropriate and related to the focus.

Sentence Structure

- Sentence structure (e.g., "At school we can join peer support which does many things to make life easier for others, and we can also contribute to food drives when asked," and "Many times throughout the year food drives are held at school or at church for those who rely on the food bank for their daily nourishment") is consistently controlled.
- Sentence type (e.g., "In the end the decision is our own and we have to do what we think is best for ourselves but sometimes we must also think about others and do something that will make life better for them") and sentence length (e.g., "There are many elderly men and women who are lonely and we brighten up their day when we arrive by reading to them or telling them about our school and friends and families" and "School is not the only place where we can volunteer") are usually effective and varied.
- Sentence beginnings (e.g., "You may be called upon," "Many times throughout the year," "A Saturday would be," and "If the weather is nice") are often varied.

Vocabulary

- Words and expressions (e.g., "give up some of our free time," "spend some one on one time," "rely on the food bank for their daily nourishment," and "cans of soup and packets of spaghetti and paper products like toilet paper") are often used accurately.
- Specific words and expressions (e.g., "participating in the community clean up," "we brighten up their day," "their memories of the good old days," and "put on rubber gloves and walk around the neighbourhood picking up old newspapers, bottles, Mc Donald's hamburger rappers, and other garbage") show some evidence of careful selection and some awareness of connotative effect (e.g., "Mc Donald's hamburger rappers").
- The tone (e.g., "It doesn't take much effort to clean the neighbour's drive at the same time as you are shoveling your own" and "A Saturday would be well spent giving your time to help collect bottles") created by the student is distinct.

Conventions

- The quality of the writing is sustained because it contains only minor convention errors (e.g., "helping with community bottle drive" and "By volunteering to bring food or help with the loading up of cars, is").
- Any errors that are present in mechanics (e.g., "it doesn't matter," "old peoples home," and "hamburger rappers") and in usage (e.g., "the peer support team go" and "for those who are not rich or unemployed") rarely reduce clarity and seldom interrupt the flow of the response.

Sample Student Response – Level 4

Tiny Ripples of Hope

Volunteering your time and talents to benefit others is one way that people can make changes that will improve the society in which they live. There are many places where a person can volunteer and by helping others who are in situations that are less than desirable will benefit the people who need the assistance and those who give their time and talents. Three ways that a person can volunteer that will help to improve society are by giving food for food drives and Christmas hampers, by volunteering to visit or read to old people in homes, and by being a part of a school's mentoring program. There is no doubt that each of these ways will benefit society.

Not everyone has enough to eat every day. It is surprising that in our society there are people who are homeless, who do not earn enough money to feed their families, or who daily go hungry. Sometimes little children go to school with empty tummies and then they can't concentrate on their school work. Well, by donating food to the food bank or by filling hampers in the supermarkets or by bringing non perishable food items to school at Christmas, people can make a difference to those who's lives is one of poverty and neglect. When everyone has enough food there is less likely to be theft and then the quality of life is improved for everyone. At school there is a peer support group that goes once a month after school to the local old people's home. At the home, students visit with the old people who are lonely because they do not have family or friends to visit them. These old people love it when the students come to talk and visit with them because the students give them a fresh perspective on life. Some of the old folk have forgotten what it is like to be young and they want the students to talk about their school work, their sports, their hobbies, and their friends. But best of all the old folk, who's eyesight is too bad for them to see properly, like it when the students read to them from books and glossy magazines. Volunteering at the local old folks home benefits the students who go to help out as well as the lonely old people who live pretty boring lives otherwise and so their society is improved.

The peer support group at school also provide volunteer programs in the school such as peer tutoring, conflict resolution, and mentoring programs. School society has improved because of these programs since they have benefitted every person in the school from the teachers to the students. Peer tutoring enables students who have difficulties in a subject to match up with a partner who is a wiz at that particular subject. The wiz then helps the struggling student to have a better understanding of the subject and to do better in tests and homework. The peer tutor must not though do the work for the student. When a conflict resolution team gets to work there can be positive results. The team hears every side of the arguement and then helps those who are in conflict to make decisions about their behavior and how they can avoid conflict in the future. Obviously, conflict resolution leads to big improvements in the school society as there are less fights and bullying. Those who give up their time to mentor others spend time trying to make school a safer and better society.

There is no doubt that society has improved because of those people who volunteer their time and talents to make life easier for others. It doesn't matter whether it is by donating to the food bank and making up Christmas hampers, or by spending time with the elderly at their old folks home, or by being a part of
the school's peer support team as long as the purpose of volunteering is to improve the society in which you live. Whatever a person decides to do, society will be improved by those who selflessly dedicate their time and talents to make life easier and better for others.

Rationale for Student Exemplar Level 4 Essay

Content

- The student's exploration of the topic in the analysis of the ways in which "Volunteering your time and talents to benefit others…" by "giving food for food drives," "volunteering to visit or read to old people in homes," and "by being a part of a school's mentoring program" is insightful.
- The student's purpose to examine the ways volunteering can improve the society in which we live is deliberate.
- The ideas presented by the student are perceptive (e.g., "It is surprising that in our society there are people who are homeless, who do not earn enough money to feed their families, or who daily go hungry") and carefully chosen (e.g., "These old people love it when the students come to talk and visit").
- Supporting details (e.g., "Some of the old folk have forgotten what it is like to be young") are precise and original (e.g., "the students give [the old people] a fresh perspective on life").
- The writing is confident (e.g., "society will be improved by those who selflessly dedicate their time and talents to make life easier and better for others") and holds the reader's interest through the suggestions of how society can be improved through volunteering.

Organization

- The introduction is engaging ("Volunteering your time and talents to benefit others is one way that people can make changes that will improve the society in which they live") and skillfully establishes a focus on how volunteering improves society for everyone that is consistently sustained.
- Details are developed in paragraphs in a judicious order, (evident in how the various examples of how volunteering can benefit society) and coherence is maintained throughout the essay by the elaboration of how each type of volunteering can benefit society.
- Transitions fluently connect details within sentences (e.g., "It is surprising that in" and "because the students give them a fresh perspective on life") and between paragraphs (e.g., "At school there is…" and "There is no doubt…").
- Closure is effective (e.g., "There is no doubt that society has improved because of those people who volunteer their time and talents to make life easier for others") and related to the focus that "the purpose of volunteering is to improve the society in which you live."

Sentence Structure

- Sentence structure is effectively and consistently controlled (e.g., "Well, by donating food to the food bank or by filling hampers in the supermarkets or by bringing non perishable food items to school at Christmas people can make a difference to those who's lives is one of poverty and neglect" and "These old people love it when the students come to talk and visit with them because the students give them a fresh perspective on life").
- Sentence type (e.g., "Whatever a person decides to do, society will be improved by those who selflessly dedicate their time and talents to make life easier and better for others") and sentence length (e.g., "Well, by donating food to the food bank or by filling hampers in the supermarkets or by bringing non perishable food items to school at Christmas, people can make a difference to those who's lives is one of poverty and neglect") are consistently effective and varied.
- Sentence beginnings (e.g., "Not everyone has enough to eat every day," "When a conflict resolution team gets to work," and "Those who give up their time") are consistently varied.

Vocabulary

- Words and expressions are used accurately (e.g., "little children go to school with empty tummies," "non perishable food items," and "a fresh perspective on life") and deliberately (e.g., "quality of life" and "Some of the old folk have forgotten").
- Precise words and expressions (e.g., "poverty and neglect," "glossy magazines," and "The wiz then helps the struggling student") are used to enrich details.
- The tone created by the student (e.g., "lonely old people who live pretty boring lives" and "Obviously, conflict resolution leads to big improvements in the school society") is convincing.

Conventions

- The quality of writing is enhanced because it is essentially error-free (e.g., "Some of the old folk have forgotten what it is like to be young and they want the students to talk about their school work, their sports, their hobbies, and their friends").
- Any errors that are present in mechanics (e.g., "arguement") and usage (e.g., "who's eye-sight," "old folks home," and "peer support group at school also provide") do not reduce the clarity and do not interrupt the flow of the response.

ANSWERS AND SOLUTIONS—WRITING UNIT TEST

Sample Student Response – Level 3 Narrative

TIME TO GROW UP

Grandpa was planning his next chess move. As she looked across the table at Grandpa, Leah was reminded that things hadn't always been this comfortable between them…

Leah remembered when her parents told her that Grandpa was moving in, soon after Grandma died. Leah was upset when they moved him in to the room that she and her mother had spent hours decorating. That room was Leah's special place. She didn't even take her friends in there. Leah had rushed outside before her parents could see her tears.

Leah was an only child. She wasn't a complainer, so Leah didn't argue when Mom announced that they had to repaint her room. One day Dad asked her to help them switch the furniture. They wanted Grandpa to have a new room, different from the apartment he had shared with Grandma Jenny.

The fall and winter passed. Lots of things were different. Grandpa snored. Left his teeth in the hall bathroom, which was embarrassing if Leah had a friend over. Grandpa was a diabetic, so he needed special meals. Leah and her mom didn't go as many places together, and Dad postponed the trip to Disneyland. Otherwise, Grandpa was very quiet and didn't say much. He would eat his meals with his family, then he would go straight to his room.

Leah entered the kitchen one Saturday morning during Spring Break. Leah was an early riser on the weekends. Usually she would make some toast, and watch TV in the family room. Leah loved the peace and quiet of early morning, with the sun shining through the bay window.

She was surprised to see Grandpa sitting at the kitchen table, reading the Saturday paper.

"Uh, Grandpa," Leah asked nervously from the doorway, "would you like some coffee?"

At the sound of Leah's voice, Grandpa turned with a twinkle in his eye. "You must be a better cook than me! Your grandma claimed I was the only person she knew who could burn water! Your dad told me that you were an early riser like me…I've been staying in my room to watch TV in the morning because I didn't want to bother anyone." Grandpa had thought it was too fine a day to waste in bed when the sun was shining and the grass was green again.

Leah giggled, because finally Grandpa was feeling good enough to tease her again. The following Saturday, Grandpa suggested a game of chess after he and Leah finished their breakfast. With a happy smile, he went to get his chess set from his room. Grandpa was a patient teacher, and Leah was a quick learner. The first time Leah won a game, Grandpa pretended to be upset, but he was actually proud of what he had taught her.

Grandpa was still planning. Of course he would try his best to win, but even if she lost again, Leah didn't mind. Grandpa's arrival had altered her life for the better, and she didn't mind at all.

Rationale for Student Exemplar Level 3 Narrative

Content

- The student's exploration of the topic is clear and logical. A teenager copes with the impacts of a grandparent moving in with the family.
- The student's purpose (to show how a significant experience alters a young person's life) is implied but evident.
- The ideas presented by the student (when a girl's grandmother dies, she has to give her room to Grandpa, who moves in with her family) are appropriate and predictable.
- Supporting details (e.g., "Leah was upset" and "He would eat his meals with his family") are relevant but general.

The writing is straightforward and generalized (e.g., "Lots of things were different") and occasionally arouses the reader's interest through details (e.g., "Dad postponed the trip to Disneyland").

Organization

- The introduction is functional and establishes a focus by presenting a happy situation immediately followed by a flashback to Grandpa moving in. That focus is generally sustained.
- Events are developed in a discernible order with the girl being upset at losing her room but gradually coming to accept Grandpa's presence in the home as a positive change. Coherence may falter occasionally as a result of the cursory progression of the plot and absence of details.
- Transitions (e.g., "The fall and winter passed" and "one Saturday morning") are generally used to connect details within sentences and between paragraphs but tend to be mechanical.
- Closure is related to the focus but is mechanical ("Grandpa's arrival had altered her life for the better, and she didn't mind at all").

Sentence Structure

- Sentence structure is generally controlled.
- Sentence type and length are sometimes effective and/or varied ("Leah giggled, because…" and "Grandpa was still planning").
- Some variety of sentence beginnings is evident (e.g., "As she looked" and "Usually she would make").

Vocabulary

- Words and expressions are generally used appropriately throughout the story.
- General words and expressions are used adequately to clarify meaning (e.g., "things hadn't always been this comfortable" and "which was embarrassing").

The voice/tone created by the student is discernible (e.g., "Leah loved the peace and quiet of early morning"). It is somewhat uneven, because the minimal dialogue sounds convincing, but the third person narration is objective rather than distinctive in style or vocabulary choices.

Conventions

- The quality of the writing is sustained through generally correct use of conventions
- Errors occasionally reduce clarity and sometimes interrupt the flow of the response (e.g., "left his teeth in the bathroom, which was embarrassing if Leah had a friend over").

Sample Student Reponse – Level 3 Narrative

TIME TO GROW UP

Leah gazed fondly across the table at her Grandpa, as he planned his next chess move. Who would have thought that Grandpa would actually have to be planning a chess move to beat the granddaughter he had taught to play his favorite game? Things hadn't always been this comfortable between them…

Leah thought back to the snatches of conversation that she had overheard between her parents, a few days after her Grandma's funeral:

"…can't look after himself. Grandma never let him in the kitchen…"

"…know he likes his independence, but I just don't see…"

"…have to move Leah downstairs…Your dad can't do stairs."

That was when Leah had fled out the back door. What were they thinking? It was one thing to have Grandpa over for Sunday dinner, but moving him in to the room that she and her mother had spent hours decorating was unthinkable. That room was Leah's perfect sanctuary. She didn't even take her friends in there, because Leah didn't want them to move anything.

So, one thing led to another. Like her dad, Leah was an only child. She wasn't a complainer, so Leah didn't argue when Mom announced that they had to repaint her room. Leah didn't even ask why. She also didn't argue the day Dad asked her to help them switch the furniture. They wanted Grandpa to have a new room, free of reminders of the apartment he had shared with Grandma Jenny.

Leah overheard them talking, again, shortly before Grandpa moved in.

"…can't believe she's been so good about it…do you think…"

"…always been such a quiet, co-operative child…hope this isn't upsetting her…"

Without waiting around to hear more, Leah fled again. Once she felt calmer, she returned to the house.

The fall and winter passed. Lots of things were different. Grandpa snored. Grandpa left his teeth in the hall bathroom, which was embarrassing if Leah had a friend over. Every meal required careful planning, because Grandpa was a diabetic. Leah and her mom didn't go as many places together. Dad decided to postpone the Christmas trip to Disneyland, because Grandpa wasn't ready to be left home alone yet. Otherwise, Grandpa was very quiet and didn't say much. He would eat his meals with his family, then go straight to his room.

One Saturday morning during Spring Break, Leah entered the kitchen. Unlike her parents, Leah was an early riser on the weekends. Usually she would make some toast, get the newspaper, read the comics, or watch some TV in the family room. Leah loved the peace and quiet of early morning, with the slanting of the sun's rays through the bay window in the kitchen.

To her surprise, Grandpa was sitting at the kitchen table, reading the Saturday paper.

"Uh, Grandpa," Leah stammered from the doorway, "would you like some coffee?"

At the sound of Leah's voice, Grandpa turned in her direction, with a hint of a twinkle in his eye "You must be a better cook than me! Your grandma would never let me near her kitchen…she claimed I was the only person she knew who could burn water! Your dad did tell me that you were an early riser like me…I've been staying in my room to watch TV in the morning because I didn't want to bother anyone. Today, I woke up and thought it was too fine a day to waste in bed when the sun was shining and the grass was getting green again."

Leah giggled, because this was the teasing grandpa she remembered. For the second time, *one thing led to another*. The following Saturday, Grandpa suggested a game of chess after he and Leah finished their breakfast. He ignored Leah's weak protests that she would be "no good," bringing his chess set from his room. Grandpa was a patient teacher, and Leah was a quick learner who seemed to be a natural for the game. The first time Leah triumphantly said "Checkmate" sometime in April, Grandpa pretended to be horrified, but he was actually proud of what he had taught her.

Grandpa was still planning. "Come on, Grandpa, make up your mind…anyhow, I haven't beat you yet this week!"

Even if she lost again, Leah didn't mind. She was amazed at how Grandpa's arrival had not only changed, but enriched her life.

Rationale for Student Exemplar – Level 3 Narrative

Content

- The student's exploration of the topic (how an experience shapes a life) is both adept and plausible. A teenage girl develops maturity in relationships when a grandparent moves in with her family.
- The student's purpose (to show positive changes in a young person brought about by a life-altering experience) is intentional, as implied by the story.
- The ideas presented by the student (struggling to deal with unexpected change, intergenerational relationships) are thoughtful and sound.
- Supporting details (e.g., "snatches of conversation" and "they had to repaint her room") are relevant and specific.

The writing is elaborated with sufficient details, like the snatches of overheard conversation, to draw the reader's interest.

Organization

- The introduction is purposeful and clearly establishes a focus by beginning with a companionable scene before relating the series of events that had led to the scene at the beginning. The focus on the grandfather's arrival in the home is capably sustained through a progression of related events.
- Details are developed in paragraphs in a sensible order that follows Leah's initial dismay through the gradual adjustments to having Grandpa living with her family. Coherence is generally maintained because the chronological sequence of events is clear, despite the flashback technique used.
- Transitions, both explicit (e.g., "So, one thing led to another") and implicit (e.g., "At the sound of Leah's voice…") clearly connect events and details within sentences and between paragraphs.
- Closure is appropriate and related to the focus (e.g., "She was amazed at how Grandpa's arrival had not only changed, but enriched her life").

Vocabulary

- Words and expressions are often used accurately (e.g., "likes his independence" and "fled out the back door").
- Specific expressions show some evidence of careful selection (e.g., "unthinkable" and "every meal required careful planning") and some awareness of connotative effect (e.g., "with a hint of a twinkle in his eye").
- The voice/tone created by the student is distinct and the most effective when the student re-creates earlier conversations in italics or other dialogue that is worked into the narrative.

Conventions

- The quality of the writing is enhanced because it is essentially error-free.

Sample Student Response – Level 4 Narrative

TIME TO GROW UP

Leah gazed fondly across the table at the old man bent thoughtfully over his next chess move. Grandpa. Her only Grandpa. Beside him, the mug of coffee Leah had just poured was sending gentle fronds of steam wafting across an early morning sunbeam. Grandpa was so funny. Who would have thought that he would actually have to ponder a chess move? That a misplay might cause him to lose, first thing Saturday morning, to the granddaughter he had taught to play his favorite game? Things hadn't always been this comfortable between them…

Leah lay sprawled across her "thinking rock," at the far end of her parents' acreage, staring sightlessly at fluffy clouds which drifted aimlessly across the blue eternity of the August sky. One lucky mosquito had landed on the smooth expanse of Leah's upper arm, where it was enjoying a substantial meal, totally ignored by the arm's owner. "Is this what 'depressed' feels like?" Leah asked herself. Grandma Jenny's funeral earlier that day hadn't been depressing. It had really been quite pretty and nice, with all the flowers, and kind words about Grandma. The lunch had been ok. Even when they had dropped Grandpa off at his apartment, Leah hadn't minded. Everything seemed quite normal…almost like the times they would drop Grandpa off when he had come for dinner those weekends when Grandma Jenny used to go visit her sister. The permanence of the change in the family hadn't really set in yet.

Leah hadn't meant to eavesdrop on her parents' conversation back home after the funeral. She had gone to her room to relax and read, because the day had been quite exhausting…thanking people who spoke sympathetically to her, bringing coffee and sandwiches to her two great-aunts, Grandma's sisters, getting more Kleenex for her dad, who had been Grandma Jenny's only son…It was when Leah emerged from her room to walk to the washroom in the hallway that she overheard them talking in the kitchen. It was just snatches, but Leah could immediately see where the conversation was leading.

"…can't look after himself. Grandma never let him in the kitchen…"

"…know he likes his independence, but I just don't see…"

"…have to move Leah downstairs…Your dad can't do stairs."

That was when Leah had fled out the back door. What were they thinking? It was one thing to have Grandpa over for Sunday dinner, but her room that she and her mother had spent hours decorating in July? Next to the rock, that room was Leah's perfect sanctuary. She didn't even take her friends in there, because Leah didn't want them to move anything.

So, one thing led to another. If her parents wondered at Leah's silence over supper that night, they wisely didn't comment. They probably thought she was grieving for Grandma in her own way, which was true, to a certain point. However, Leah was grieving more for herself; there was no doubt about it.

Like her dad, Leah was an only child. She wasn't a complainer, so Leah didn't throw tantrums and she didn't argue when Mom announced that they had to repaint her room. Leah didn't even ask why. She *knew*. Leah didn't argue the day Dad asked his daughter to help them switch the furniture, moving Leah's downstairs to the guest room, to be replaced with the single bed, green recliner, computer desk, and TV stand they had purchased for Grandpa. They wanted Grandpa to have a new room, free of reminders of the apartment he had shared with Grandma Jenny. Leah obediently helped with the garage sale, where strangers bartered over Grandma and Grandpa's furniture, as well as the furniture from the guest room downstairs. That room would now be Leah's.

The fall and winter passed, awkwardly. Lots of things were different. Grandpa snored, and sometimes kept her parents awake across the hall. Grandpa left his teeth in the hall bathroom, which was embarrassing if Leah had a friend over. Every meal required careful planning, because Grandpa was a diabetic. Leah and her mom didn't go as many places together, because Mom had to leave work early some days to take Grandpa to the doctor. Dad decided to postpone the Christmas trip to Disneyland, Florida, that he and Mom had promised, because "Dad isn't ready to be left home alone yet," he told Leah. Otherwise, Grandpa was very quiet and didn't say much. "He's still sad about Grandma and he misses her," Mom told Leah when Grandpa went to his room again, right after supper.

One Saturday morning during Spring Break in late March, Leah climbed the stairs to the kitchen and opened the door. It was about 7:00 AM, but Leah, unlike her parents, was an early riser on the week-ends. Usually she would make some toast, get the newspaper in, read the funnies, go on the computer in the kitchen nook, or watch some TV in the family room off the kitchen. Leah loved the peace and quiet of early morning, the slanting of the sun's rays through the bay window in the kitchen, the view out over the deck to the lawn and pond. Sometimes a squirrel would be scampering along the railing of the deck, or a couple of birds would be busily devouring breakfast from the raised feeder that Dad had installed out of reach of the squirrels.

His back to the basement door, Grandpa was sitting at the kitchen table, reading the Saturday paper, which he had obviously retrieved from the mailbox at the end of the acreage driveway.

"Uh, Grandpa," Leah stammered nervously from the doorway, "would you like some coffee?"

At the sound of Leah's voice, Grandpa turned in her direction. Was that a hint of a twinkle in his eye? "You must be a better cook than me! Your grandma would never let me near her kitchen…she claimed I was the only person she knew who could burn water!" He chuckled at the memory. "You know, your dad did tell me that you were an early riser like me…I've been staying in my room to watch TV in the morning because I didn't want to bother anyone, but I woke up this morning, and I thought to myself, 'What the heck, it's too fine a day to waste in bed when the sun is shining and the grass is getting green again. Might even spot my first robin out on the back forty there!'"

Leah giggled. This was the teasing grandpa she remembered. "How about bacon? And I can whip up a mean omelet…I have to fend for myself, or I'd starve on Saturdays. Mom and Dad are never up till at least 10!"

So, one thing led to another. The following Saturday, Grandpa proposed a game of chess after he and Leah finished their breakfast. He overcame Leah's weak protests that she would be "no good," and fetched his chess set from his room. Grandpa was a patient teacher, and Leah was a quick learner who seemed to have a natural affinity for the game. The first time Leah triumphantly said "Checkmate" sometime in April, Grandpa looked over at her in mock horror and pushed his chair back. "Guess we can't play anymore…you're getting too good for an old geezer like me!"

…Grandpa was still pondering. "Come on, Grandpa, make up your mind…anyhow, I haven't beat you yet this week!"

Grandpa looked up with a sly wink as he moved his wrist slightly to maneuver a knight that Leah had somehow missed noticing. "Checkmate," he smiled.

Rationale for Student Exemplar Level 4 Narrative

Content

- The student's exploration of the topic is insightful (an empathetic story about the challenges of living with an aging relative) and imaginative.

- The student's purpose (to narrate a realistic experience and the challenges faced by the participants) is deliberate. The story is intended to show how a life-altering challenge can bring out the best in everyone involved.
- The ideas presented by the student (an only child finds out that her Grandpa will be coming to live with her family) are carefully chosen and perceptive.
- Supporting details (e.g., "Leah lay sprawled across her 'thinking rock'" and "single bed, green recliner") are precise and original.

The writing is confident, creative, and holds the reader's interest with italicized flashbacks and a well-developed main character who faces some realistic conflicts.

Organization

- The introduction, which presents the main character some time after the event that has altered her life, is engaging and skillfully establishes a focus on the topic that is consistently sustained through the rest of the narrative.
- Events and details are developed in paragraphs in a judicious order (the student writer uses flashback and dialogue to carry some of the plot forward), but coherence is maintained at all times through a clearly evident chronological sequence of events.
- Transitions, both explicit (e.g., "earlier that day") and implicit (e.g., "So, one thing led to another") fluently connect events and details within sentences and between paragraphs.

Closure is effective and related to the focus (e.g., "Grandpa looked up with a sly wink as he moved his wrist slightly to maneuver a knight that Leah had somehow missed noticing. 'Checkmate,' he smiled."). Not only does this ending complete the game introduced at the beginning, but it reflects the amazing attitudinal changes that have occurred in both Leah and her grandfather

Sentence Structure

- Sentence structure is effectively and consistently controlled throughout the story.
- Sentence type and length are consistently effective and varied (e.g., "Leah giggled," "How about bacon," and "The following Saturday,…").
- Sentence beginnings are consistently varied (e.g., "If her parents wondered…," "However, Leah was…," and "His back to the basement door").

Vocabulary

- Words and expressions are used accurately and deliberately throughout the story (e.g., "bent thoughtfully over his next chess move" and "staring sightlessly at fluffy clouds").
- Precise words and expressions are used to create vivid images and to enrich details (e.g., "where strangers bartered," "fall and winter passed, awkwardly," and "slanting of the sun's rays through the bay window").
- The voice/tone created by the student is convincing. The use of the italics to recall earlier events and emotional responses creates empathy for the main character as she struggles to adapt to changes that are beyond her control.

Conventions

- The quality of the writing is enhanced because it is essentially error-free.
- Any errors that are present do not reduce clarity and do not interrupt the flow of the response. Occasional sentence fragments (e.g., "That a misplay might cause him to lose…") seem to be deliberate because of the overall quality of the writing.

NOTES

KEY Strategies for Success on Tests

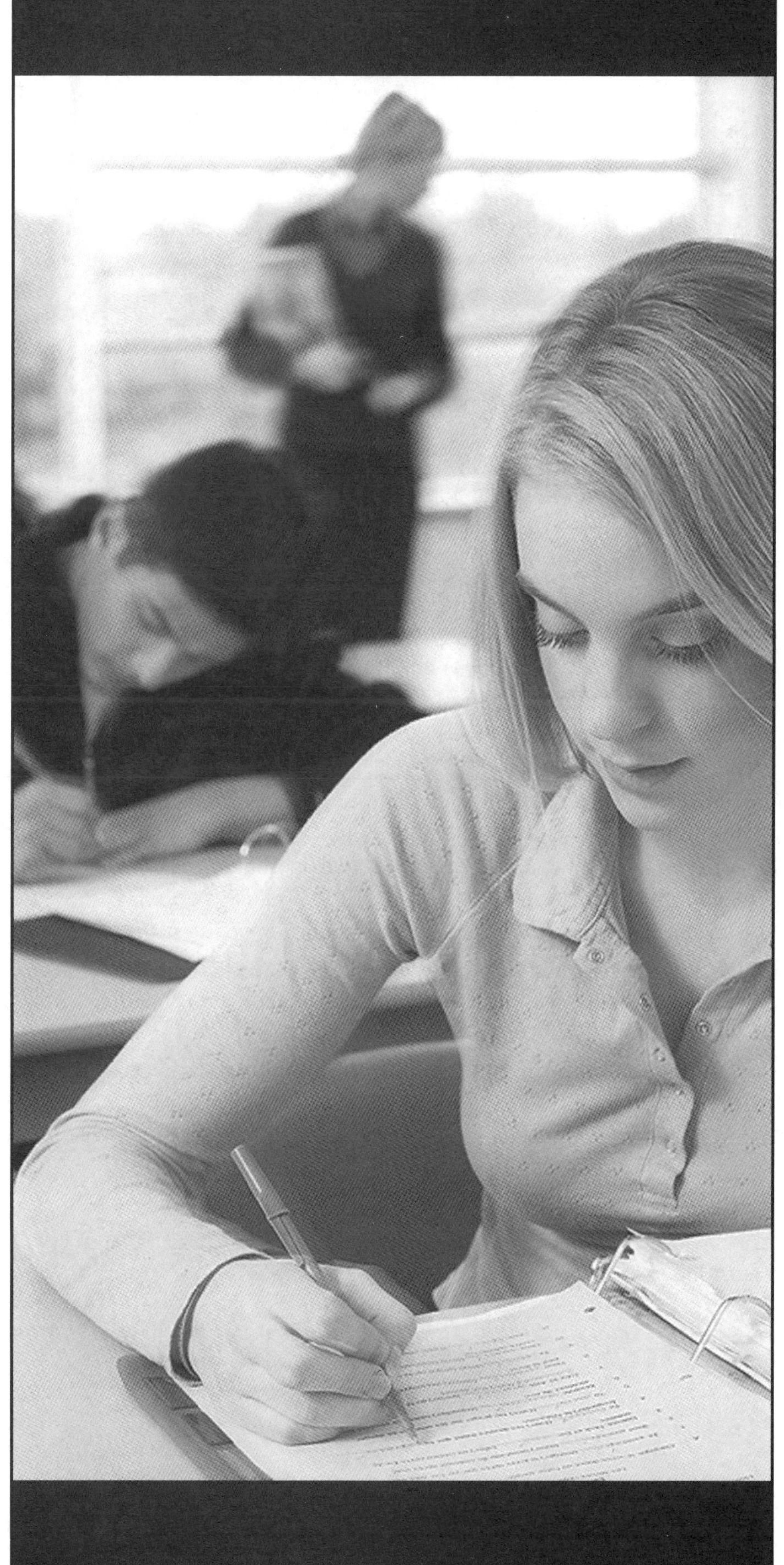

KEY STRATEGIES FOR SUCCESS ON TESTS

Having a good understanding of effective test-taking skills can help your performance on any test. Being familiar with question formats can help you in preparing for quizzes, unit tests or year-end assessments.

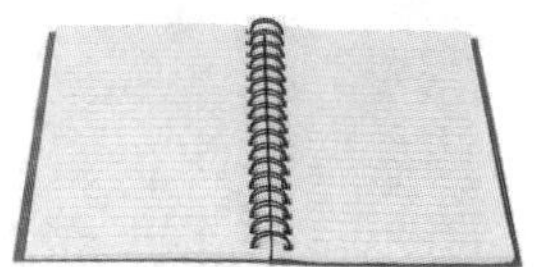

Test Preparation and Test-taking Skills

THINGS TO CONSIDER WHEN TAKING A TEST

- It is normal to feel anxious before writing a test. You can manage this anxiety by thinking positive thoughts. Visual imagery is a helpful technique to try.
- Make a conscious effort to relax by taking several slow, controlled, deep breaths. Concentrate on the air going in and out of the body.
- Before you begin the test, ask questions if you are unsure of anything.
- Jot down key words or phrases from any oral directions.
- Look over the entire test to assess the number and kinds of questions on the test.
- Read each question carefully and reread it if necessary.
- Pay close attention to key vocabulary words. Sometimes these words are bolded or italicized, and they are usually important words in the question.
- Mark your answers on your answer sheet carefully. If you wish to change an answer, erase the mark and then ensure that your final answer is darker than the one that you have erased.
- On the test booklet, use highlighting to note directions, key words, and vocabulary that you find confusing or that are important to answering the question.
- **Double-check** to make sure you have answered everything before handing in your test.

When taking tests, some words are often overlooked. Failure to pay close attention to these words can result in an incorrect answer. One way to avoid this is to be aware of these words and to <u>underline</u>, circle, or **highlight** these words while you are taking the test.

Even though the following words are easy to understand, they are also easy to miss and can change the meaning of the question and/or answer significantly.

all	**always**	**most likely**	**probably**	**best**	**not**
difference	**usually**	**except**	**most**	**unlikely**	**likely**

Example

1. During the race, Susan is **most likely** feeling

A. sad

B. weak

C. scared

D. determined

HELPFUL STRATEGIES FOR ANSWERING MULTIPLE-CHOICE QUESTIONS

A multiple-choice question provides some information for you to consider and then asks you to select a response from four choices. There will be one correct answer. The other answers are distracters, which are incorrect.

Here are some strategies to help you when answering multiple-choice questions.

- Quickly skim through the entire test. Find out how many questions there are and plan your time accordingly.
- Read and reread questions carefully. Underline key words and try to think of an answer before looking at the choices.
- If there is a graphic, look at the graphic, read the question, and go back to the graphic. Then, you may want to circle the important information from the question.
- Carefully read the choices. Read the question first and then each answer with it.
- When choosing an answer, try to eliminate those choices that are clearly wrong or do not make sense.
- Some questions may ask you to select the best answer. These questions will always include words like **best**, **most strongly**, and **most clearly**. All of the answers will be correct to some degree, but one of the choices will be "best" in some way. Carefully read all four choices (**A**, **B**, **C**, **D**) before choosing the answer you think is the best.
- If you do not know the answer or if the question does not make sense to you, it is better to guess than to leave it blank.
- Do not spend too much time on any one question. Make a mark (*) beside a difficult question and come back to it. If you are leaving a question to come back to later, make sure that you also leave the space on the answer sheet.
- Remember to go back to the difficult questions at the end of the test; sometimes clues are given throughout the test that will provide you with answers.
- Note any negatives, such as **no** or **not**, and be sure your choice fits the question.
- Before changing an answer, **be sure** you have a very good reason to do so.
- Do not look for patterns on your answer sheet.

HELPFUL STRATEGIES FOR ANSWERING OPEN-RESPONSE QUESTIONS

An open-response question requires you to respond to a question or directive such as **explain, predict, list, describe, use information from the text and your own ideas; provide the main idea and supporting details**. In preparing for open-response tasks you may wish to:

- Read and re-read the question carefully.
- Recognize and pay close attention to **directing words** such as **explain, predict, and describe.**
- **Underline** key words and phrases that indicate what is required in your answer, such as explain, summarize, mainly about, what is the meaning of, best shows…
- Write down rough, point-form notes regarding the information you want to include in your answer.
- Think about what you want to say and organize information and ideas in a coherent and concise manner within the time limit you have for the question.
- Be sure to answer every part of the question that is asked.
- Stick to the question, be brief, and only answer what is asked.
- Answer in full and correctly written sentences keeping your answer within the space provided.
- Re-read your response to ensure you have answered the question.
- **Think:** Does your answer make sense?
- **Listen:** Does it sound right?
- Use the appropriate subject vocabulary and terminology in your response.

TEST PREPARATION COUNTDOWN

If you develop a plan for studying and test preparation, you will perform well on tests.

Here is a general plan to follow seven days before you write a test.

Countdown: Seven Days Before the Test

1. Review important areas in which to gather information:
   - areas to be included on the test
   - types of test items
   - general and specific test tips
2. Start preparing for the test at least seven days prior to the test-taking day. Develop your test preparation plan and set time aside to prepare and study.

Countdown: from Six to Two Days Before the Test

1. Review old homework assignments, quizzes, and tests.
2. Rework problems on quizzes and tests to make sure you still know how to solve them.
3. Correct any errors made on quizzes and tests.
4. Review key concepts, processes, formulas, and vocabulary.
5. Create practice test questions for yourself and then answer them. Work out lots of sample problems.

Countdown: The Night Before the Test

1. The night before the test is for final preparation, which includes reviewing and gathering material needed for the test before going to bed.
2. Most important is getting a good night's rest, knowing that you have done everything within your means to do well on the test.

The Day of the Test

1. Eat a nutritious breakfast.
2. Ensure that you have all the necessary materials.
3. Think positive thoughts: "I can do this!" "I am ready!" "I know I can do well!"
4. Arrive at your school early so that you are not rushing. A stressful, rushed morning can set a hurried or anxious pace for the test.

SUCCESS TIPS DURING THE TEST

The following strategies can be useful to use when writing your test.

- Take two or three deep breaths to help you relax.
- Read the directions carefully and underline, circle, or highlight any key words.
- Survey the entire test to get a flavour of what you will need to do.
- Budget your time.
- Begin with an easy question or a question that you know you can answer correctly rather than following the numerical question order of the test.
- If you draw a blank on the test, try repeating the deep breathing and physical relaxation activities first. Then move to visualization and positive self-talk to get you going.
- Write down anything that you remember about the subject on the reverse side of your test paper. This activity sometimes helps you to remind yourself that you do know something and you are capable of writing the test.
- Look over your test when you have finished and double-check your answers to be sure you did not forget anything.

NOTES

Practice Tests

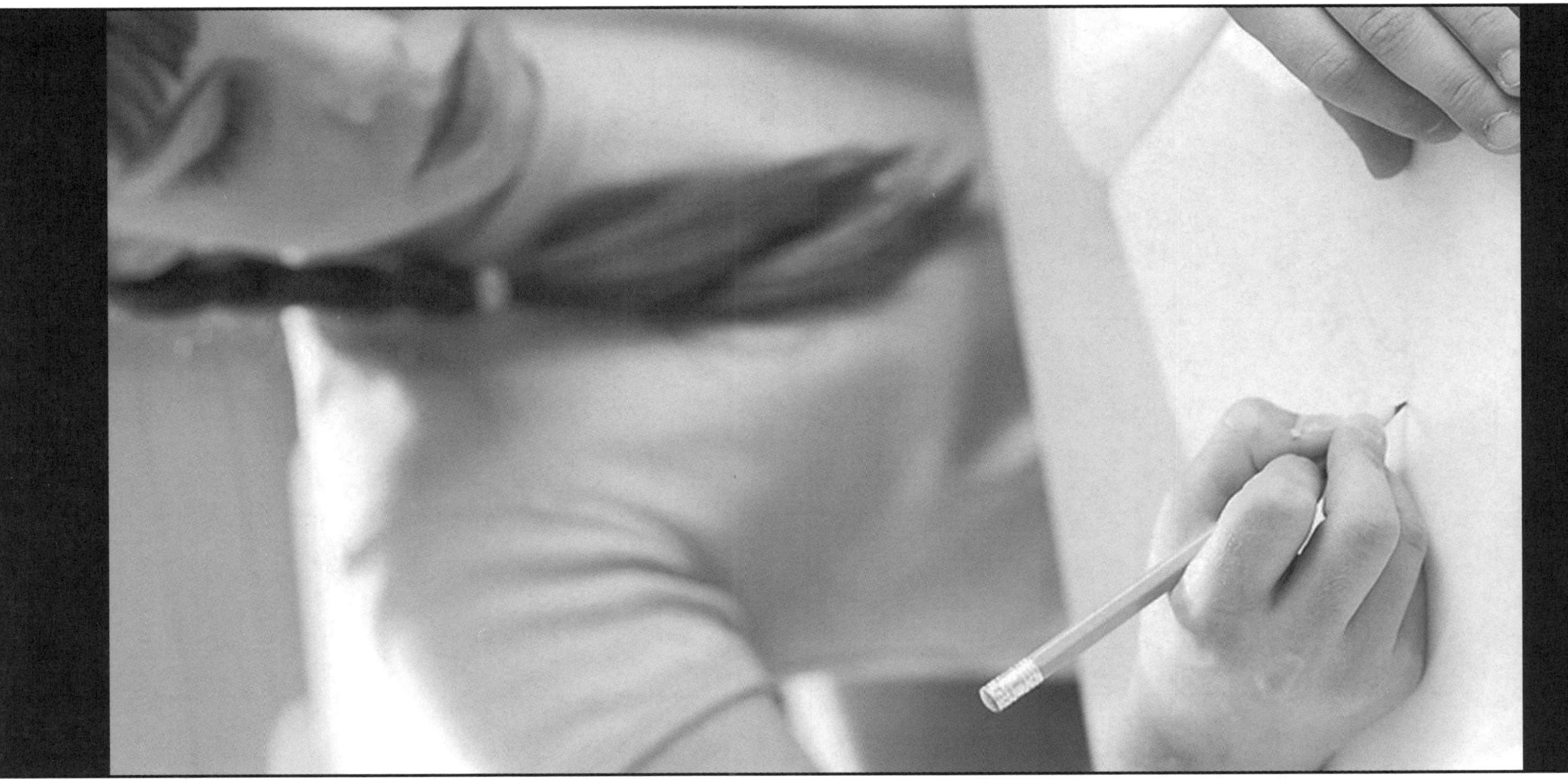

TABLE OF CORRELATIONS			
General Expectation	**Specific Expectation**	**Practice Test One**	**Practice Test Two**
Students are expected to:			
10R1.0 read and demonstrate an understanding of a variety of literary, informational, and graphic texts, using a range of strategies to construct meaning. (Reading for Meaning)	*10R1.1* read a variety of student- and teacher-selected texts from diverse cultures and historical periods, identifying specific purposes for reading. (Variety of Texts)	13, 21	
	10R1.2 select and use appropriate reading comprehension strategies before, during, and after reading to understand texts, including increasingly complex texts. (Using Reading Comprehension Strategies)		
	10R1.3 identify the most important ideas and supporting details in texts, including increasingly complex texts. (Demonstrating Understanding of Content)	2, 3, 5, 7, 8, 15, 16, 18, 19, 23, 24, 25, 26, 32	9,15, 20, 30
	10R1.4 make and explain inferences about texts, including increasingly complex texts, supporting their explanations with well-chosen stated and implied ideas from the texts. (Making Inferences)	6, 11, 17, 27, 28, 33	7, 16, 17, 19, 24, 27, 28, 31, 32,

	10R1.5 extend understanding of texts, including increasingly complex texts, by making appropriate connections between the ideas in them and personal knowledge, experience, and insights; other texts; and the world around them. (Extending Understanding of Texts)	14. 29	
	10R1.6 analyse texts in terms of the information, ideas, issues, or themes they explore, examining how various aspects of the texts contribute to the presentation or development of these elements. (Analysing Texts)	1, 22	1, 22
	10R1.7 evaluate the effectiveness of texts, including increasingly complex texts, using evidence from the text to support their opinions. (Evaluating Texts)		
	10R1.8 identify and analyse the perspectives and/or biases evident in texts, including increasingly complex texts, and comment on any questions they may raise about beliefs, values, identity, and power. (Critical Literacy)		10, 21

10R2.0 Recognize a variety of text forms, text features, and stylistic elements and demonstrate understanding of how they help communicate meaning. (Understanding Form and Style)	*10R2.1* identify a variety of characteristics of literary, informational, and graphic text forms and explain how they help communicate meaning. (Text Forms)	9, 20	6, 13, 23
	10R2.2 identify a variety of text features and explain how they help communicate meaning. (Text Features)		
	10R2.3 identify a variety of elements of style in texts and explain how they help communicate meaning and enhance the effectiveness of the texts. (Elements of Style)	10, 12, 30, 31, 34, 35	2, 4, 11, 12, 18, 25, 26, 29
10R3.0 Use knowledge of words and cueing systems to read fluently. (Reading With Fluency)	*10R3.1* automatically understands most words in a variety of reading contexts. (Reading Familiar Words)		5, 8, 33
	10R3.2 use appropriate decoding strategies to read and understand unfamiliar words. (Reading Unfamiliar Words)	4	3, 14
	10R3.3 identify and use a variety of strategies to expand vocabulary (Developing Vocabulary)		

PRACTICE TEST ONE

Read the following passage to answer questions 1 to 7.

from EMMA

Emma Woodhouse, handsome, clever, and rich, with a comfortable home and happy disposition, seemed to unite some of the best blessings of existence; and had lived nearly twenty-one years in the world with very little to distress or vex her.

She was the youngest of the two daughters of a most affectionate, indulgent father; and had, in consequence of her sister Isabella's marriage, been mistress of his house from a very early period. Her mother had died too long ago for her to have more than an indistinct remembrance of her caresses; and her place had been supplied by an excellent woman as governess, who had fallen little short of a mother in affection.

Sixteen years had Miss Taylor been in Mr. Woodhouse's family, less as a governess than a friend, very fond of both daughters, but particularly of Emma. Between them it was more the intimacy of sisters. Even before Miss Taylor had ceased to hold the nominal office of governess, the mildness of her temper had hardly allowed her to impose any restraint; and the shadow of authority being now long passed away, they had been living together as friend and friend very mutually attached, and Emma doing just what she liked; highly esteeming Miss Taylor's judgment, but directed chiefly by her own.

The real evils, indeed, of Emma's situation were the power of having rather too much her own way, and a disposition to think a little too well of herself; these were the disadvantages which threatened alloy to her many enjoyments. The danger, however, was at present so unperceived, that they did not by any means rank as misfortunes with her.

Sorrow came—a gentle sorrow—but not at all in the shape of any disagreeable consciousness. Miss Taylor married. It was Miss Taylor's loss which first brought grief. It was on the wedding-day of this beloved friend that Emma first sat in mournful thought of any continuance. The wedding over, and the bride-people gone, her father and herself were left to dine together, with no prospect of a third to cheer a long evening. Her father composed himself to sleep after dinner, as usual, and she had then only to sit and think of what she had lost.

The event had every promise of happiness for her friend. Mr. Weston was a man of unexceptionable character, easy fortune, suitable age, and pleasant manners; and there was some satisfaction in considering with what self-denying, generous friendship she had always wished and promoted the match; but it was a black morning's work for her. The want of Miss Taylor would be felt every hour of every day. She recalled her past kindness—the kindness, the affection of sixteen years—how she had taught and how she had played with her from five years old—how she had devoted all her powers to attach and amuse her in health—and how she nursed her through the various illnesses of childhood. A large debt of gratitude was owing here; but the intercourse of the last seven years, the equal footing and perfect unreserve which had soon followed Isabella's marriage, on their being left to each other, was yet a dearer, tenderer recollection. She had been a friend and companion such as few possessed: intelligent, well-informed, useful, gentle, knowing all the ways of the family, interested in all its concerns, and peculiarly interested in herself, in every pleasure, every scheme of hers—one to whom she could speak every thought as it arose, and who had such an affection for her as could never find fault.

Continued

[1] valetudinarian—someone who is weak or sickly

How was she to bear the change?—It was true that her friend was going only half a mile from them; but Emma was aware that great must be the difference between a Mrs. Weston, only half a mile from them, and a Miss Taylor in the house; and with all her advantages, natural and domestic, she was now in great danger of suffering from intellectual solitude. She dearly loved her father, but he was no companion for her. He could not meet her in conversation, rational or playful.

The evil of the actual disparity in their ages (and Mr. Woodhouse had not married early) was much increased by his constitution and habits; for having been a valetudinarian[1] all his life, without activity of mind or body, he was a much older man in ways than in years; and though everywhere beloved for the friendliness of his heart and his amiable temper, his talents could not have recommended him at any time.

—*by* Jane Austen

1. Which of the following statements gives the **main** theme of the passage?
   A. Best friends often desert each other.
   B. Employees might become family members.
   C. It is sometimes difficult to accept life's changes.
   D. Parents do not always relate well to their children.

2. According to this passage, the "real evils" (paragraph 4) of Emma's situation are related to the fact that
   A. she lives in the countryside
   B. she has no brothers to protect her
   C. her mother passed away at an early age
   D. she has gotten used to getting her own way

3. About how old is Emma when Miss Taylor gets married?
   A. 5 years of age
   B. 7 years of age
   C. 16 years of age
   D. 21 years of age

4. As it is used in the quotation "Even before Miss Taylor had ceased to hold the nominal office of governess," the word "nominal" **most likely** means
   A. in name only
   B. insignificant
   C. to nominate
   D. costly

5. What is "the change" (paragraph 7) that Emma finds nearly unbearable?
   A. Her sister is gone.

B. The governess has married.

C. Her father has decided to marry the governess.

D. She cannot visit her friend now that she has gotten married.

6. Which of the following phrases **best** describes Mr. Weston's character?

A. Easy-going and well-to-do

B. Relaxed and basically lazy

C. Irritable and high-strung

D. Energetic and boisterous

7. The relationship between Emma and Miss Taylor is **best** described as

A. close

B. sisterly

C. self-serving

D. deteriorating

Read the following passage to answer questions 8 to 12.

STARS

Now in the West the slender moon lies low,
And now Orion[2] glimmers through the trees,
Clearing the earth with even pace and slow,
And now the stately-moving Pleiades,[3]
In that soft infinite darkness overhead
Hang jewel-wise upon a silver thread.

And all the lonelier stars that have their place,
Calm lamps within the distant southern sky,
And planet-dust upon the edge of space,
Look down upon the fretful world, and I
Look up to outer vastness unafraid
And see the stars which sang when earth was made.

—*by* Marjorie Pickthall

[2] Orion—a constellation taking the form of a hunter with a belt and a sword

[3] Pleiades—in Greek myth, the seven daughters of Atlas and a group of stars in the constellation Taurus, not far from Orion

8. Which of the following statements gives the **main** idea of the poem?
   A. The moon and the stars light up the sky at night.
   B. Nature has a powerful effect on humans.
   C. Constellations are named after humans.
   D. The moon calms people's fears.

9. What is the rhyme scheme of the poem?
   A. abab
   B. abba
   C. abcabc
   D. ababcc

10. The purpose of the personification of Orion and Pleiades is to illustrate
    A. how slowly they moved
    B. how much these constellations are like people
    C. the beauty of the lights shining out of the dark sky
    D. the grace and majesty of the constellations as they move across the sky

11. What does the description of the "slender moon" lying low (line 1) indicate about the moon?
    A. It was full.
    B. It was about to set in the west.
    C. It was not in a vertical position.
    D. It was waning rather than waxing.

12. Which of the senses is **most strongly** evoked in this poem?
    A. Touch
    B. Smell
    C. Taste
    D. Sight

Read the following passage to answer questions 13 to 19.

CLOSET OF THE FUTURE PICKS OUT CLOTHES

TOKYO—Japan's leading electronics companies are hard at work trying to make the country's notoriously cramped houses smarter—and more convenient—with a high-tech touch.

At its new Tokyo showroom, Matsushita Electric Industrial Co., maker of the Panasonic brand, is enticing Japan's gadget lovers with two model "houses of tomorrow."

On show are a toilet that analyzes your urine and automatically sends suspicious results to the doctor via the Internet, and a closet that picks out clothes according to weather forecasts—and whether you need to impress the boss.

Not sure what to wear for that high school reunion? Just ask your closet. Wondering how to get rid of that pimple on your chin? Consult the mirror for advice on clear skin.

"These are ideas that in a few years we'll be able in some way to sell," Matsushita spokesman Wilson Solano said. "This is market potential."

The products went on display last week. They aren't even priced yet, and are slated to go to market in 2005 or beyond.

Meagre Japanese abodes are infamous for paper-thin walls and tight quarters. Floor space averages only 32.5 square metres, which is barely half a storey in a typical North American house.

But the trend is clear. What they lack in size, some are trying to make up in smarts. Toilets flush by remote control and have motorized seats that adjust to your height.
Lights are primed to switch on when someone walks in a room. And the Japanese have been adopting high-speed Internet access much faster than Americans.

Part of Matsushita's push are products that afford extra elbow room.

That includes the all-in-one washer-dryer, especially useful in Japan where the typical washing machine is only half as big as its American counterpart and where most people hang clothes outside.

Matsushita also introduced a kitchen table with a touch-screen computer built into it that doubles as a flat-screen television.

It's not the only company trying to tap cravings for creature comforts.

Sharp Corp. presently unveiled an air conditioner that supposedly kills the flu bug, while Sanyo Electric Co. has a bed sheet that monitors a sleeper's breathing, heart rates and body movement to adjust the room's heat and lighting for a good night's rest.

Back at Matsushita's showroom, some gadgets actually take up more space than their forerunners. There's the oversized refrigerator with a built-in camera that beams pictures to your mobile phone so you can check if you're low on milk while cruising the dairy aisle.

Continued

The company also offers an electromagnetic stove and countertop. Its heating elements won't burn fingers on touch but will warm up pans when covered, while the counter automatically powers a special line of cordless kitchen appliances.

There is also the "laboratory toilet" that tests your urine to measure blood sugar, protein and body fat.

Not to be outdone is the automated closet. Users simply punch in today's weather and preferred clothing style—such as casual or formal—and let the computer sort out the rest. Between wearings, the wardrobe also treats your garments to a steam cleaning.

And for those in need of a live-in beautician, there's the Matsushita bathroom sink ensemble. Its mirror takes infrared pictures of your hair and skin, keeps the record in its data banks and recommends the treatment to bring out that shine. It also dispenses mineral waters in varying degrees of acidity to best suit your ailment.

The developments are similar to luxuries being dabbled with in the United States but mostly reserved for the privileged few.

Microsoft mogul Bill Gates' multi-million mansion outside Seattle features a computer system that changes music, temperature, lighting and even digital artwork to match visitor preferences as people move from room to room.

Japanese consumers are similarly renowned for being gizmo-crazy, and line up for the latest in everything from mobile phones to digital cameras.

That's just the kind of customer Matsushita is banking on.

"The strength of this company is they know what the consumers want," Solano said. "They want to have it simple, where you can just press a button."

—*by* Hans Greimel

13. The **main** purpose of this article is to

A. describe new and unusual high-tech products

B. persuade readers to buy more electronics

C. market luxurious products to the masses

D. explain what life is like in Japan

14. What is the companies' **main** purpose in displaying these products?

A. To advertise their products

B. To stimulate sales of their products

C. To inform the public about their products

D. To educate the public about their products

15. According to the article, one reason that Japanese companies are trying to develop these high-tech products is to

A. make cramped houses more comfortable

B. win international awards in innovation

C. allow houses to be larger and warmer

D. make the country more efficient

16. For what reason would an all-in-one washer and dryer be beneficial?

A. It could be placed outside.

B. Most people in Japan do not have dryers.

C. Most people in Japan do not have washers.

D. It could hold twice as much as an American model.

17. How would the new toilet described in paragraphs 3, 8, and 16 benefit the consumer?

A. It would detect health problems.

B. It would advise the user of skin ailments.

C. It would take up less space in the bathroom.

D. It would switch on when the bathroom is entered.

18. Which of the leading-edge products described in the article uses photos as part of the technology?

A. The table and the television

B. The refrigerator and the closet

C. The refrigerator and the mirror

D. The washer and the digital camera

19. The computer system in Bill Gates' mansion is designed to change the artwork

A. to adjust to different people's tastes

B. when it gets tired of the same pictures

C. when visitors press the buttons on the walls

D. because different artwork requires different lighting

Read the following passage to answer questions 20 to 25.

PERCENTAGE OF INTERNET USERS, AGED 15 AND OVER, BY SELECTED TYPES OF INTERNET ACTIVITY, CANADA AND PROVINCE, 2000[1]

	Total users	E-mail	E-banking	Purchased goods or services	Information about goods and services	Health information	Chat service	News-groups or listserv	News sites
	(000's)	%							
Canada	12 981	83.6	22.7	23.7	74.3	45.9	30.0	15.7	54.7
Newfoundland	192	81.3	17.4	19.6	73.5	56.8	35.7	16.4	52.9
Prince Edward Island	53	82.3	16.9	18.2	71.5	55.5	28.1	16.9	46.5
Nova Scotia	396	85.9	23.6	23.4	74.8	54.0	33.8	19.2	55.0
New Brunswick	272	78.8	16.6	19.3	72.2	49.2	33.3	14.6	53.5
Quebec	2 723	78.2	21.9	19.3	73.9	40.4	34.0	11.6	55.7
Ontario	5 103	84.5	23.6	25.6	73.1	46.7	29.2	16.8	56.9
Manitoba	412	78.7	16.6	19.8	71.2	46.6	30.2	12.8	51.5
Saskatchewan	396	81.1	16.3	20.3	73.4	45.2	26.2	13.5	44.8
Alberta	1 418	86.9	23.4	25.9	78.2	43.6	30.5	16.1	53.0
British Columbia	2 016	87.8	25.1	26.2	76.2	49.2	25.1	18.5	51.9

[1] Percentage that has ever used the Internet for these activities, except e-mail, which has been used in the past 12 months.

Note: Totals exclude "Not stated."

Source: Statistics Canada, General Social Survey, Cycle 14

20. The format in which the given information is presented is known as a

A. line graph

B. bar graph

C. pie chart

D. table

21. What is the purpose of this information?

A. To show areas in which the Internet could be improved

B. To convince more people to use the Internet

C. To show how the Internet is used

D. To promote uses of the Internet

22. According to this information, what was the **most popular** use of the Internet in Canada in the year 2000?

A. To access e-mail

B. To view news sites

C. To purchase goods or services

D. To get information about goods and services

23. In which of the following provinces do Internet users bank online the **least**?

A. Prince Edward Island

B. British Columbia

C. Saskatchewan

D. Alberta

24. In which of the following provinces do Internet users do the **most** online shopping?

A. Prince Edward Island

B. British Columbia

C. Quebec

D. Ontario

25. How many Internet users does Quebec have?

A. 2 723

B. 272 000

C. 782 000

D. 2 723 000

Read the following passage to answer questions 26 to 35.

PANTOUM[4] FOR A MOTHER IN NUNAVUT

The landscape is stark and colorless,
small-town gossip follows you everywhere.
Even in the dingy hotel room, you can't be alone.
The natives hunt fox and their voices carry for miles.

Small-town gossip follows you everywhere.
What they say is foreign, is different.
The natives hunt fox and their voices carry for miles.
They covet your expensive laptop, your briefcase.

What they say is foreign, is different:
your smile, your naïve thin gloves,
They covet your expensive laptop, your briefcase.
And the telephone is your only escape.

The way you smile, your naïve thin gloves,
lonely in the white of snow.
The telephone is your only escape,
on the other end of the line there is warmth.

Lonely in the white of snow,
your hair still smells of west-coast weather.
On the other end of the line there is warmth
soft, like cherry blossoms in Victoria's spring.

Your hair still smells of west-coast weather
embroidered wolves on parkas,
soft, like cherry blossoms in Victoria's spring.
You are trapped in a sea of fur-lined hoods.

Embroidered wolves on your parka
Don't make you any warmer.
Trapped in a sea of fur-lined hoods,
dreaming of cotton and silk.

—*by* Claire Battershill
First Place National Winner
Senior Category
in *Reverse, a Zine for Youngpoets*

[4] pantoum—a poetic form in which the second and fourth lines of each four-line stanza become the first and third lines of the next stanza

26. This poem is **mainly** about

A. the cold weather in Nunavut

B. a child phoning her mother

C. a person away from home

D. hunters in a small town

27. What does the speaker mean when she says that she "can't be alone" (line 3)?

A. There are foxes all around.

B. She has too many meetings to attend.

C. When she is by herself, she becomes very anxious.

D. Even when she is by herself, she knows what people are saying about her.

28. The detail "naïve thin gloves" (lines 10 and 13) reveals that the mother

A. did not know much about her work

B. left her fancy gloves at home

C. was unprepared for the cold

D. has expensive taste

29. The **main** reason the mother is lonely is that she

A. feels out of place

B. has to work on her laptop

C. can see no cherry blossoms

D. must phone home every day

30. The phrase "Your hair still smells of west-coast weather" contains an example of the poetic device of

A. imagery

B. paradox

C. oxymoron

D. personification

31. Which of the following phrases reveals that the mother wishes she were elsewhere?

A. "The natives hunt fox"

B. "Your hair still smells of west-coast weather"

C. "Embroidered wolves on your parka"

D. "Dreaming of cotton and silk"

32. How does the mother escape from her situation?

A. She phones people she knows.

B. She packs her briefcase.

C. She returns to Victoria.

D. She goes fox hunting.

33. Which of the following words **best** describes the feeling the mother is experiencing?

A. Overburdened

B. Alienated

C. Impatient

D. Anxious

34. The phrase "there is warmth / soft, like cherry blossoms" contains an example of

A. simile

B. metaphor

C. hyperbole

D. oxymoron

35. Which of the following words **best** describes the tone of the poem?

A. Gentle

B. Serious

C. Sarcastic

D. Forgiving

PRACTICE TEST TWO

Read the following passage to answer questions 1 to 8.

ON THE FUTURE OF POETRY

Bards[5] of the Future! you that come
With striding march, and roll of drum,
What will your newest challenge be
To our prose-bound community?

What magic will you find to stir
The limp and languid listener?
Will it be daring and dramatic?
Will it be frankly democratic?

Will Pegasus[6] return again
In guise of modern aeroplane,
Descending from a cloudless blue
To drop on us a bomb or two?

I know not. Far be it from me
To darken dark futurity;
Still less to render more perplexed
The last vagary,[7] or the next.

I hold it for a certain thing,
That, blank or rhyming, song must sing;
And more, that what is good for verse,
Need not, by dint of rhyme, grow worse.

I hold that they who deal in rhyme
Must take the standpoint of the time—
But not to catch the public ear,
As mountebank[8] or pulpiteer;[9]

That the old notes are still the new,
If the musician's touch be true—
Nor can the hand that knows its trade
Achieve the trite and ready-made;

That your first theme is Human Life,
Its hopes and fears, its love and strife—
A theme no custom can efface,
Common, but never commonplace.

—*by* Henry Austin Dobson

---

[5] bards—a literary, old-fashioned word for poets, especially important, well-known poets

[6] Pegasus—a flying horse from ancient Greek mythology

[7] vagary—a strange or unpredictable change in ideas or actions

[8] mountebank—deceiver

[9] pulpiteer—propagandist

1. Which of the following statements **best** summarizes the **main** theme in this poem?
   A. Poetry should rhyme.
   B. Poetry should be about human experience.
   C. Poetry should have a magic that stirs the reader.
   D. Poetry should be about unusual topics that excite the reader.

2. Which of the following words **best** describes the mood of the poem?
   A. Lively
   B. Strained
   C. Triumphant
   D. Celebratory

3. Whom does the speaker of "On the Future of Poetry" address?
   A. Literary historians
   B. Fellow readers
   C. Writers
   D. Poets

4. The poetic technique demonstrated in lines 1 and 2 is
   A. simile
   B. metaphor
   C. hyperbole
   D. personification

5. The phrase "prose-bound community" (line 4) refers to people who
   A. love to read stories
   B. like television talk shows
   C. dislike reading in general
   D. enjoy clubs and other community organizations

6. What is the verse structure of "On the Future of Poetry"?
   A. Quatrains
   B. Octaves
   C. Sonnets
   D. Sestets

7. Which of the following words **best** summarizes the speaker's feelings about the future of poetry?
   A. Ambivalent
   B. Pessimistic
   C. Optimistic
   D. Terrified

8. As it is used in the phrase "That, blank or rhyming, song must sing," the word "blank" refers to words that
   A. rhyme
   B. do not rhyme
   C. are confusing
   D. have a distinct rhythm

Read the following passage to answer questions 9 to 19.

from EYE OF THE MOON

Someone had dropped a chocolate-covered ice cream bar in the middle of the sidewalk. Impact with the pavement had flattened it into an off-white oval splat with an irregular brown centre that bled into the creamy mess. The whole thing looked a bit like a sloppy flower, the wooden stick its short stem. Over time the whole thing would grow more murky. Pedestrians on their way to work or to the bus stop, cyclists who insisted on using the sidewalk, joggers like me, all had to make a detour around the splat or jump over. Never once that summer did anyone step into it. When the sun rose the sweet substance attracted an obscene buzz of flies.

The end of the school year always coincided with my birthday and in my seventeenth year it coincided also with my grandmother's corneal implant.... Nineteen tiny, tiny stitches, the eye surgeon told my mother, and five times a day they would have to be lubricated with medicated drops. Like watering a seedling.

I had just finished grade eleven and the plan had been to get a summer job. "No reason she can't help with her university costs," Mother said, thinking of my future, and Dad, who ever since my fifteenth birthday had become convinced that all youth was headed for hell in a hand basket, said, "Won't hurt her one bit to get a feel for work." They had a habit of speaking about me in the third person, as if I wasn't there. Or as if I was deaf. Or still a child. The habit had solidified; maybe the indirectness offered Dad a buffer against the awkwardness of dealing with an adolescent in the volatile process of becoming a woman.

A job was okay with me. Jody and Claire, my closest friends at that time, had found jobs after grade ten, and the benefits of time away from parents and extra money weren't lost on me. I put in applications at Domo Gas and Wendy's and the library, but before anyone wanted me for an interview the hospital called to say a cornea had become available and Nana had to be there right away.... She was a tough bird, Nana, and within a week she was back in her apartment in the seniors' high rise. The public health nurse would come first thing in the morning, but that left four more applications of eye drops daily for five weeks.

Continued

5 Nana, at eighty, kept track of her arthritis medicine, time of day, the changing seasons, birthdays. "I've got all my marbles, thank God," she'd say. But the nurse couldn't get her to squeeze the eyedropper without first shutting her eye, and my mother couldn't change her vacation which she'd booked for September.

"She'll have the rest of her life to work." Dad was looking at me, talking to Mother. "Why does she have to start this summer?"

To be fair, my parents didn't force me into doing the eye drops. They let me choose — a job or Nana. And they would pay me, though not as much as a job, if I chose Nana. If she'd been a complainer and fussy like Dad's mother, I might have balked. But Nana and I got along. It would be a fifteen-minute jog each way. That appealed to me. And I could take the stairs to the sixth floor. Maybe by the time school resumed in fall my body would be in some sort of shape I could maintain for graduation. Besides, the stretches of free time between eye drops held tempting possibilities.

"Weekends you'll be off," Mother said. "That's when your Dad and I will take care of Nana."

The splat on the sidewalk must have been new my first day of duty. It was a morning in late June, the sun brooding redly through the smog that hung above the shopping mall. There was no wind, and I felt sticky. I didn't see the mess staring up at me like a large eye until the last minute and had to take a flying leap over it to save my new runners from getting mucked up. In spite of the heat it felt good to be up and running and I imagined the unwanted flesh melting from my thighs. The chickadees were nervously busy in the trees, kids lounged in front of the Seven Eleven and on the south side of a small white bungalow a cat lay stretched out in the sun.

10 "What are you doing for summer holidays?" Nana asked after I'd made her tip her head way back, then pulled her eyelid up with my thumb the way the nurse had shown me, positioned the dropper correctly above the bloodshot, sutured eye, steadied my hand and squeezed out a tiny globule of liquid that fell more or less on target. I removed my thumb and the wrinkled eyelid fell shut like a china doll's. I dabbed away the moisture pearling from the corner of the eye with a cotton swab and taped gauze over it, proud of myself and relieved I'd actually done it alone for the first time.

"I said, what are you doing this summer, Julia?"

As I said, Nana was pretty sharp, but it hadn't registered that this year, she was my summer. In the beginning I didn't think of myself as locked into a schedule. Starting before ten every day, wind or calm, humidity or unrelenting sun, I would jog at three hour intervals the two blocks down our street, across the highway at Springfield Avenue, then along that winding stretch of the Donwood Drive sidewalk past the brown and white splat to Donwood Manor where Nana lived. The route would be familiar as my own breathing before summer was over, a summer when everything would become desperate for rain.

"There's lots to do in summer, Nana," I said. "Fringe Festival starts next week, I might go. They're doing King Lear."

"Hmm," she said. Nana hadn't read much Shakespeare.

15 No point in telling her that Brendan Gorlick, who had just graduated from River East High and therefore stood on the threshold of the future, was playing the part of the fool or that the tragedy would be condensed—ninety minutes was max for the Fringe. This was all beyond Nana's world.

Continued

Last winter Brendan played John Proctor in The Crucible in our school production. He always got big parts and I always got, “Julia, you’ll be one of the stage hands, OK?”

“That’s important,” Brendan would say. “Stage hands are important.” His earnestness melted my inexperienced heart. Brendan was kind, and at that point in my life any kindness I encountered made me stop short. It comforted me, as if I’d come home.

A teenager playing John Proctor is bound to be at a disadvantage. I doubt if Brendan had ever grappled with questions of betrayal and integrity any more than I had. But everyone said he’d been great in the role, and now he had a small part in King Lear.

I wasn’t expecting Nana to be filled with gratitude every time I came to do the drops. Still, when you think you’re making a sacrifice, you want it to be noticed. Nana simply assumed I had come for a long visit. “Leaving already?” she’d say, totally astonished.

By the time the Fringe opened, the nurse said Nana’s eye was doing fine, keep up the good work, these next weeks would be crucial. The splat on the sidewalk had shrunk a little and I had begun to fantasize running in cool rain. Dad spoke of global warming. “Scientists agree on that. There’s evidence. By the time our offspring grows up, who knows.” He’d be speaking to Mother, looking sideways at me.

Mother, when she came home from work at five-thirty, went directly to the basement, the coolest place, and spent the evening watching TV. Nobody but Dad felt like eating. “Go ahead, make yourself something. Pasta. Salad,” Mother said sipping a cold beer.

The opening of the Fringe was scheduled for Friday, more or less all day. I decided to bike down to Market Square between the ten o’clock and one o’clock drops, not only because Brendan might be there, but because the novelty of the four daily trips to Donwood Manor was beginning to wear thin. Jody and Claire always seemed to be working when I was free and the days of summer vacation were running past without anything happening. That was the summer I first began reflecting on time, how it slips like water through the cracks of the day. How irretrievable it is. As impossible to rewind as to fast forward.

—*by* Sarah Klassen

9. Julia does not get a summer job because

A. her parents pay her to look after Nana

B. her friends had already taken all the good jobs

C. she is too young, and she has the rest of her life to work

D. none of the places she applied to phone her for an interview

10. Julia’s father is characterized as a stereotypical dad in that he

A. thinks Julia should exercise more

B. wants Julia to help with university costs

C. likes to relax in the basement and drink beer

D. is awkward in dealing with an adolescent girl

11. What literary device is exemplified by the phrase "buzz of flies"?

A. Onomatopoeia

B. Alliteration

C. Symbolism

D. Irony

12. The phrase "'I've got all my marbles'" contains an example of

A. personification

B. propaganda

C. metaphor

D. simile

13. The type of writing used in the passage can **best** be described as

A. satirical

B. narrative

C. persuasive

D. argumentative

14. As it is used in the phrase "If she'd been a complainer and fussy like Dad's mother, I might have balked," the word "balked" means

A. rejoiced

B. refused

C. agreed

D. moped

15. For Julia, working with Nana includes all of the following benefits **except**

A. being able to see more plays

B. earning some money

C. having free time

D. getting in shape

16. For what reason is Nana surprised when Julia leaves so quickly?

A. She does not understand how important the play is to Julia.

B. She does not realize that Julia has just come to do her job.

C. She still needs more help.

D. She is expecting visitors.

17. For what reason does Julia begin reflecting on the passage of time?

A. She sees her Nana aging more quickly.

B. She realizes that time is impossible to rewind.

C. She is positive that she will not connect with Brendan.

D. She realizes that things are going on around her, but she herself is not doing anything.

18. The phrase "the wrinkled eyelid fell shut like a china doll's" contains an example of

A. simile

B. metaphor

C. alliteration

D. personification

19. Which of the following words **best** describes Nana's character?

A. Hardy

B. Confused

C. Squeamish

D. Demanding

Read the following passage to answer questions 20 to 26.

WORLD CUP 1998

This soaring game in which every player
wears concentration like a skin,
his body like Nureyev's[10], flying
higher each time than the next man
(he hopes) toward that desperately sought after
firefly, the soccer ball.

France vs. Norway, Brazil vs. Spain,
their bodies speak an old familiar language
of men in action—fierce competition
for a symbol, a ball, for anything,
this head-knocking race for mastery and at the end,
a grudging respect
for the pure muscle of it,
the head-cracking, joint-knocking, ball-kicking explosion
of strength and skill and even luck they will celebrate later.

But now
it's the purest pleasure of the doing in a race for the best
and men who finally, in this ultimate celebration
of the body
can afford to embrace and cry, in love
at last.

—*by* Kate Braid

20. Which of the following aspects of the game of soccer is this poem **mainly** about?

A. The passion of the game

B. The emotions of the fans

C. The injuries of the players

D. The technique of the athletes

21. The contrast of "men in action—fierce competition" with "embrace and cry, in love / at last" serves to

A. describe the foolishness of the men

B. break a stereotypical image

C. show the high level of play

D. create suspense

[10] rudolf Nureyev was a famous ballet dancer

22. Which of the following statements **best** describes the theme of the poem?

A. Soccer is similar to dancing in some ways.

B. Competition is often aggressive and can cause people to get upset.

C. When people are passionate about what they do, their emotions soar.

D. People celebrate with all their might when their country's team wins.

23. The comparison of the soccer player to the ballet dancer suggests that the

A. dancer is like an athlete

B. player leaps through the air with beauty

C. game of soccer is intricately choreographed

D. player must practice as much as a dancer does

24. The lines "France vs. Norway, Brazil vs. Spain, / their bodies speak an old familiar language" suggest that

A. even though the players' native tongues are different, the jargon of soccer is familiar to them all

B. the action on the field is difficult for the players from different countries to understand

C. the players' speak different languages, but their motivation and actions are the same

D. the players are aging and compete fiercely to win the World Cup for their countries

25. The literary device contained in the lines "that desperately sought after / firefly, the soccer ball" is

A. simile

B. conflict

C. metaphor

D. oxymoron

26. When the poet refers to the ball as a "symbol" (line 10), she **most likely** means the ball is a symbol of

A. love

B. power

C. victory

D. emotion

Read the following passage to answer questions 27 to 33.

from EVE'S RANSOM

An hour later he was at Old Square, waiting for the tram to Aston. Huge steam-driven vehicles came and went, whirling about the open space with monitory bell-clang. Amid a press of homeward-going workfolk, Hilliard clambered to a place on the top and lit his pipe. He did not look the same man who had waited gloomily at Dudley Port; his eyes gleamed with life; answering a remark addressed to him by a neighbour on the car, he spoke jovially.

No rain was falling, but the streets shone wet and muddy under lurid lamp-lights. Just above the house-tops appeared the full moon, a reddish disk, blurred athwart floating vapour. The car drove northward, speedily passing from the region of main streets and great edifices into a squalid district of factories and workshops and crowded by-ways. At Aston Church the young man alighted, and walked rapidly for five minutes, till he reached a row of small modern houses. Socially they represented a step or two upwards in the gradation which, at Birmingham, begins with the numbered court and culminates in the mansions of Edgbaston.

He knocked at a door, and was answered by a girl, who nodded recognition.

"Mrs. Hilliard in? Just tell her I'm here."

There was a natural abruptness in his voice, but it had a kindly note, and a pleasant smile accompanied it. After a brief delay he received permission to go upstairs, where the door of a sitting-room stood open. Within was a young woman, slight, pale, and pretty, who showed something of embarrassment, though her face made him welcome.

"I expected you sooner."

"Business kept me back. Well, my niece?"

The table was spread for tea, and at one end of it, on a high chair, sat a child of four years old. Hilliard kissed her, and stroked her curly hair, and talked with playful affection. This little girl was his niece, the child of his elder brother, who had died three years ago. The poorly furnished room and her own attire proved that Mrs. Hilliard had but narrow resources in her widowhood. Nor did she appear a woman of much courage; tears had thinned her cheeks, and her delicate hands had suffered noticeably from unwonted household work.

Hilliard remarked something unusual in her behaviour this evening. She was restless, and kept regarding him askance, as if in apprehension. A letter from her, in which she merely said she wished to speak to him, had summoned him hither from Dudley. As a rule, they saw each other but once a month.

"No bad news, I hope!" he remarked aside to her, as he took his place at the table.

"Oh, no. I'll tell you afterwards."

Very soon after the meal Mrs. Hilliard took the child away and put her to bed. During her absence the visitor sat brooding, a peculiar half-smile on his face. She came back, drew a chair up to the fire, but did not sit down.

"Well, what is it?" asked her brother-in-law, much as he might have spoken to the little girl.

"I have something very serious to talk about, Maurice."

"Have you? All right; go ahead."

"I—I am so very much afraid I shall offend you."

The young man laughed.

Continued

"Not very likely. I can take a good deal from you."

She stood with her hands on the back of the chair, and as he looked at her, Hilliard saw her pale cheeks grow warm.

"It'll seem very strange to you, Maurice."

"Nothing will seem strange after an adventure I've had this afternoon. You shall hear about it presently."

"Tell me your story first."

"All right, I'll tell you. I met that scoundrel Dengate, and—he's paid me the money he owed my father."

"He has *paid* it? Oh! really?"

"See, here's a cheque, and I think it likely I can turn it into cash. The blackguard has been doing well at Liverpool. I'm not quite sure that I understand the reptile, but he seems to have given me this because I abused him. I hurt his vanity, and he couldn't resist the temptation to astonish me. He thinks I shall go about proclaiming him a noble fellow. Four hundred and thirty-six pounds[11]; there it is."

He tossed the piece of paper into the air with boyish glee, and only just caught it as it was fluttering into the fire.

"Oh, be careful!" cried Mrs. Hilliard.

"I told him he was a scoundrel, and he began by threatening to thrash me. I'm very glad he didn't try. It was in the train, and I know very well I should have strangled him. It would have been awkward, you know."

"Oh, Maurice, how *can* you——?"

"Well, here's the money; and half of it is yours."

"Mine? Oh, no! After all you have given me. Besides, I sha'n't[12] want it."

"How's that?"

Their eyes met. Hilliard again saw the flush in her cheeks, and began to guess its explanation. He looked puzzled, interested.

"Do I know him?" was his next inquiry.

"Should you think it very wrong of me?" She moved aside from the line of his gaze. "I couldn't imagine how you would take it."

"It all depends. Who is the man?"

Still shrinking towards a position where Hilliard could not easily observe her, the young widow told her story. She had consented to marry a man of whom her brother-in-law knew little but the name, one Ezra Marr; he was turned forty, a widower without children, and belonged to a class of employers of labour. The contrast between such a man and Maurice Hilliard's brother was sufficiently pronounced; but the widow nervously did her best to show Ezra Marr in a favourable light.

"And then," she added after a pause, while Hilliard was reflecting, "I couldn't go on being a burden on you. How very few men would have done what you have—"

"Stop a minute. Is *that* the real reason? If so—"

Continued

[11] *four hundred and thirty-six pounds*—at that time, a large sum of money; skilled workers made less than a hundred pounds a year

[12] *Sha'n't*—shan't; contraction of *shall not*; the spelling was correct when the story was written

Hurriedly she interposed.

"That was only one of the reasons—only one."

Hilliard knew very well that her marriage had not been entirely successful; it seemed to him very probable that with a husband of the artisan class, a vigorous and go-ahead fellow, she would be better mated than in the former instance. He felt sorry for his niece, but there again sentiment doubtless conflicted with common-sense. A few more questions, and it became clear to him that he had no ground of resistance.

"Very well. Most likely you are doing a wise thing. And half this money is yours; you'll find it useful."

—*by* George Gissing

27. The relationship between Maurice and Mrs. Hilliard can **best** be described as

A. comfortable

B. intimate

C. distant

D. tense

28. The reason that Hilliard "did not look the same man who had waited gloomily at Dudley Port" was that since then,

A. 436 pounds had been paid to his father

B. his niece had invited him over for dinner

C. he had been paid money that was owed to him

D. he had been paid money that was owed to his father

29. By having Hilliard call Dengate a "reptile," the writer is employing the literary technique of

A. simile

B. metaphor

C. hyperbole

D. personification

30. The reason that Maurice claims to be glad Dengate did not try to thrash him in the train is that

A. Maurice would have had nowhere to run

B. everyone would have seen Maurice get a beating

C. Maurice could not have gotten the money from Dengate

D. Maurice would have strangled Dengate with everyone watching

31. Which is the following statements **best** explains Mrs. Hilliard's invitation to Maurice?

A. She was eloping with Ezra Marr.

B. She had just been paid 436 pounds.

C. She was getting married to Ezra Marr.

D. She had some strange news to tell Maurice.

32. The **main** reason that Mrs. Hilliard will not take half of Maurice's money despite his offer is that

A. she would rather have his affections

B. he has already done so much for her

C. she no longer actually needs the money

D. he does not really intend to give it to her

33. As it is used in the quotation "it became clear to him that he had no ground of resistance," the phrase "no ground of resistance" **most likely** means that Hilliard

A. felt he was losing ground to her

B. could not resist her approach

C. needed to stand his ground

D. had no reason to object

ANSWERS AND SOLUTIONS—PRACTICE TEST ONE

1. C	**8. B**	**15. A**	**22. A**	**29. A**
2. D	**9. D**	**16. B**	**23. C**	**30. A**
3. D	**10. D**	**17. A**	**24. B**	**31. D**
4. A	**11. B**	**18. C**	**25. D**	**32. A**
5. B	**12. D**	**19. A**	**26. C**	**33. B**
6. A	**13. A**	**20. D**	**27. D**	**34. A**
7. B	**14. A**	**21. C**	**28. C**	**35. A**

1. C

Beginning in paragraph 4, the passage describes the changes in Emma's life and Emma's reaction to them. "How was she to bear the change?" (paragraph 7) The main idea is that it is sometimes difficult to bear life's changes.

2. D

In paragraph 4, the "the real evils" are described: Emma has had her own way too much and she thinks too much of herself. (The word *evil* might seem strong; it might even seem to be hyperbole. Today, many people would regard these evils as independence, empowerment, and self-esteem. However, Jane Austen was a sharp-eyed observer of society and behaviour; she knew what indulgence and conceit can lead to).

3. D

The last sentence of the first paragraph gives Emma's age as nearly twenty-one. Although the sentence indicates that Emma was *nearly* twenty-one years of age, this answer is closer to any of the others.

4. A

Since Miss Taylor was "less…a governess than a friend" (paragraph 3), you can say that she was not really a governess. "Governess in name only" fits the context best. She would still be called the governess, but she was really something else.

5. B

It is Miss Taylor's marriage and move to a new home that Emma finds difficult to bear. "How was she to bear the change?—It was true that her friend was going only half a mile from them; but Emma was aware that great must be the difference between a Mrs. Weston, only half a mile from them, and a Miss Taylor in the house" (paragraph 7).

6. A

Mr. Weston was "a man of unexceptionable character, easy fortune, suitable age, and pleasant manners…" (paragraph 6). *Easy fortune* means "well-to-do." *Unexceptional character* means "good character" (good character was considered the rule and bad qualities were the exception); and *pleasant manners* suggest that he was easy to get along with—both close enough to *easy-going*.

7. B

"Between them it was more the intimacy of sisters" (paragraph 3). *Sisterly* describes their friendship.

8. B

The poem describes the speaker's experience with nature and how nature affects her. This experience is the subject of the poem.

9. D

The first four lines in each stanza have an *abab* rhyming pattern. Then, each stanza ends with a rhyming couplet, *cc*. The rhyme scheme is *ababcc*.

10. D

Personification is used to bring out some quality in the thing that is personified. By giving human attributes of movement, grace, and beauty to the stars, the poet expresses what she feels when she looks into the heavens. The personification illustrates the grace and majesty of the constellations as they move across the sky.

11. B

The moon lies low in the western sky. You can infer that the moon is about to set.

12. D

Every image in the poem is seen. There is nothing to appeal to smell, touch, or taste. The one mention of singing is not an example of imagery at all; it is an allusion. The stars are those that sang "when earth was made"—they are not singing now. An *allusion* is an indirect reference to something else, often a literary, religious, historical, or mythological subject; this allusion is to the Book of Job in the Bible.

13. A

The article is full of interesting bits of information about new high-tech products. Its most likely purpose is to entertain readers with what-will-they-think-of-next descriptions of new electronics.

14. A

"'These are ideas that in a few years we'll be able in some way to sell'" (paragraph 5). Notice that the companies do not have anything ready to sell at the moment. They are just making sure that people are interested and ready to buy in the future. The best answer is "to advertise their products."

15. A

Only one answer has any support in the article: most of the products are designed to make cramped Japanese houses more comfortable (paragraphs 1, 7, and 8).

16. B

Since Japanese houses are small, Japanese washing machines are small. Most Japanese households do not have dryers, so a combination dryer and washer would likely be beneficial (lines 44–49).

17. A

All the information about the high-tech toilets is found in paragraphs 3, 8, and 16. A toilet that tests urine to measure blood sugar, protein, and body fat and sends suspicious results to a doctor over the Internet would detect health problems.

18. C

The refrigerator (paragraph 14) uses a camera link to beam pictures to a mobile phone, and the mirror (paragraph 18) takes infrared pictures of hair and skin.

19. A

"To adjust to different people's tastes" is the only answer that has support in the article. The mansion has a "computer system that changes…digital artwork to match visitor preferences" (paragraph 20).

20. D

The information is presented in the form of a table. The format of tables, charts, and graphs should be very familiar.

21. C

The table simply presents information that shows how the Internet is used.

22. A

This question can be answered by examining the figures for Canada as a whole or by examining the figures for each of the provinces. The second method will show any variation by province or by region.

Using either method, e-mail is the most popular use of the Internet.

23. C

A glance down the "E-banking" column reveals the smallest percentage to be 16.3 in Saskatchewan.

24. B

You must look under "Purchased goods or services" to find the amount of online shopping. British Columbia had the highest percentage: 26.2.

25. D

The top of the "Total users" column shows that the numbers given are *000s*, or *thousands*. The number given must be multiplied by 1 000. The total number of users in Quebec is 2 723 000.

26. C

Each stanza speaks of the mother not fitting in. Everything is strange; she is foreign. She dreams of another place. Being away from home is what the poem is mainly about.

27. D

Look at the quotation in context: "Even in the dingy hotel room, you can't be alone." Also, consider the phrases "small-town gossip follows you everywhere" and "their voices carry for miles." It is clear that she knows that people are gossiping about her everywhere she goes and that the natives are talking about her for miles around.

28. C

Naïve means lacking in experience and judgment. The mother did not know how cold it would be in Nunavut. With her thin gloves, she is unprepared.

29. A

There are several references to the mother being an outsider, thus her loneliness likely stems from feeling out of place.

30. A

Imagery is language that appeals to the senses. This line appeals directly to the sense of smell. The image also suggests all the things that are associated with weather on the West Coast.

31. D

When she is "dreaming of cotton and silk," the mother is wishing she could be wearing lighter clothes and, therefore, could be somewhere else.

32. A

The mother escapes by phoning people she knows: "The telephone is your only escape, /on the other end of the line there is warmth."

33. B

Alienation is the feeling of being cut off from other people, the feeling of not being part of what is going on. There are several references to the mother being different, an outsider. She feels alienated.

34. A

The comparison of the cherry blossoms with a warm Victoria spring contains the word *like*; thus, it is a simile.

35. A

The tone, which is the writer's attitude toward the subject, can best be described as gentle. There is no harshness or unpleasantness of any kind. The situation described is sad, but there is no blaming of the outsider mother or of the local people.

ANSWERS AND SOLUTIONS—PRACTICE TEST TWO

1. B	**8. B**	**15. A**	**22. C**	**29. B**
2. A	**9. A**	**16. B**	**23. B**	**30. D**
3. D	**10. D**	**17. D**	**24. C**	**31. C**
4. B	**11. A**	**18. A**	**25. C**	**32. C**
5. A	**12. C**	**19. A**	**26. C**	**33. D**
6. A	**13. B**	**20. A**	**27. A**	
7. C	**14. B**	**21. B**	**28. D**	

1. B

According to lines 29 and 30, poetry's "first theme is Human Life, / Its hopes and fears, its love and strife"—in other words, poetry should be about human experience.

2. A

Try reading the poem aloud and listen to the rhythm. Notice that the poem is made up of rhyming couplets. The rhythm, the rhyme, and also the references to music give this poem a lively feeling.

3. D

It might seem reasonable to assume that the writer of a poem about the future of poetry could be addressing readers, writers, literary historians, *and* poets. However, since the first line of the poem is "Bards of the future," the best response is simply *poets*.

4. B

The phrase "… you that come / with striding march, and roll of drum" contains an example of a *metaphor*, a comparison between two things or a transfer of ideas associated with one object to another. In this case, poets are compared to marchers in a parade.

5. A

Prose is all the writing that does not include poetry. Since *prose-bound* means "limited to prose," then the "prose-bound community" must be the people who read stories.

6. A

The *quatrain* has a four-line verse structure. This poem is arranged in verses, or stanzas, of four lines each.

7. C

The speaker offers advice to future poets. The fact that he supposes that poets may benefit from his suggestions indicates that he feels some optimism about the future of poetry.

8. B

Blank verse has a regular rhythm, but no rhyme. Even though you may not be certain about the meaning, you can figure out that it refers to verse that does not rhyme because in the context of the poem, it is placed in opposition to verse that does rhyme (line 18).

9. A

Nana's eye surgery happened before the places Julia had applied to could call her. Her parents let her choose whether or not she wanted to look after Nana, and they offered to pay her if she did.

10. D

In paragraph 3, Julia's father's attitude is explained—he is not direct with her and feels awkward dealing with "an adolescent in the volatile process of becoming a woman."

11. A

Onomatopoeia is a word that represents a sound, as in the *buzz* of flies. Other examples are *hiss* and *creak*.

12. C

A metaphor is a comparison between two unlike things, or the transfer of the ideas around one object on to another. Here, Nana's state of mind is compared with the game of marbles. That she has all her marbles means that she still has her whole mind.

13. B

This is a narrative passage because it tells a story.

14. B

To balk to is to stop or to refuse. This line shows that Julia is not quite so fond of her other grandmother.

15. A

"Being able to see more plays" is the only response that is not a benefit.

16. B

In paragraph 19, Nana assumes that Julia has come for a visit, not realizing she is just there to do her job. This is the reason Nana is surprised when Julia leaves.

17. D

In paragraph 22 the narrator says "... the days of summer vacation were running past without anything happening. That was the summer I first began reflecting on time..."

18. A

A simile is a comparison using *like* or *as*. The phrase "like a china doll's" contains a simile.

19. A

Hardy best describes Nana. She is described as being a "tough bird" who takes care of herself for the most part.

20. A

There are many words in the poem that focus the reader on the passion of the game—"desperately," "fierce competition," "purest pleasure," "embrace and cry," and "love."

21. B

A stereotype is when a person is portrayed as conforming to a set image; for example, "Women are emotional," or "Teenagers are terrible." In the beginning of this poem, men are shown as the stereotypical strong athletes, but at the end of the poem, this stereotype is broken when they embrace and cry.

22. C

Theme is the universal idea that is the focus of the poem or story. A theme is contained in a literary work, such as a poem, but it also applies to life and to readers' experiences. The speaker shows how passionate the players are and how emotional they become. This idea applies not only to the soccer players, but to anyone who has ever been passionate about something.

23. B

The speaker intends the reader to see soccer as an art form, in which the players' bodies leap or fly through the air just as beautifully as ballet dancers do.

24. C

"France vs. Norway, Brazil vs. Spain" shows that the languages spoken by the teams are different. The phrase "their bodies speak an old familiar language" shows that what they do physically and without thinking is the same regardless of where they are from.

25. C

A metaphor is a comparison between two unlike things, or the transfer of the ideas around one object on to another. Here, the soccer ball is compared with a firefly, because fireflies are quick and flash around a field.

26. C

The players are in "fierce competition" for the symbol, so it follows that the thing they are in competition for is victory. There are several references in the poem to the desire to win.

27. A

Note the statement "her face made him welcome" (paragraph 5). This suggests that Hilliard and his sister-in-law have a comfortable relationship.

28. D

Maurice Hilliard tells Mrs. Hilliard that he has received a cheque that covers a debt owed his father by Dengate. You can safely infer that the money is the reason he seems a different man. (Remember the information in the footnote: it was a large amount of money.)

29. B

Hilliard says that Dengate is a reptile: "I'm not quite sure I understand the reptile" (paragraph 25). This direct statement is a metaphor comparing Dengate's character with the qualities of a reptile.

30. D

"'I told him he was a scoundrel, and he began by threatening to thrash me. I'm very glad he didn't try. It was in the train, and I know very well I should have strangled him. It would have been awkward, you know.'" (paragraph 28)

The only problem here is that a careful reader will notice that Hilliard is not serious. His tone gives him away. It was in the train (meaning there were witnesses) and "it would have been awkward, you know" (awkward being one way of describing the consequences of murder). Then his sister-in-law cries, "Oh, Maurice, how can you—?" (*Can*, not *could*. She is reacting to his jesting words and his tone.) However, this is still the only possible answer, even though Hilliard does not mean what he says.

31. C

The news that she tells Maurice is that she intends to marry Ezra Marr.

32. C

Mrs. Hilliard is reluctant to accept half the money because Hilliard has already done so much for her, but she is able to refuse because "I sha'n't want it" (paragraph 31). *I shall not want it*—although she may be short of money now, she will not be in the future. The reason, which Hilliard immediately guesses, is that she is getting remarried. She might not like to take more from Hilliard, but she is able to refuse because she will soon be married.

33. D

In this context, *ground* means reason. Hilliard thinks about her marriage and realizes that his objections are not sensible. The marriage is a good idea and he has no reason to object to it.

NOTES

Appendices

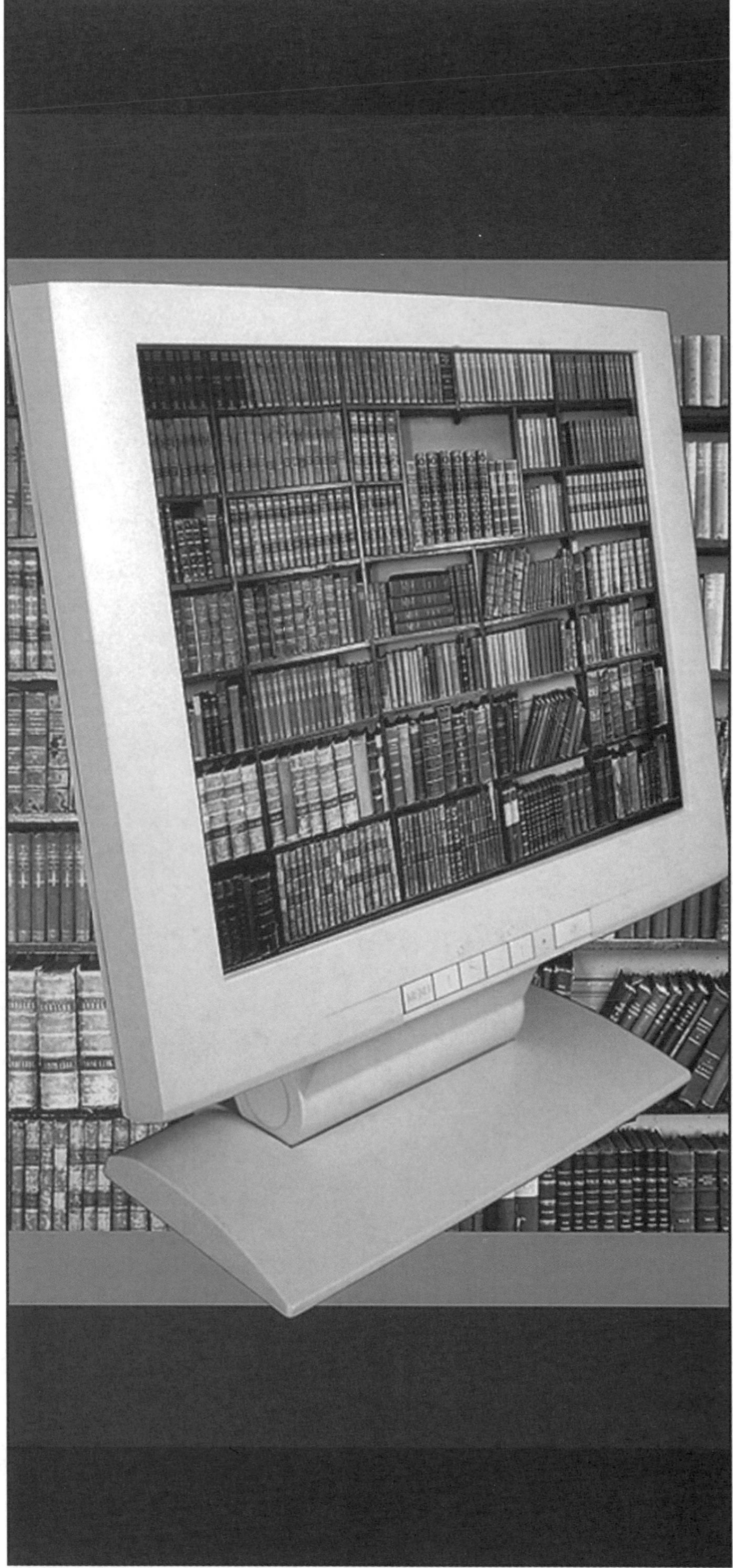

NOTES

Glossary of Relevant Terms

Abstract	Abstract terms and concepts name things that are not knowable through the senses; examples are love, justice, guilt, and honour.
Alliteration	The repetition of initial consonants.
Allusion	A reference to a pre-existing work of art or literature or to a person or event.
Ambiguity	A vagueness or lack of clarity of meaning or expression that makes more than one interpretation possible.
Analogy	A comparison that is made to explain something that is unfamiliar by presenting an example that is similar or parallel to it in some significant way.
Anecdote	A brief story telling an interesting incident; often used as an introduction to a related topic for an essay.
Antagonist	The character in a drama or novel who presents the greatest opposition to the central figure. Antagonists can be sympathetic, like Macduff in *Macbeth*, or villainous, like Claudius in *Hamlet*.
Antecedent Action	Action that takes place before the story opens.
Apostrophe	A figure of speech in which animate or inanimate objects are addressed in the second person as if the object were able to understand being addressed.
Aside	A brief, often sarcastic or revealing comment made by an actor to the audience and not meant to be heard by the other characters. It allows the spectators to hear significant and sometimes foreshadowing remarks. An example of this is Iago's aside in *Othello*: "With as little a web as this will I ensnare as great a fly as Cassio."
Assonance	The repetition of similar or identical vowel sounds.
Atmosphere	The emotional tone and overall effect of a narrative or descriptive passage.
Ballad	A folk song or story in poetic form.
Blank Verse	Poetry possessing rhythm but not rhyme.
Chronological	In order of time.
Cliché	An overused expression; one that has become stale through overuse.
Colloquial	Informal writing suitable for everyday speech but not for formal writing.
Connotative Meaning	The suggested meaning of words because of personal experience and association.
Consonance	The repetition of a consonant sound within a series of words to produce a harmonious effect.
Denotative Meaning	The specific dictionary meaning of words and terms.
Diction	The choice of words in literature, usually classified using such descriptive terms as *slang* or *colloquial*, *informal*, *formal*, *elevated*, *technical*, *ordinary*, *figurative*, *archaic*, *abstract*, *concrete*, *connotative*, or *denotative*.
Discrepancy	Distinct difference between two things that should not be different or that should correspond.

Dissonance	Harsh sound or discordance; in poetry, a harsh, jarring combination of sounds.
Dramatic Monologue	A poem involving an uninterrupted speech by a character to a silent second figure. It is meant to reveal the personality of the speaker through his manner of speech, the attitudes his remarks disclose, and the implied reactions of his listener.
Dynamic Character	A character that undergoes a permanent change in some aspect of his or her character, personality, or outlook.
Epic	A long narrative poem that recounts the deeds of a legendary or historical hero or group of heroes.
Flashback	The recounting, in fleeting or extended form, of past incidents in a character's life, usually for the purpose of clarifying present events.
Flat Character	A character with only a few traits; often plays a minor role.
Foil	Any character whose contrast to another character brings out the personality of the latter. Banquo is a foil of Macbeth in *Macbeth.*
Foreshadowing	Any indication or hint of a later event in a story.
Hyperbole	A figure of speech that uses exaggeration for effect.
Imagery	Language that uses imagery evokes sensory impressions.
Irony	The result of a statement's saying one thing while meaning the opposite, or of a situation developing contrary to expectation. Verbal irony refers to a statement in which the opposite of what is said is meant. Dramatic irony is based on the principle of opposition between appearance and reality. The speaker is unaware of the opposition, but the audience recognizes the ironic implications. Irony of situation is embedded in circumstances themselves and does not depend on the spoken word.
Jargon	Special vocabulary of a particular group or activity; sometimes used to refer to confusing or unintelligible language.
Metaphor	A comparison made by referring to one thing as another.
Monologue	A literary form; an oral or written composition in which only one person speaks.
Mood	In a story, the atmosphere; when a writer creates the setting, action, and characters of a story so as to suggest a dominant emotion or patterns of emotions. This emotional pattern is the mood of the story. Also can refer to a person's state of mind or complex of emotions at any given time.
Ode	A poem expressing lofty emotion. Odes often celebrate an event or are addressed to nature or to an admired person, place, or thing; an example is "Ode on a Grecian Urn" by John Keats.
Onomatopoeia	The use of words that suggest the sound of the thing they describe.
Oxymoron	Two words that contradict each other used together for effect; for example, *wise fool.*
Parable	A short, simple story that teaches or explains a lesson—often a moral or religious lesson.
Paradox	An apparently self-contradictory statement that is, in fact, true.

Parallelism	Refers to the grammatical or structural similarity between sentences or parts of a sentence.
Pathos	A term used to describe an element in literature that evokes pity or sorrow.
Personification	The attribution of human characteristics to non-human things.
Point of View: First Person	The story is told by one of the characters in the story (*I*). The narrator is in the story. First person narrators can only narrate what they can perceive.
Point of View: Objective	The story is told without describing any characters' internal thoughts and feelings. Only the characters' actions and words are told. This point of view is a lot like the camera's point of view in a movie.
Point of View: Third Person	The story is told through the eyes of one or more characters (*he*, *she*, and *they*). The narrator is outside the story and describes what the characters think, feel, and do. Omniscient narrators know everything that happens and what any character thinks and feels. Limited omniscient narrators only know about one character and the things that one character thinks and feels.
Prologue	An introduction to a play, often delivered by the chorus (in ancient Greece, a group, but in modern plays, usually by one actor) who plays no part in the action of the play that follows.
Protagonist	The central character of a drama or narrative.
Pun	A humorous expression that depends on a double meaning, either between different senses of the same word or between two similar sounding words.
Rhetorical Question	A question that is not posed to be answered seriously. Instead, it is used to draw attention to a point.
Rhyme	Rhyme is, loosely, the repetition of the same vowel sounds in poetry.
Ridicule	Contemptuous mocking or derision; ridicule may be an element of satire.
Round Character	A complex, many-sided, and fully developed character.
Satire	A form of writing that exposes the failings of individuals, institutions, or societies. Satire uses ridicule or scorn in order to correct or expose some evil or social injustice.
Simile	A comparison using the words *like* or *as*.
Sonnet	A lyric poem fourteen lines long and usually written in iambic pentameter. The Shakespearean sonnet consists of three quatrains (four-line stanzas) and a couplet (two lines), all written to a strict end-rhyme scheme (abab cdcd efef gg). The Italian sonnet has the following more complex structure: a b b a a b b a c d e c d e. The last six lines of an Italian sonnet structure can vary in structure. The development of the poet's thoughts is also structured. There are several methods: one is to use each quatrain for different points in an argument and the couplet for the resolution of the argument. Because of the complexity of the sonnet, poets sometimes find it a suitable form for expressing the complexity of thought and emotion.
Static Character	Remains the same sort of person at the end of the story as he or she was at the beginning of the story.

Stock Character	A stereotyped figure who has occurred so often in fiction that his or her nature is immediately known.
Symbol	Anything that stands for or represents something other than itself. In literature, a symbol is a word or phrase referring to an object, scene, or action that also has some further significance associated with it. For example, a rose is a common symbol of love. Many symbols, such as flags, are universally recognized. Other symbols are not so universally defined. They do not acquire a meaning until they are defined by how they are used in a story. They may even suggest more than one meaning. For example, snow could be used to symbolize goodness because of its purity. Snow could also be used to symbolize cruelty because of its coldness. Symbols are often contained in story titles, in character and place names, and in classical, literary, and historical allusions and references. They are found in images or figures that appear at important points in a story and in images that either receive special emphasis or are repeated.
Symbolism	The use of one thing to represent something else.
Synecdoche	A figure of speech in which a part of something is used to represent the whole.
Thesis	A statement that is made as the first step in an argument or a demonstration.
Tone	The attitude toward both subject matter and audience implied in a piece of literature.

CREDITS

Every effort has been made to provide proper acknowledgment of the original source and to comply with copyright law. However, some attempts to establish original copyright ownership may have been unsuccessful. If copyright ownership can be identified, please notify Castle Rock Research Corp so that appropriate corrective action can be taken.

23	"I Am a Native of North America" by Chief Dan George, from "My Heart Soars", Hancock House Publishers Ltd., Reprinted by permission of Hancock House Publishers Ltd.
25	"Ex-Basketball Player", from COLLECTED POEMS 1953-1993 by John Updike, copyright © 1993 by John Updike. Used by permission of Alfred A. Knopf, a division of Random House, Inc.
27	Excerpt from "Tell Tale Heart" by Edgar Allen Poe
27	Excerpt from "Island of the Blue Dolphin", by Scott O'Dell. published by Houghton Mifflin Company, 1990.
34	Sonnet II by William Shakespeare
37	"Insolence" by Nancy Neff. Published in LITERARY CAVALCADE, May 1972. Copyright © 1972 by Scholastic Inc. Reprinted by permission of Scholastic Inc.
52	"Dragon Night" by Jane Yolen. Copyright © 1980 by Jane Yolen. Currently appears in HERE THERE BE DRAGONS, published by Harcourt Brace and Company. Reprinted by permission of Curtis Brown, Ltd.
57-8	"A Purple World" by Richard Wagamese, published in The Calgary Herald, June 9, 1991, p. C3
60-2	"Circus in Town" from "The Lamp at Noon and Other Stories" by Sinclair Ross, published by McClelland & Stewart Ltd., Copyright © 1968 by Sinclair Ross
65-8	"Of Frogs and Fairy Godmothers" by Harold Horwood, from "The Magic Ground", Nimbus Publishing, Limited (1996), Copyright © Harold Horwood
69-70	"The Joy of Family Vacations" by Natalie Cooper
72	"One Man's Ceiling is Another Man's Floor" by Paul Simon
76-7	"You Had Two Girls", by Duncan Campbell Scott
79-80	"Schools use daily gym class in battle with child obesity", by Heather Sokoloff, published in The National Post, January 10, 2004, page A1
81	"When to Her Lute Corinna Sings", by Thomas Campion
83	"Where the Reids Lived", by Mary Bowen, published in The National Post, March 22, 2004, p. AL 10
144	from "Romeo and Juliette" by William Shakespeare
191-2	Excerpt from "Emma", by Jane Austin
193	"Stars" by Marjorie Pickthall
195-6	"Closet of the Future Picks Out Clothes", by Hans Greimel, published in The National Post, September 10, 2002

202 Table: Percentage of Internet users, aged 15 and over, by selected types of Internet activity, Canada and province, 2000, from Statistics Canada, General Social Survey, Cycle 14

204 "Pantoum for a Mother in Nunavut", by Claire Battershill, published on Re: Verse, a Zine for Young Poets

207 "On the Future of Poetry", by Henry Austin Dobson

209-11 "Eye of the Moon", by Sarah Klassen, from *A Feast of Longing*, published by Coteau Books. Used by permission of the publisher.

214 "World Cup 1998", by Kate Braid, published in The Canadian Journal of Poetry and Critical Writing (Vol. 26, Issue 1, Summer 2003)

216-8 Excerpt from "Eve's Ransom", by George Gissing

NOTES

NOTES

NOTES

NOTES

RESOURCE INFORMATION Order online at www.castlerockresearch.com

THE KEY Study Guides assist in preparing students for course assignments, unit tests, and final or provincial assessments.

KEY Study Guides – $29.95 each plus G.S.T.

SECONDARY	ELEMENTARY
Biology 12, University Prep (SBI4U)	Science 8
Canadian and World Politics 12, University Prep (CPW4U)	Math 7
Chemistry 12, University Prep (SCH4U)	Science 7
English 12, University Prep (ENG4U)	Language 6 Reading & Writing
Math 12 Advanced Functions, University Prep (MHF4U)	Mathematics 6
Math 12 Calculus and Vectors, University Prep (MCV4U)	Science 6
Physics 12, University Prep (SPH4U)	Math 5
World History 12, University Prep (CHY4U)	Science 5
Biology 11, University Prep (SBI3U)	Mathematics 4
Chemistry 11, University Prep (SCH3U)	Science 4
English 11, University Prep (ENG3U)	Language 3 Reading & Writing
Math 11, Foundations for College Mathematics (MBF3C)	Mathematics 3
Math 11, Functions and Applications, U/C Prep (MCF3M)	Science 3
Math 11, Functions, University Prep (MCR3U)	
Physics 11, University Preparation (SPH3U)	
World History 11, University/College Prep (CHW3M)	
Canadian History 10, Academic (CHC2D)	
Canadian History 10, Applied (CHC2P)	
Civics 10, (CHV2O)	
English 10, Academic (ENG2D)	
Math 10, Academic, Principles of Mathematics (MPM2D)	
Math 10, Applied, Foundations of Mathematics (MFM2P)	
OSSLT, Ontario Secondary School Literacy Test	
Science 10, Academic (SNC2D)	
Science 10, Applied (SNC2P)	
English 9, Academic (ENG1D)	
Geography of Canada 9, Academic (CGC1D)	
Math 9, Academic, Principles of Mathematics (MPM1D)	
Math 9, Applied, Foundations of Mathematics (MFM1P)	
Science 9, Academic (SNC1D)	
Science 9, Applied (SNC1P)	

The **Student Notes and Problems (*SNAP*)** student workbooks provide complete lessons for course expectations, detailed explanations of concepts, and exercises with complete solutions.

SNAP Workbooks – $29.95 each plus G.S.T.

SECONDARY
Physics 12, University Preparation (SPH4U)
Physics 11, University Preparation (SPH3U)
Math 9, Academic, Principles of Mathematics (MPM1D)
Math 9, Applied, Foundations of Mathematics (MFM1P)

ORDERING OPTIONS

Visit our website at www.castlerockresearch.com

Schools are eligible for an education discount—for more information, contact Castle Rock Research Ontario.

5250 Satellite Drive, Unit 11
Mississauga, ON L4W 5G5
E-mail: Ontario@castlerockresearch.com

Phone: 905.625.3332
Fax: 905.625.3390

Castle Rock
Research Ontario